Better Homes and Gardens®

step-by-step Yard & Garden Basics

Better Homes and Gardens® Books
Des Moines, Iowa

Better Homes and Gardens® Books
An imprint of Meredith® Books

Step-By-Step Yard & Garden Basics
Writer: Liz Ball
Project Editor: David Haupert
Art Director: Lyne Neymeyer
Creative Consultant: Karen Weir-Jimerson
Copy Chief: Catherine Hamrick
Copy and Production Editor: Terri Fredrickson
Contributing Copy Editors: Chardel Blaine, Barbara Feller Roth
Contributing Proofreaders: Mary Duerson, Sue Fetters, Mary Pas, Nancy Ruhling, JoEllyn Witke
Contributing Photographers: Derek Fell, Dency Kane
Design Assistant: Beth Ann Edwards
Indexer: Jana K. Finnegan
Electronic Production Coordinator: Paula Forest
Editorial and Design Assistants: Kaye Chabot, Mary Lee Gavin, Karen Schirm
Production Director: Douglas M. Johnston
Book Production Managers: Pam Kvitne, Marjorie J. Schenkelberg

Meredith® Books
Editor in Chief: James D. Blume
Design Director: Matt Strelecki
Managing Editor: Gregory H. Kayko
Executive Garden Editor: Cathy Wilkinson Barash

Director, Retail Sales and Marketing: Terry Unsworth
Director, Sales, Special Markets: Rita McMullen
Director, Sales, Premiums: Michael A. Peterson
Director, Sales, Retail: Tom Wierzbicki
Director, Sales, Home & Garden Centers: Ray Wolf
Director, Book Marketing: Brad Elmitt
Director, Operations: George A. Susral
Director, Production: Douglas M. Johnston

Vice President, General Manager: Jamie L. Martin

***Better Homes and Gardens®* Magazine**
Editor in Chief: Jean LemMon
Executive Garden Editor: Mark Kane

Meredith Publishing Group
President, Publishing Group: Christopher M. Little
Vice President, Finance & Administration: Max Runciman

Meredith Corporation
Chairman and Chief Executive Officer: William T. Kerr

Chairman of the Executive Committee: E. T. Meredith III

All of us at Better Homes and Gardens® Books are dedicated to providing you with information and ideas to enhance your home and garden. We welcome your comments and suggestions. Write to us at: Better Homes and Gardens® Books, Garden Editorial Department, 1716 Locust St., Des Moines, IA 50309-3023.

If you would like to purchase any of our books, check wherever quality books are sold. Visit our website at bhg.com or bhgbooks.com.

First Edition—01

Library of Congress Catalog Number: 00-134297
ISBN: 0-696-21288-9

contents

introduction

Whether you're just starting to garden or have been maintaining your yard for several years, *Step-by-Step Yard and Garden Basics* is the book for you. Within these pages are all the techniques and tips needed to make your yard and garden beautiful. The first two chapters inspire with different types of gardens and show you how to create a great front yard. Then you can turn directly to the chapter on the plants you are working with—lawns and lawn alternatives, flowers (including bulbs, annuals, and perennials), edibles (vegetables, herbs, and edible flowers), vines, or trees and shrubs. Each is filled with easy-to-follow step-by step projects. At the end of each chapter, you'll find a seasonal checklist of related chores for both northern and southern gardens. The final chapters show how to use ornaments as finishing touches and explain which tools to use for each task. With more than 80 step-by-step projects and 200 timesaving and weather-related tips to guide you, you'll have a beautiful garden before you know it. There's even space to record your successes.

Happy gardening!

Cathy Wilkinson Barash
Executive Garden Editor

WELCOME TO
MY GARDEN

welcome to my garden

cutting gardens

For many gardeners, the greatest luxury is to have an abundance of flowers for indoor arrangements. One way to ensure such bounty is to set up a cutting garden so you don't rob your ornamental garden every time you want to cut some flowers for indoor enjoyment. Although cutting gardens are as diverse as the gardeners who tend them, their main purpose is production rather than landscape display. Often tucked into sunny spaces off the beaten track, cutting gardens are filled with plants that flower exuberantly and dependably. Unlike their ornamental counterparts, these gardens are usually planted in no-nonsense rows for easy maintenance and harvest. They may include flowering plants of all kinds—bulbs, perennials, and roses—yet their mainstay is annuals, because they generally bloom for the entire season. The more you cut annuals, the more they bloom. Fill your cutting garden with your favorite plants for bouquets. Include those with a variety of textures and heights and add a few that offer foliage accents. And don't overlook those fragrant blooms.

This small patch of flowers is actually a cutting garden. Its jumble of jaunty blossoms with strong stems will continue through most of the summer. You'll stimulate more bloom by taking regular cuttings. You don't have to worry about having a harmonious design and a neat-as-a-pin appearance. Some perennials, such as lilies and coral bells, are so useful in arrangements that they're included with the many annuals. Annual standbys for cutting include nicotiana, phlox, feverfew, cleome, statice, and gomphrena.

ornamental gardens

The best ornamental gardens are a marriage of good design and attractive, appropriate plants. They enhance a residential landscape, setting off the house and other special features of the property. Ornamental gardens may feature perennials, annuals, bulbs, vines, shrubs, or foliage plants—singly or in a pleasant combination. An ornamental garden may take the form of a border or an island bed, and it may be formal or informal, in the sun or in the shade, and parallel or perpendicular to the nearest property line. Choose plants that are adapted to the prevailing conditions in your yard because these plants will require the least maintenance. And strive for variety—for the many textures and colors and to host a range of beneficial insects and other creatures to control pests and diseases. Year-round ornamental gardens will provide enjoyment in every season if you select plants with different bloom times. Start with spring bulbs and flowering shrubs and end with asters, goldenrod, and trees aglow with fall foliage. Dried grasses and plants with interesting seedpods, cones, bark, and branching patterns continue their show throughout the winter.

Not all ornamental gardens feature plants with colorful blossoms. Here, the site and soil are best served with foliage plants that share a tolerance for dry soil. The garden's stone edging and the floppy, casual habits of most of the plants create a comfortable, informal style. Wintercreeper, used in the front, provides a bit of color interest with its variegated foliage. As the season progresses, the grasses will change color and develop feathery seedheads. Notice that the taller plants are at the back, the shorter ones in front.

formal gardens

Formal gardens are characterized by symmetrical design and repetition of plants. The simplest gardens are often the most elegant. A formal garden usually features four similar beds arranged in a geometric pattern around a central focal point. The focal point is usually a statue, fountain, birdbath, or container of plants. Neat, permanent paths of stone, brick, or pavers define the beds as well as direct foot traffic to the center of the garden. The total effect is one of order and neatness. Whether the theme of your garden is herbs, water, or roses, the overall feeling of the formal planting is one of sophistication and tranquillity.

The plants in formal gardens are neatly arrayed within low, tightly clipped hedges that outline each bed. The choice of plants reinforces the restful, elegant tone. Use only a few different plant types and choose subtle (rather than bright) colors. Strive for compact, low-growing shrubs, flowers, or groundcovers and place them around a taller shrub or tree in the center of the bed. For utmost formality, repeat exactly the same layout design in each bed.

Formal gardens don't have to imitate the rigid style of huge 18th- or 19th-century English or French estate gardens. They may reflect the surrounding environment and have a regional feeling. Random-size native stone—laid here as a small dry wall to edge the beds—softens the formality while effectively evoking a sense of place. The use of different plants in each bed also contributes to a relaxed country look. Notice how the similar colors of the stone, the house, and many of the plants reinforce the unity of the formal layout.

kitchen gardens

Kitchen gardens are small food gardens conveniently located in a sunny spot, usually near the kitchen door. They may contain herbs, vegetables, salad greens, and flowers for cutting. Unlike large, classic vegetable gardens, which may be planted far from the house, kitchen gardens are a convenient source of small amounts of fresh-picked food destined for immediate use on the stove or table. Their small scale keeps maintenance at a manageable level. As a bonus, these practical gardens are often ornamental. Whether formal or informal, they can delightfully decorate an entrance—front or back—to the house. Use perennial crops to provide multiseason interest and structure to the garden. The soft, ferny foliage of ripening asparagus stems is a perfect backdrop for the reds and purples of salad greens, basil, and eggplant. A blueberry hedge can shelter the beds while providing flowers and berries, then fall color. Strawberries supply fruit and discourage weeds. How handy it is to duck out the back door to pinch a few sprigs of herbs, such as parsley or oregano. And chives and sage—when allowed to bloom—contribute beauty as well as edible flowers.

This fairly large kitchen garden has a formal layout. Within its brick-edged beds, you'll find globe basil, onions, peppers, many different salad greens, and other crops, all neatly arrayed in rows. The effect is softened by the occasional vertical accent such as the central arch supporting climbing beans and clematis. Containers filled with herbs and flowers punctuate the paths. An attractive fence encloses the garden. You could install a more substantial fence than the one shown here to keep out rabbits, deer, and other critters who like to visit food gardens.

island bed

An island bed stands alone. Unlike flower beds that border walls, hedges, or buildings, an island bed has no back or front. It is often oval, teardrop, free-form, or kidney-shaped. The addition of an island bed can reduce a huge expanse of lawn, unify the plantings on a property, and make good use of limited space and available sunlight. Spacious properties require fairly large beds; otherwise the beds will appear overwhelmed by lawn. Though you may be tempted to carve your island bed out of an open, sunny lawn, you might consider developing it around existing trees or shrubs. It's a simple matter to extend the mulched area under a tree well beyond its canopy and create

The pink flowers in the border complement those in the island bed to unify the landscape. Even though the plants are tall, they don't overwhelm the island, because the lawn between them is wide.

The lower-growing annuals that edge the bed neatly define its gently curving edge. Notice how the lawn path echoes the shape of this side of the bed.

This island bed is planted asymmetrically. Unlike most, it has a definite back and front. Sometimes an east-west orientation is the best way to ensure that the tall plants won't shade the low ones.

a bed that has both shade and sun areas. In large beds, incorporate an unobtrusive path, such as stepping-stones, so you can get to the center.

Proportion plays a role in bed size and plant selection. Big beds are suited to large plants, often in mass plantings. Site the tallest plants toward the center of the bed. They should be no taller than half the width of the bed to maintain a balanced design. Working from the center to the edge of the bed, fill in with medium, then smaller plants—small trees, shrubs, perennials, and annuals. In fall, plant hardy bulbs—daffodils, tulips, Greek windflowers, snowdrops, and crocus—for color and interest in early spring. To minimize root disturbance under trees, grow shallow-rooted perennials and groundcovers.

You can view an island bed from any vantage point, so move your yard furniture every once in a while. When you do, you'll have a new perspective to enjoy while relaxing or meditating.

A brick walk along this side of the bed provides easy access and a neat edge. Some island beds have bricks, stones, or pavers of some sort along all sides to define the edges and make lawn mowing easier.

In this asymmetrical bed, the taller plants are on one side rather than in the center, creating a less formal look and making it easier to pick the roses.

Island gardens reduce lawn size and typical maintenance chores to a more manageable level. Surrounding an island with lawn or greenery sets off the flowers effectively.

edible flower garden

An edible flower garden is a double delight: It lets you have your beauty and eat it, too. The trick here is to select only the specific plants whose flowers are documented as safe for humans to eat. Sometimes they're the blossoms of traditional food plants, such as squash, or culinary herbs such as chives. In most cases they're plants that are considered in our culture to be strictly ornamental. Lilacs, pansies, and tulips are good examples. By growing edible flowers yourself, you can ensure that they're never treated with toxic pesticides. Because more than 70 familiar plants bear edible flowers, you have lots of leeway in creating and planting your own edible flower garden. What's more, it's fun

Nasturtiums are renowned edibles. Their flowers add color and spice to salads, cooked vegetables, oils, and vinegars. Their foliage is tasty, too. Use either dwarf or trailing types.

'Lemon Gem' marigolds are the tastiest of the marigolds, and their foliage has a lemony scent. Sprinkle the flower petals lightly over potato salad or cooked vegetables to create a citrusy, tarragon flavor.

Dianthus, or cottage pinks, are lovely perennials with a sweet clovelike scent and flavor. Chop the petals and mix them into softened sweet butter and spread on bread for attractive tea sandwiches. For a pretty accent, toss petals in with fruit salad.

Thyme is already an herb garden standby. Its foliage is useful in many dishes, and its white, pink, purple, or magenta flowers are good in fish sauces, cheese fillings, and dips.

and easy. Choose a garden style that suits you—formal or informal, island or border, even containers—and dedicate it to ornamental plants that bear edible blooms. It's a good idea to grow several varieties of roses and daylilies, for example, because their flowers vary in flavor. Select and site plants as you would in any garden. Taller ones go toward the back, smaller ones more forward. Don't forget to include vines such as honeysuckle for vertical interest. Use trees and shrubs that bear edible flowers, such as citrus, roses, and rose of Sharon, to anchor the bed or border. Include herbs, such as sage, borage, mint, and anise hyssop, that have blooms as tasty as their foliage. Use tiny Johnny-jump-ups, 'Lemon Gem' marigolds, violets, or sweet woodruff for edging.

Chamomile flowers look like miniature daisies, with white petals and yellow centers. Chamomile reseeds easily and can be used as a groundcover where it will not be stepped on often, or between stepping-stones of a path. The flowers and foliage smell like green apples. Traditionally, chamomile is used to make a calming tea.

Scarlet runner bean flowers easily climb up trellises to provide vertical interest. Use the flowers before they develop into beans. They add a beany flavor to salads and to potato and vegetable dishes.

Calendula, or pot marigold, bears yellow or orange flowers. Chop the petals (fresh or dried) and use them as a substitute for pricey saffron; the flavor is slightly bitter. Calendula petals impart a lovely color to cheese, rice, and potato dishes.

entry garden

Entry gardens are growing in popularity because new house designs frequently feature a garage protruding from the front of the home. An area planted around the front entrance to the house softens the impact of the obtrusive driveway and garage and reclaims the landscape from the dominance of the automobile. Regardless of the architecture of the home, an entry garden also establishes the front yard as a welcome transition from the busy world to a tranquil sanctuary. If you decide to add an entry garden, you will find that the same garage that tends to dominate the approach to your house suddenly can become your ally. Its bulk not only

This entry garden is located in California where water resources are limited. The plants—all drought-tolerant and self-reliant—attractively fill an area that otherwise might be a thirsty, high-maintenance lawn.

Attractive lighting fixtures add visual interest to your entry garden—even in the daytime—and highlight the plantings at night. They also augment the light coming from your entry and improve security at the front of your house.

defines a space for a garden, it shelters the area to create a protected niche for plants. Its walls are handy for mounting trellises to support attractive climbing vines or espaliered shrubs. Design your garden to reflect the style of your home. Use similar materials, such as brick or stone, to blend with the surroundings. Choose plants that will be able to handle the soil and light conditions that prevail at the front of the house. If your entry faces south, you know how hot the interior can be in summer, thanks to direct sunlight radiating heat into your walls. You can add beauty outside—and reduce heat gain inside—by planting a small deciduous tree to shade your entry in summer. In winter, after the leaves drop, the sun is a welcome visitor once again.

Use evergreens to anchor an entry garden and provide year-round color. Place taller ones near the back, shorter ones closer to the walkway. Keep the shrubs from crowding the doorway, where they could hide an intruder from view.

Plan to use hardscape materials that harmonize with the plants and the house. Here natural stone forms the walkways. The switch to wood indicates the edge of each step, marking the transition to the next level.

Rosemary, a popular culinary herb that is used here as a groundcover, has soft, needled, green to gray-green foliage year-round in Zones 6 and warmer. The plant bears tiny blue or white edible flowers in spring that add color to this bed.

country garden

A country garden expresses freedom. In days gone by, wealthy people had a formal city home where they lived during the business week. Plantings there reflected the cramped, disciplined, formal life in the city. These people also had a country place for weekend relaxation and informal entertaining. Their gardens in the country reflected a sense of escape from the confines of city life. They were informal, and because they were likely to be neglected during the week, they often appeared undisciplined and overgrown. Today country-style gardens are perfect for anyone who loves the relaxed, seemingly carefree abundance of plants and who enjoys memories of bygone eras. There are no

This bluestone path contributes to the informal tone of the garden. Stepping-stones, wood chips, or gravel—typically materials at hand—are also common in country gardens. Place landscape fabric beneath them to discourage weeds.

In a country garden, profusion and abundance reign supreme. Here lady's mantle and other low-growing plants spill lazily out of the bed onto the path. They soften its edge, creating the impression that it meanders.

Ornaments or planted containers randomly placed along an expanse of wall or a hedge create variety. Here a pedestal breaks up the stretch of ivy-covered wall. Be sure to include a birdbath in the garden.

special design rules to follow. Country gardens can be any color, size, or shape, and they can be anywhere on your property. However, the best ones have two things in common: color and crowding. Country gardens are all about flowers—as many as possible. Their trademark is a profusion of color, and they're usually jam-packed with exuberant annuals and perennials. Clumps of towering hollyhocks, phlox, larkspur, and cleome with midheight daisies, zinnias, and purple coneflowers are stitched together with luxuriant vines to form an unruly tapestry. Here's an opportunity to experiment with all kinds and colors of plants. Remember: Although they may look carefree, healthy country gardens take the same conscientious care that others do.

Tall plants, especially foxglove, are fixtures of country gardens. Their dramatic vertical spires provide a narrow profile and height in the garden that trees usually bring to a landscape. Flowering vines on a trellis or fence post also add height.

Landscape (shrub) roses, rather than more formal hybrid tea roses, casually billow over fences and climb crumbling walls. They provide wonderful color all season long. Cutting the blooms to bring indoors encourages the plants to flower more.

A rustic post-and-rail fence defines the tone and space of this garden. By serving as an extension of an ivy-covered wall and hedge, the fence completes the enclosure. It also provides support for plants growing on either side.

border

A border grows along a boundary of some sort. It follows a fence, retaining wall, deck, building, hedge, walk, or driveway, all of which define the growing bed and provide a backdrop for the plantings. The border softens the edges of the boundary and brightens its appearance. Borders are the most familiar and traditional residential garden, probably because they're practical as well as beautiful. Flowering borders solve lots of landscape problems. They effectively obscure the unattractive foundations of a house, deck, porch, or garage. They can beautify the edge of a property and create a sense of privacy. Tall borders—either flowers or ornamental grasses—

The solid expanse of wall behind this flower border creates a sheltering backdrop for colorful plants. The wall protects them from wind and provides structure for vines. In winter, it absorbs and holds heat from the sun.

Colorful annuals, such as this snapdragon, bridge the periods between the peak bloom of perennials when green foliage dominates in the border. If you consistently deadhead the annuals, most of them will bloom steadily all season.

At the front of the garden, use flowering groundcovers such as this sweet alyssum. As they fill in between larger plants, they weave together the elements of the border to provide a more cohesive appearance.

screen out unpleasant views and reduce noise and dust from a busy street. Midheight beds can moderate the harsh lines of a swimming pool or parking area. And borders that flow along both sides of a front walkway provide a wonderful welcome. Use all kinds of flowering plants in a border. Mix annuals and perennials (including spring bulbs) to ensure color throughout the growing season. Choose plants that will thrive in the soil and light conditions at the site, remembering that borders work well in both sun and shade—sometimes some of each. Include small flowering shrubs as fillers and trees as anchors for the bed through the entire year. If the border is wide, set stepping-stones or make a narrow path inside the border for access to the back.

Tall, vertical plants normally go toward the back of a flower border. This gladiolus is only a temporary resident near the front. It is grown for cutting and will be harvested soon.

Cut down on weeding chores and neaten flower borders by spreading 2 to 3 inches of organic mulch around all plants. It helps retain soil moisture and contributes nutrients as it gradually decomposes.

Border gardens often face a lawn. A small stretch of well-maintained grass beautifully frames the colorful flowers. Maintain a neat, sharp edge between the lawn and garden.

color in the garden

All plants contribute unique ornamental features to a garden. Their leaves, flowers, shapes, and growth habits have their own individual charm and beauty. Many plants produce attractive post-season seedheads, pods, and cones that add even more visual interest. But when it comes to designing an ornamental garden, it's the color—of both flowers and foliage—that matters most. Gardens are more than random assortments of plants you find in nature or orderly rows of merchandise like those you see at the garden center. Instead, they're artful arrangements of plants that you purposely select and carefully site to enhance their health and celebrate their beauty. Although you might make your choices for an ornamental garden based on other factors—annual versus perennial, edible versus decorative, woody versus soft-stemmed—flower and foliage color will greatly influence your decision. The goal of some gardeners is simply to assemble a variety of colors in joyous profusion. On the theory that plants of many colors jostle one another everywhere in nature, these

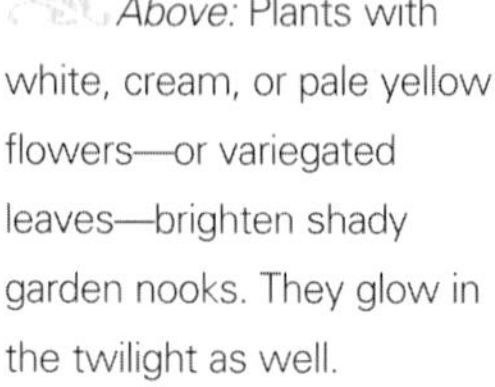

Above: Plants with white, cream, or pale yellow flowers—or variegated leaves—brighten shady garden nooks. They glow in the twilight as well.

Above right: Various patterns of variegation on plant foliage combine with a variety of leaf textures to create an interesting garden that has no flowers at all.

Right: Monochromatic beds—whether developed from flowers or foliage—offer an attractive contrast to a variety of colors. Shades of green do the trick here.

gardeners are comfortable with random color, even though they use other criteria to position the plants.

Other gardeners prefer to create a specific effect by using color in a more painterly way. For example, they might choose hot colors such as red, orange, yellow, chartreuse, and gold for a border garden that receives full afternoon sun. By combining plants with bright-colored foliage and flowers, they create a garden that visually echoes its hot site.

Above: The intensity of colors makes a difference. In this garden, the pale flowers—white with yellow highlights—combine with the fine foliage texture to create a lacy, misty effect.

Above right: Plants with bold, highly saturated colors complement one another. When these spring tulips and daffodils fade, the garden may have an entirely different color palette.

bold plants for highlights

Some plants have brightly colored flowers. Others have tall, lush habits. Bold plants have both. Their size and sassy color usually make them loners instead of team players. They are best used as special effects. Bold plants make excellent exclamation points in a border, providing height, vertical interest, or contrast. They're particularly handsome around pools and patios. Many bold plants, such as taro, canna, banana, and ginger, are tropicals. They boast wonderful purple, chartreuse, or striped foliage, and many are topped by flowers in warm, bright oranges, reds, salmons, and yellows. Bring these tender tropicals indoors for the winter in northern regions.

color in the garden

Conversely, these garden "painters" might use cool colors—pink, white, magenta, blue, lavender, or purple—for a bed that receives bright but indirect light a lot of the time. In both cases, however, the colors are harmonious. Contrasting colors work just as well. Punctuate a flower bed of warm colors with plants in cool tones. Pair various plants in warm and cool colors, such as chartreuse and purple, in beds or containers. Color plays a key role in special situations such as shade and evening gardens, where plants with pale, luminous flowers or foliage dominate. To attract hummingbirds or butterflies, choose plants with bright, saturated colors.

Above: Nothing says sunshine like a bed of yellow flowers. Single-color gardens (monochromatic) are an interesting novelty. The challenge is to select plants of similar hue and to maintain bloom through the season.

Above right: Nasturtiums are cheery in shades of red, orange, and yellow. They make an edible vignette, sparkling as they climb up a cobalt blue trellis and contrasting with lavender flowers.

Right: A harmonious collection of bright, hot-colored flowers brings spirit and liveliness to its part of the garden, whether on the ground or scaling the fence. Gray foliage and the bee skep cool things down a bit.

Below: The blue-based pinkish-purple colors of anise hyssop and cleome set a cool tone for this section of the flower bed. Many herbs, such as sage, lavender, and chives, have flowers in the same color range.

Above: Lilies come in such a wide range of colors that they are naturals for any monochromatic garden scheme. Here, pink and white rubrum lilies are paired with hollyhocks and bee balm.

Left: Large properties can handle a tapestry of big, richly colored plants. Clumps of cool- and warm-colored flowers successfully play off one another to produce a powerful scene that becomes a major player in this landscape.

height in the garden

Flowers growing at graduated heights display the full charm of plants of various sizes. The resulting layers affect proportion and scale in the garden. The flatter the terrain, the more important it is for the garden to have some strikingly upright plants to break the horizon, link the sky with the ground, and relieve the one-dimensional effect of a flat flower bed. The bigger and broader the bed, the taller and bolder the vertical accent plants should be. Their presence forces the eye to move upward and around the garden to take in the dynamic view. In larger landscapes, trees do this. In a garden, tall flowering plants and climbing shrubs and vines accomplish the same purpose. Permanent (hardscape) elements help you create strong vertical lines in your garden. Of course, they add height by

Above: As with most climbing vines, white clematis visually continues the upward reach of flowering plants—in this case the straight, tall foxgloves. The contrasting color and habit of the elements keep the pink foxgloves from blending into the brick wall.

Right: Wisteria can be trained as a self-supporting shrub or as a vine. Notorious as a reluctant bloomer when young, it becomes a real showstopper when it matures. It requires a sturdy support.

themselves, and they make it possible for plants to grow vertically. The wall that defines a border garden, the tepees in a kitchen garden, and the arbor or pergola over a walkway—all enable vines to climb upward. So do statuary and lampposts. Small trees and large shrubs support vines, too. Nothing perks up a ho-hum needled evergreen like a jaunty clematis roaming among its branches all summer.

Tall plants, especially vines, soften the edges of a garden. Vines either cling, twine, or grab onto their supports, so choose them carefully. They can hide landscape eyesores and create attractive transitions between softscape and hardscape elements around decks, garages, and patios. Evergreen vines on the north side of a house insulate it during cold weather. Deciduous vines covering a south wall provide shade, reduce heat gain, and cut glare during the hot summer months.

Left: Rustic, handmade supports are decorative in themselves. Until the peas cover the tepee, it will add height and pleasing proportion to the kitchen garden.

Right: The beauty of roses climbing over an arbor in a flower garden is self-evident. Climbing roses add elegance and height to the scene. Be sure to fasten their canes securely to the support.

making a cutting garden

In their prime, cutting gardens are as colorful and lovely as any garden. However, the flowers in this garden are intended to be cut down at the peak of their bloom. Therefore, cutting gardens aren't for display and are usually located off to the side or in the back of the property where they won't detract from the appearance of the yard when the flowers are cut. They exist to provide flowers, foliage, and various seedpods for indoor displays, floral crafts, and gift bouquets. And they provide a generous supply of cut flowers so you don't need to raid the more visible flower border.

Choose a site that receives sun most of the day. Because you'll be placing great demands on the soil,

YOU WILL NEED

- soaker hose
- seeds or seedlings
- gloves
- trowel
- hand pruners
- black plastic
- bucket
- tepid water

1 To ensure regular moisture, lay drip irrigation lines on the planting rows. Soaker-hose (leaky-pipe) systems slowly deliver water directly to roots.

2 Place seeds in furrows, then thin later to correct the spacing. Plant young nursery plants on a cloudy day or at least when the sun isn't bright.

4 In cool regions, warm the soil so annuals can go in earlier. Spread black plastic over the planting rows to absorb the heat from the sun.

5 Start harvesting flowers when plants reach mature size. Be sure to take as much stem as possible and place them in a container of tepid water immediately.

be sure to prepare it thoroughly by adding organic material such as compost before you plant each year. Annuals are heavy feeders because they produce flowers all summer, so dig granular, slow-acting fertilizer into the soil at the beginning of each season. Perennials also benefit from a sprinkling of fertilizer on the soil around the emerging plants in spring to provide consistent, uniform nutrition for several months. Supplement by spraying dilute liquid fertilizer periodically during the summer on the leaves of plants that need a boost. Mulch between plants to discourage weeds and retain moisture.

3 Cut off any flowers from young nursery plants. This delays flowering so the plants can channel their energy into building strong roots and stems.

6 Stimulate most annuals and some perennials to produce more flowers by cutting flowering stems as they begin to open. Cut off faded flowers, too.

best cutting-garden flowers

- Baby's breath
- Cleome (spider flower)
- Cockscomb
- Cornflower
- Cosmos
- Dahlia
- Geranium
- Larkspur
- Lily
- Lisianthus
- Marigold
- Mealy-cup sage
- Peony
- Petunia
- Poppy
- Snapdragon
- Sweet pea
- Tulip
- Zinnia

planning for paths

Be sure to lay out rows or boxed beds so the paths between them are wide enough to walk on or accommodate a wheelbarrow. As plants grow, they tend to bush out into the paths. Allow enough space so you can lug tools past the plants without harming them. It's important to have easy access to each row for spraying, deadheading, staking, and cutting as well as for replanting with fall bloomers.

creating a great front yard

assessing your options

Your front yard is your public face—an extension of your home. It's also a transition zone, easing you, your family, and guests from the outside world into your sheltered, private domain. Good design helps you create an attractive and inviting welcoming area that doesn't require much effort to maintain. It also enhances the value of your property and creates the necessary curb appeal when it's time to sell your home. Think of your yard as a series of outdoor rooms—each with one or more functions, which may include storage, entertainment, circulation (getting from point A to point B), children's play, food production, or beauty. Because front yards typically concentrate on two of these—beauty and

A white, south-facing wall reflects light and heat from the sun onto nearby plantings in summer. Set up trellises or other supports and train vines to climb them to reduce the harsh glare and heat. Their foliage softens and shades the wall.

Using the same shrub repeatedly limits diversity in your yard. Many kinds of shrubs provide color and texture year-round. They also help keep the landscape healthy because they host many kinds of beneficial creatures. Those that bear colorful berries in the fall attract birds, as well.

Grass competes with tree roots for nutrients and water. And whenever you mow close to the tree, you risk injuring the trunk. But if you mulch the area under the tree canopy, you can improve the tree's health. Living mulch—a groundcover planting—is the ideal choice.

circulation—choose a plan that combines both. Keep your options open so you can make changes easily when you decide to redecorate each room. Let your front yard complement the style of your house. The hardscape (permanent, non-plant features) and softscape (plantings) must work well together to create a congenial setting. If your house has a formal look, stick with a more formal front yard, featuring straight paths, symmetrical plantings, and elegant gates and fences. Manicure the planted areas, deliberately prune hedges and shrubs, and concentrate on using green foliage plants throughout.

Roof overhangs keep rain from foundation plantings. Save time and precious water by planting out from the overhang so they catch the rain.

Shrubs that threaten to block windows and walks are problems. Move them to a spot where they're free to grow naturally. Plant dwarf shrubs in the more restricted areas.

Many groundcovers spread aggressively by underground runners, encroaching on the lawn and nearby garden beds. Choose types that grow in clumps and spread gradually. Use sturdy edging around beds to restrain the exuberant ones.

Save time, energy, and money by limiting high-maintenance lawn areas. Use a premium mixture of grass varieties suited to your climate. Minimize water, herbicide, and pesticide use by mowing the grass about 3 inches high.

assessing your options

If your house doesn't have a formal style, let the landscape have a more natural look. Curve the paths and driveways; build gates and fences that have a rustic flair. Make sure other hardscape features have natural elements, such as hewn wood and stone, rather than iron and painted lumber. Choose lots of colorful plants, and spread them around randomly. Carefully plan the circulation of traffic—for people and vehicles. For example, you'll want to install walks in places where people need to walk, build gates wide enough to accommodate machinery and deliveries, and design driveways to suit your family's parking patterns. Use plants and fences to screen utility boxes, outdoor outlets, and hose faucets. Design other planting areas to provide shade where it's

Plants in containers dry out quickly in the summer sun. Those in clay pots and containers that are elevated dry out even faster. Place pots where you can conveniently water them daily—perhaps twice a day during hot summer months. Group containers to save work and to create an attractive effect.

Shrubs, such as this azalea, that need acidic soil may fail to thrive near masonry or mortared walls. Over time, rain and snow can cause lime to leach from the wall and enter the soil, reducing its acidity. Add powdered sulfur or aluminum sulfate to correct the balance.

Most plants, especially bulbs, do best in soil that drains well, yet holds moisture. To improve the soil in areas where clay soil is the norm, build a boxed, raised bed over the clay base. Fill it with good soil, amended with lots of organic matter.

needed and outline the edges of walks to guide visitors. Locate outdoor lighting for safety as well as beauty so it illuminates walks and steps and enhances security near the front door. Be sure to think low maintenance, too. The right plant in the right place copes well without constant pruning, watering, and spraying. Limit lawn size to reduce time, energy, and money spent on herbicides and pesticides. Beds of groundcovers under trees and shrubs save water and protect the soil. A diversity of plants hosts beneficial insects, birds, and other allies that control pest problems.

Trees that are too close to the house can cause roof problems. Check periodically to see that branches don't rub the shingles, drop debris, or clog the gutters. Prune back any that threaten.

Tree roots must remain at their natural depth in the soil. If you build a planting bed beneath a tree or otherwise change the grade of the property near a tree, don't pile soil over the root zone or against the trunk.

Design your yard so you can view the plantings from inside. Check the sight lines from windows before you plant.

Perennial plants return year after year, but bloom for a relatively short time. For color in the yard all summer, plant bright annuals, such as geraniums, petunias, coleus, and impatiens, among the permanent shrubs and perennials.

choosing walk materials

It's easy to take walkways for granted, even though they're critical elements of your front yard. They make it work as an outdoor room, a welcoming area, and a transition zone, simultaneously defining an area and carrying people past it. In short, they're the backbone of your front yard—hard at work creating spaces for lawns and gardens and facilitating traffic. If you give them pleasing proportion and use interesting materials to create them, they automatically become a decorative element as well. But their basic role is to move people, and the guiding principle to consider is "location, location, location." Put walks and paths where people want to travel on their journeys from

walk-design hint

Create a custom look for your walkway by combining different paving materials. Set concrete stepping stones in a bed of colored gravel. Or dress up an asphalt walk by laying worn bricks along its edges. They provide a contrasting color and neater appearance.

Concrete "log" pavers resemble the real ones but last much longer. Use them as stepping stones in a garden bed, woodland area, shallow creek, or in an informal walk across your lawn.

A light-colored gravel path is more functional than attractive. Placing landscape fabric underneath discourages weeds but still allows water to drain into the soil. Install an edging to control the gravel.

Special paints and stains can dress up concrete steps. Coordinate the color with those of the siding and trim.

Shell and gravel paths lend a bright, informal feel to the front entrance. Spread them directly over level, firm soil or compacted sand. Though this loose fill is easy and economical to install, it erodes in heavy rains. As a result, occasionally you may need to add more.

place to place. Anticipate the most popular routes. Consider, for example, what the shortest pathway between a car parked in your driveway and the front door is, and the one between your side door and the barbecue area. Before laying down a walk, you might want to define it with stakes and string for a week to see whether people use it or they choose an alternate path. Choose an appropriate style. Straight paths are more efficient, economical, and formal, while curved paths are less formal and more pleasing visually. An incline approaching your house requires special treatment if the grade is steeper than 10%.

Wood chips are soft underfoot and are easy to lay down quickly. Eventually, the wood decomposes, requiring a new layer of fresh chips.

Plank paths work especially well over areas where the ground is not level and where water collects. Use pressure-treated wood or other weather-resistant lumber such as redwood or cedar.

A brick walk is durable, elegant, and easy to maintain. Lay it—in one of many patterns—over a base of sand or mortar. Use a complementary edging.

choosing walk materials

Use steps or a curve to ease the problem. Ramps work, too, and are especially helpful for those who have mobility difficulties. Proportion and scale are important in the design of a walkway; it shouldn't dominate the landscape. Make the walkway as wide as the steps or landing to the house at that point, even if it's narrower earlier in its route. Narrow walks slow people down; use them in gardens where you want guests to linger and enjoy the views. A wide walk is utilitarian and moves people faster, so it's suitable for the main thoroughfare in front of your house. Typically, front walks are 36 to 54 inches wide. Make them—and the structures alongside them, such as arbors—at least wide enough for two people walking abreast, one person carrying a bag

discouraging weeds from walkways

One of the problems with walkways made of loose material—wood chips, pebbles, nut hulls, or pine needles—is that weeds can penetrate them. Discourage perennial weeds by laying down landscape fabric first. It allows water to penetrate into the soil but blocks emerging weeds. Then pour at least 2 inches of the loose material over the fabric.

A red-brick path complements the somewhat formal look of the straight picket fence that runs parallel to it. The color of the path sets off the pink plants that spill out of the bed.

Organic material, such as ground or shredded bark, makes a good walking surface for small paths that meander through informal planting areas. Any leftover material may be used to mulch the plants.

stairway planting

This rock garden—fashioned from a stone stairway—is a perfect example of the functional and attractive fusion of hardscape and softscape. To duplicate this design, buy or collect several large pieces of natural stone. Set them in the soil so they'll be stable underfoot. Be sure to have some friends with strong backs help you move them. Then tuck lots of low-maintenance plants—ones that don't need special soil, generous water, or constant grooming—into the spaces between levels to soften the harsh edges of the stone and dot the area with color and texture. The result is a natural garden that harmonizes beautifully with its surroundings.

of groceries in each arm, or for someone in a wheelchair. Opt for the narrow end of this range if your property is small, the house is narrow, or the distance to the front door is quite short. Be sure that it's sturdy, not slippery, and is as level as possible.

Use edging to give all of your walks a finished look. A firm edge also keeps the sides of your walks from being damaged. And if the edging material is a contrasting color or pattern, it also helps guide the eye of visitors and keeps them from straying off to the side. Set any decorative fencing at least a foot from the edge of the walk or driveway.

edging

Bricks, in various colors and sizes, create crisp, finished edges along walkways. Experiment with them: Try them on edge, on end, or at an angle. You can use them to edge planted beds, too.

Wood edging continues the informal style and color of a walk that features log stepping stones. Use wood that's decay-resistant. Drive stakes into the soil every few feet to keep the wood from moving.

Concrete edging is similar to curbing, except that it's usually narrower. Install this durable and inconspicuous edge the same way you would curbs.

Plastic edging and similar products made from recycled car tires or other materials will last many years. Some are available in several colors.

using walls & fences

Walls and fences can be significant hardscape elements of your yard. Because one of their main functions is to define space, they literally can create a front yard for you by carving out a private space and separating it from the public world. In the process, they contribute character and beauty to your entire landscape. Of course, the purpose of a wall or fence influences its design. One common use is to establish a degree of privacy from the public. This is especially important if your property fronts a busy street, or if the neighboring houses crowd you. Design is critical in these cases. Typically, privacy fences are 6 feet tall. A fence along property lines taller than that or a stockade or other

weather

Weather takes its toll on fences. Humidity promotes rust on iron and mildew and decay on wood. Harsh sun causes paint to peel. Soil heaved by frost loosens posts and topples rails. Be sure to use sturdy materials and solid construction techniques to minimize upkeep and repair.

This picket fence features narrow slats with wider than usual spacing. The more open style gives the fence a light, airy feeling and permits a clear view of the plants on the other side.

A wood gate set in an imposing stone wall makes an attractive contrast. The design is strong enough to blend well with the stone yet light enough to mitigate the massiveness of the wall.

Ornamental gates add elegance to virtually any style of fence or wall. Buy one from a supplier, or design and build your own.

Most municipalities require that you surround a swimming pool with a security fence. There's no reason it can't be attractive as well as utilitarian.

solid-surface fence—although a more effective screen—sends a negative message and is often regarded as a spite fence. Check with local authorities to determine height restrictions, if any.

As you plan your front yard, you may want to temper your inclination for privacy with the desire to present a welcoming view. You can do this by using walls or fences that are only about 4 feet high or that have open spaces, like picket, split-rail, and wrought-iron fences. They still define boundaries and offer an inviting glimpse inside, yet they discourage shortcuts across your lawn.

Rustic fences have a country charm. Use materials at hand, such as the unpainted scrap wood shown here or bare branches of willow or other trees. They don't have to be a uniform width.

A wattle fence made of kudzu, grape, or other flexible, woody plant stems encloses beds as it simultaneously showcases low-growing plants.

An unpainted picket fence requires much less maintenance than a painted one. Here the rustic color harmonizes with the siding on the house.

using walls & fences

Openings in fences and walls are especially important if they enclose—or serve as a border for—plantings of any kind. They admit light and encourage good airflow that keeps flowers and shrubs from overheating or developing mildew. Fences and walls separate the children's play area or the dog's territory from the main yard. They establish space for specialty gardens or for a sheltered microclimate for certain plants such as edibles. Specially designed fences keep undesirable wildlife out of vegetable patches. And many types of walls and fences support plants that like to climb and ramble. Roses covering a fence—or plants growing from the cracks in a stone wall—soften their architectural lines and help them blend into the surrounding softscape. Build your walls

gates

Gates are decorative features as well as practical devices that provide passageways through a fence or wall. Choose interesting designs that coordinate with the style of your fence. Locate them in places that are convenient; gates don't necessarily have to accompany a walkway. The longer you make the fence or wall—or the larger the area it encloses—the more gates you'll need.

The charming design of an arbored entry gate combines with the beautiful plants it frames to create a doubly ornamental entrance.

A fence with mirrors mounted in strategic places opens up a limited space and adds an element of fun and whimsy to a yard or garden. The mirrors reflect extra light and create a sense of depth.

Brick or stone walls give any yard a sense of permanence and security. Cutouts in the wall encourage air circulation and add a decorative touch.

and fences with materials that complement those of the house. Use native stone or weather-resistant wood from trees indigenous to the region to add character and a sense of place to the landscape. If you opt for a brick wall—and your house has a brick exterior—make sure the wall brick matches that of the house. Proportion is important, too. If you plan to parallel a walk or path with a new wall or fence, limit its height to no more than 2 feet so you can maintain a sense of space, as well as allow room for swinging arms. And keep it at least 2 feet away from the traffic path to avoid a crowded effect.

Bamboo fencing is particularly appropriate for Asian-themed yards and gardens but is also practical and adaptable for other areas. Its relatively fine-textured format provides good privacy screening.

There's nothing more classic than a white picket fence surrounding a garden or the entire property. It sets off the colors and textures of all kinds of plants and gives them good air circulation.

Fenced screens partition rather than enclose an area. This white, airy structure is decorative—with or without a colorful cover of climbing plants.

Living wall of plants

Prune a row of shrubs to create a living wall. Hedges make useful and attractive enclosures for yards or gardens. Their foliage absorbs sound and provides a soft backdrop for colorful gardens. Hedges made of thorny shrubs are also very effective barriers.

a great entryway

Entryways are opportunities for gardens. What better way to welcome guests than with plants? One of the loveliest and longest traditions in old cities and rural areas is to use plants to soften and enhance the architectural lines of utilitarian walkways, steps, railings, and front doors. For city homes, a windowbox full of pansies or a pot of geraniums on the *front stoop* effectively produces a garden atmosphere. In the country, families often greet their guests with a personalized *dooryard*—generally an area filled with an entertaining jumble of flowering plants or herbs that's enclosed by a picket fence, low wall, or arbor over which roses ramble. Until recently, most

plant placement

Put plants where they won't get in the way when you need to work on the exterior of your house. Keep shrubs away from the foundation so the outdoor faucet and electrical outlets are always accessible. Train climbing plants on trellises so you can reach steps, railings, and siding to repair and repaint them.

A climbing rose over the door suggests the informality of rural life. Add annual vines to provide continuous color after the roses have faded.

Containers full of brightly colored flowers and foliage welcome guests. Strategic placement of the flowers warns visitors about steps and landings.

homeowners in the exurbs and suburbs overlooked the potential of the space approaching the front door as a garden area. Big expanses of high-maintenance green lawn, dotted with the occasional island of groundcover, sweep practically to the front door. And, almost uniformly, you'll still find row upon row of evergreen shrubs, originally intended to hide the concrete of the poured foundation where it emerges above the soil surface. Unfortunately, many of these serviceable shrubs invariably survive to grow as tall as the house—or at least high enough to cover the front windows. This brings visibility and

Low-growing flowers spill onto this stepping-stone entry walk. The color and foliage soften the edges of the walk and provide a cheerful greeting.

security problems. However, things are changing in the suburbs and exurbs. These days, the approach to the front door is called an *entryway* (or *front courtyard*, if it's tucked between the front entrance and a garage that protrudes from the front of the house). Along with the change in name is a change in perception. Owners are suddenly appreciating this area for its potential as an outdoor room—or, more accurately, an outdoor foyer. Why not develop this entryway into an area that will decorate the house and welcome visitors? Plant a garden there. Replace the tired shrubs and lots of lawn around the front

using edibles as ornamentals

One way to make the entryway doubly useful is to plant vegetables there. An edible landscape can be as colorful and varied as a flower garden. Plant vines (tomatoes and scarlet runner beans), ground covers (red and green lettuces), shrubby plants (peppers, red cabbage, and white, purple, or striped eggplant), and containers full of herbs. The result is a garden that's as tasty as it is ornamental.

This neat flagstone walk is flanked by large, sheltering trees. The impatiens, azaleas, and ferns nestling in their shade make the approach to the house a delightful walk in the woods.

walk with lively plants that look better and take less care than grass does. Add hardscape features, such as paths, lighting, raised beds, steps, and terraces, to showcase the plants. Use traditional annual and perennial flowers, plus bulbs and a small ornamental tree or two if there's enough space. Plant ornamental grasses or evergreen and flowering vines. Hang baskets of flowers from the lamppost or porch. If the area has the best sun, put the rose garden or the vegetable garden there.

This new walkway defines a perfect area for planting ornamental plants that like sun. The color and texture of the bright flowers draw visitors' eyes away from the newness of the walk.

Successful entryways reflect the style of the home. This geometric walkway and the linear rows of small shrubs alongside it echo the clean lines and straight edges of this contemporary house.

Here, the approach to a traditional home is lined with period plantings, including hostas, ivy, and impatiens. Welcoming ferns in hanging baskets soften the architectural lines of the porch.

suit the planting to the site

The most attractive entry gardens blend best with the style and scale of the home. And those that also take into account the conditions that exist on the site are bound to be the most successful. Plants look best and are healthiest when they're happy—free from stress and the factors that cause it. Choose plants that will be happy in the soil and in the light around the entrance to your home. Consider the exposure. The area around a south-facing front door will get heated up by the harsh sun during the summer, and that heat will be intensified by reflections from nearby paving. Choose plants that like sun and don't need constant watering. Plant a small tree or two to create some shade for plants as well as visitors. Consider your soil, too. If it's clay or sand, choose plants that can cope with these difficult soils. It's much easier to change the plant than to change the soil.

outdoor lighting

Today, lighting the yard is much more than turning on the outdoor light so visitors can see their way to the door at night. While these lights are still important for safety and security, they're only part of the story. Thanks to technology, most families can afford to buy low-voltage landscape lighting. It extends outdoor living on the deck or patio well into the night and makes plants glow dramatically after sundown. On winter nights, this system marks the walkways and highlights the beautiful landscape. Low-voltage outdoor lighting is powered by regular 115-volt household current, but it's channeled through a transformer that reduces it to 12 volts—so weak it won't shock you even if you

light sensitivity

Some trees are sensitive to night lighting, especially bright streetlights. If lights are on every night, all night, they may disrupt the growth cycle of basswood, birch, black locust, catalpa, cottonwood, dogwood, elm, goldenrain tree, hemlock, honeylocust, maple, redbud, silverbell, sumac, sycamore, and zelkova.

safety lighting

Low-voltage accent lights along the walk help augment the front-door light. And during rainstorms, the low-placed fixtures highlight puddles and slippery spots to improve the safety of family and guests.

These low-voltage accent lights reveal the uneven texture in this paving at night. The cheery yellow marigolds brighten the walk during the day and reflect the lights' glow after dark.

Low-voltage post lights do a good job of illuminating potential hazards, such as high curbs, changes in grade, and steps. This light keeps nighttime walkers from running into the corner of a raised garden bed. Note that the fixture is placed inside, rather than outside, the bed to avoid lawn mower or weeder damage.

Rectangular deck lights recessed snugly between the railing posts in this installation. You could move the mounting point lower to direct the light closer to the railing, or place it at the top to spread the light farther out onto the decking. A small light on the end post calls attention to the transition to steps.

touch the bare wires. Also, you don't need to bury the wires that connect the light fixtures. Just hide them under some mulch or string them along a railing or fence. They're easy to install, and a set of six lights costs only pennies a day to operate, even if you use them 12 hours at a stretch. Design the

Deck lighting casts light downward onto stairs to ensure safe passage at night. You can easily install the fixtures by stapling their cables onto the wooden risers or along the base of the railing.

These deck lights clearly indicate the change in height from one railing to the next and signal a corner and grade change.

two types of lighting

Downlighting from capped fixtures, called tiered or mushroom lights, casts a soft glow. It lights the walk for safety and accents the nearby groundcover. Because it's directed downward from a low position, the light doesn't dissipate the darkness enough to compromise night vision.

Most uplighting is for effect. Strategically placed flood or spotlights illuminate special features of the landscape such as a specimen shade tree or statue. The resulting shadows make their own contribution to the nighttime scene. Use uplighting sparingly to avoid creating distractions.

outdoor lighting

placement of your landscape lighting fixtures with three thoughts in mind—security, safety, and beauty. To increase security and safety around your property, use unobtrusive fixtures that direct their light downward along walks and steps. The lights cast a glow that defines a walkway or driveway and reveals any potential hazards such as surface roots, planted containers, fallen branches, children's toys, or patches of ice or gravel. Position floodlights to illuminate dark areas in groves of trees or among shrubs, where an intruder might hide. Some sets include motion-detector lights with infrared sensors. Use these to light the driveway and property boundaries. They turn on automatically when anyone approaches the house on foot or by car after dark. To enhance the

siting electrical outlets

If you plan to set up low-voltage lights in several areas of the yard, install outdoor electrical outlets on each side of the house. This arrangement will give you more flexibility and save you money on cable. You'll need a transformer for each outlet.

decorative lighting

Once you have the low-voltage equipment, you can personalize or modify the lights. A California gardener shows off his seashell collection by mounting them on stakes with low-voltage lights.

Illuminating the garden with electric lights doesn't have a long history. In fact, the first garden to be lighted at night was in East Hampton, New York in 1916. Old fixtures are highly collectible.

This oversized streetlamp uses a conventional light bulb, but it's a real eye-catcher, nevertheless. It's on a pedestal, surrounded by cannas.

Flower-shaped fixtures are certainly appropriate to downlight a garden path at night. During the day, they nod unobtrusively above their plant companions.

beauty of your yard after dark, place fixtures as if you were painting with light. Experiment with post lights, accent lights, and floodlights. Create a mood by carefully locating fixtures around planted beds, under vines and trees, and in or near a water feature. Showcase special plants, dramatize bark and foliage texture, and create exotic shadows. Because low-voltage lights accent the features of the subject they are lighting, rather than draw attention to themselves, most are made of black polymer plastic. Exceptions are higher-end Chinese lanterns and other stylized or antique fixtures that are ornamental day and night.

Although most lights used for safety and security are unobtrusive, others, such as this mission-style lantern, add a decorative touch during the day and complement the style and flavor of the garden.

Fish lights cleverly extend the effects of low-voltage lighting to water-garden areas. Special fixtures can set all kinds of moods, create drama or mystery, encourage reflection, or just introduce whimsy.

Lanterns are naturals for garden light fixtures. They're sturdy and weatherproof, and you can mount them easily on posts, fences, and railings.

seat yourself

Lighting along a garden path conducts you safely through it at night. However, fixtures that accent plants, water, and ornaments—and make pale flowers glow luminously—encourage you to stay and enjoy the mood. Be sure to include a comfortable seat so you can pause to enjoy the special experience that is a garden after dark. Lighting reveals the magnificent moths visiting moonflowers and yucca at night. Its reflection on water and the shadows it casts on walls and walks change the entire character of the garden.

outdoor lighting

Depending on their design, low-voltage fixtures emit light in slightly different ways. You can configure them to produce any of these three effects: downlighting, uplighting, and sidelighting. *Downlighting* imitates nature, illuminating items from above. Flood or spotlights mounted high in trees, on posts, or under roof eaves cast light downward—as the moon would—to create a pale glow in the garden or on the lawn or pool. *Uplighting* creates a more dramatic effect. The same flood or spotlights positioned on the ground—but aimed upward—can give gnarled tree branches, statuary, and special architectural features a stark relief. *Sidelighting* emphasizes details. Because the light is softer, it doesn't cast such harsh shadows. Set lights on two or more sides of the feature you want to light

lighting tips

A little lighting goes a long way. That's the principle behind the two major rules of landscape lighting: (1) Don't overdo the lighting in your yard. The result will be confusing and garish. (2) Take pains to ensure that your lighting doesn't disturb your neighbors. Make sure it doesn't shine into nearby windows or eliminate darkness that neighbors prefer.

decorative lighting

Have some fun with your landscape lighting. Use accent fixtures as features in and of themselves. Deliberately overdo small areas for effect. Colored panes increase the options for unconventional decor.

Globe lights are versatile. Mounted them overhead, they do an excellent job of lighting a walk for the safety of those using it after dark. And when you use them individually as accent lights in areas throughout your property, their full-moon shape and soft glow create a mood of mystery and wonderment, .

Fixtures that downlight have covers over the bulb that simultaneously direct the light toward the ground and prevent it from escaping upward to cause glare in people's eyes. In this installation, form follows function as the drooping petals of this decorative flower-light fixture cast their glow onto the plants and the path below.

The manufacturer of these wall blocks/pavers produces matching blocks with low-voltage lighting embedded within them to produce a subtle glow.

so their beams merge as they pass over the object for a three-dimensional effect. A fourth term called *grazing* refers to a procedure you can use with the three types of lighting effects. As the name implies, you aim a fixture so its beam of light just skims the subject. For example, highlight the surface textures of tree bark or rough stucco by stretching the light all across the surface to make it glow. Before installing a set of lights, connect them and lay them out on the ground. Then try them after dark to find out whether they create the effect you want.

Underwater lights—encased in waterproof mounts and professionally installed—add a special dimension to a water garden or pool. This installation accents the waterfall for nighttime visitors.

Sparkle lights strung on trees, deck railings, and other supports immediately cheer up a nocturnal scene. Most familiar at Christmastime, they bring their same fairyland beauty to a summer landscape.

These portable novelty flower lights are powered by batteries in their hollow plastic stems. Just twist the blossom to light the bulb in the center.

You can create your own decorative fixtures in a variety of styles from recycled objects. These are made from an upside-down can and a shell.

getting started

climate: understanding

Plants grow most successfully when they are adapted to the climate where they are planted. Based on measurements of the lowest recorded temperatures across the country, the United States Department of Agriculture has designated a series of geographic climate zones. They are numbered 1 to 11, coldest to warmest. When you shop for perennials, shrubs, or trees, check the plant tags to determine whether they can tolerate winter in your zone. The tags usually indicate a cold-hardiness range by listing two numbers. If there's only one number, it identifies the coldest area where the plant will survive winter.

Local garden centers and nurseries should carry those plants that are suited to the local climate. Your property has microclimates—small pockets where prevailing temperatures vary—often within a few feet of each other. Near the house, which offers shelter and radiates heat, conditions are warmer—by as much as one zone—than slopes that experience harsh wind and sun. Be aware of these variations when siting your plants.

USDA hardiness zone map

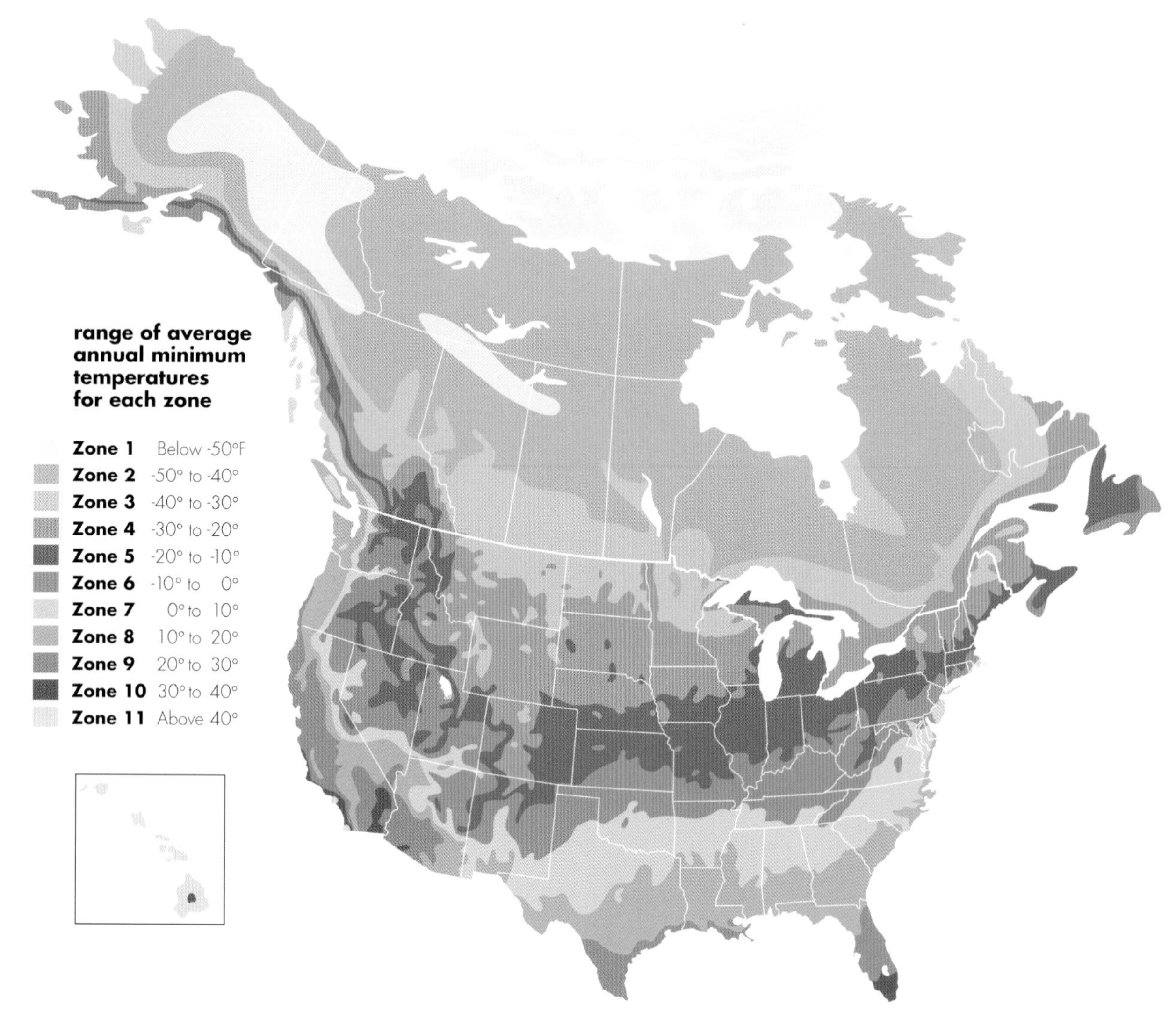

your zone

spring frost dates

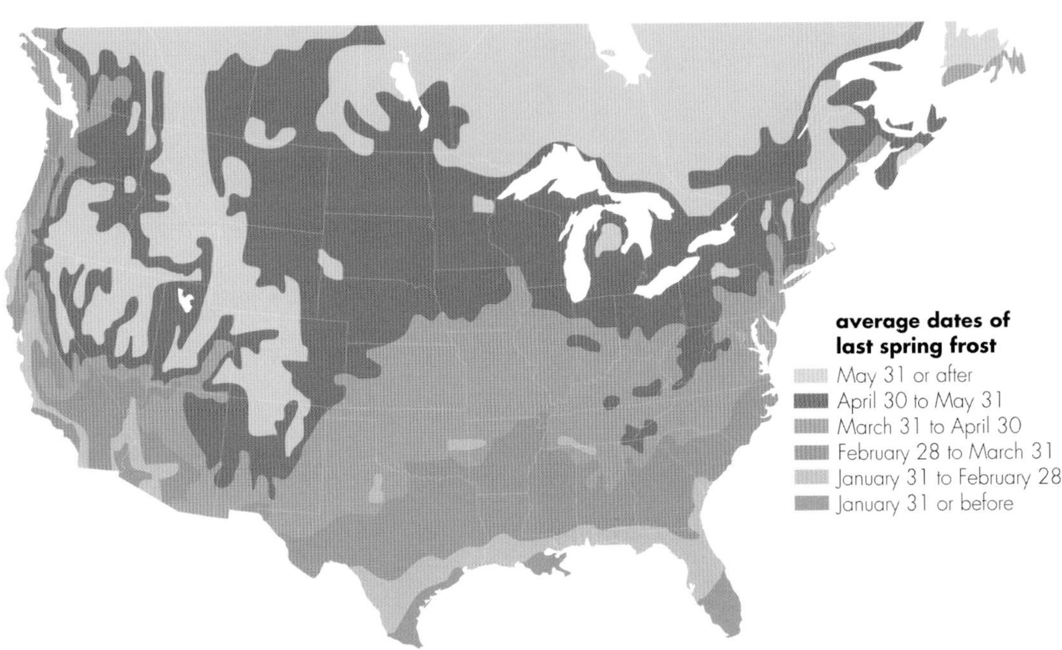

autumn frost dates

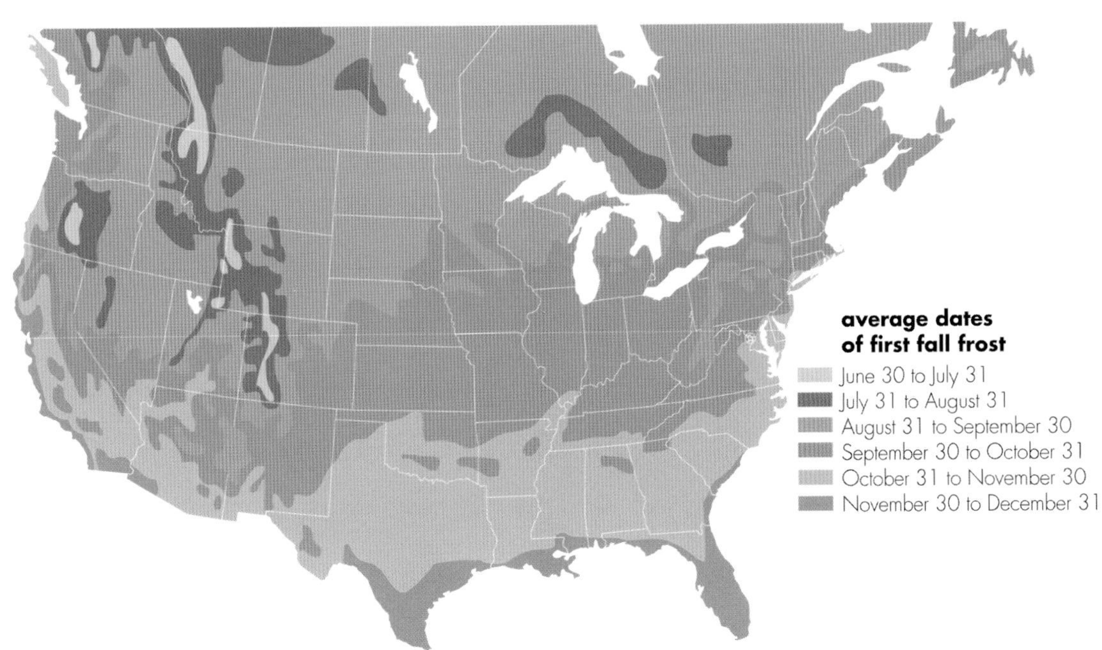

how to read a plant tag

Plant tags are full of information to help you make the best choice at your garden center or nursery. Take the time to examine them and learn about the specific requirements of the plants they accompany. By means of symbols and pictures, growers pack as many facts and details as possible onto the small plastic tag—to help you successfully grow and nurture your plants.

The front of a tag usually lists the common and scientific names and summarizes key information about it. An accompanying closeup color photo usually shows the plant's flowers and foliage as they appear at maturity. The photo might show the entire plant in a garden setting to help you

appearance at maturity
The color photo shows you how the plant will look when it's full-grown. This is important because the best time to buy plants is when they are young—often before flowers are visible.

lighting preferences
Look for a symbol to indicate the type of light the plant requires. This one means full sun. Other symbols are used to indicate partial shade and shade.

special details
Check the description of the plant's characteristics, foliage, and the type of soil and climate it prefers. Special qualities, such as drought tolerance, may be mentioned.

Full sun | 10' Tall 5' Wide | Easy to grow | Low maintenance

- Attractive and colorful evergreen shrub
- Showy leaves with golden margins
- Tolerant of high heat and unfavorable soil conditions
- Nice foundation or mass planting

5 GAL.
GLEAF

plant names
Labels provide a plant's common and botanical (in Latin) names. The common name can vary from region to region, check the botanical name to be sure of the plant's true identity.

size at maturity
Note the plant's expected height and width (or spread) at maturity. These details will help you avoid the need to prune it constantly or to move the plant because it's too large for its space.

expertise required
Some plants are more difficult to grow than others. Check the label for an icon that indicates that the plant is appropriate to your gardening skill and interest level.

judge its relative size and potential use in your yard. Symbols on the tag give size information, as well as sun, soil, and water requirements. And you might find desirable features, listed as bulleted phrases. The reverse side of the tag usually provides specific details about how to transplant and care for the plant—information that's important to the survival of perennials, trees, and shrubs. The tags that accompany plants you buy will be a valuable reference over many seasons as the plants grow and bloom. Save, date, and store the tags somewhere handy.

cold-hardiness range
Perennial plants, trees, and shrubs vary in their ability to withstand winter weather. Check the label for their geographical cold-hardiness range, indicated by zone numbers.

planting instructions
Because plants often have specific planting needs, read and follow the step-by-step planting instructions. For instance, various bulbs need to be planted at specific soil depths.

COLD HARDINESS

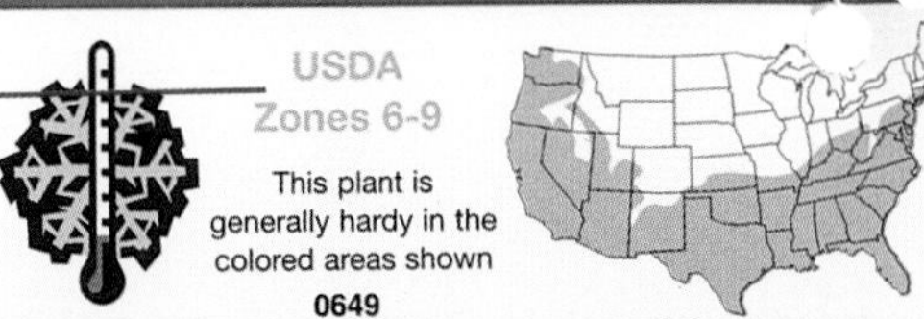

USDA Zones 6-9

This plant is generally hardy in the colored areas shown

0649

PLANTING GUIDE

Plant in full sun in moist, well-drained, fertile soil. A 2-4" layer of mulch is beneficial.

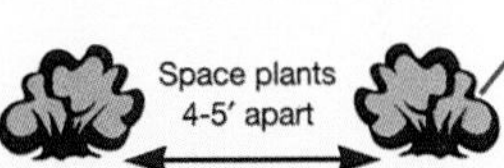

1. Dig hole slightly larger than plant's root mass or pot size.
2. Backfill hole with a finely crumbled mound of freshly dug soil. To remove plant, tap pot edge on a hard surface, then ease plant out of pot. If root mass is tightly tangled, loosen exposed surface with fingers or a sharp knife.
3. Place root mass on top of backfilled soil so that it is high enough to place plant's main stem at its original soil depth. Backfill with remaining soil. Tamp soil gently.
4. Water deeply immediately. Apply a root-stimulator solution according to package directions.
5. Mulch around plant leaving breathing space between mulch and plant base.

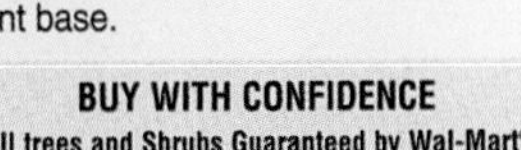

BUY WITH CONFIDENCE
All trees and Shrubs Guaranteed by Wal-Mart®

CARE AND MAINTENANCE

Water in the morning with a hose or drip system that saturates the area around the drip line. Water when the soil is dry 3–4" deep.

Prune before new growth begins in spring or in late fall.

Apply fertilizer in early spring just before new growth begins.

proper spacing
Spacing information is very helpful when you make your buying decisions—especially for plants you intend as groundcovers or hedges.

other helpful products
Some tags suggest products that reduce plant stress during transplanting and afterward. A few examples are water-saving crystals, kelp or seaweed tonics, and mycorrhiza products.

care advice
Plant tags often offer guidance on care of the plant after you've planted it. Proper watering, fertilizing, and pruning are critical to its vigor and beauty.

assessing the soil

The relative acidity or alkalinity of the soil—its chemical environment—affects the availability of the nitrogen, phosphorus, and potassium for the plants. And the plants' ability to take full advantage of the nutrients in the soil depends on how well their chemical environment suits them. Some plants, such as azalea and holly, need soil that's on the acidic side. Others need the soil to be sweeter—more alkaline. The soil's degree of acidity or alkalinity is referred to as its pH. Soil pH is expressed on a scale of 1.0 (acid) to 14.0 (alkaline), with pH 7.0 being neutral. In certain regions of the country, soils are usually more acid or more alkaline. To a great extent, this affects the

soil pH testing

YOU WILL NEED

- pH test kit
- trowel
- soil

1 Fill tube from a pH test kit with soil taken 3 to 4 inches below the soil surface in the test area. Don't touch the soil with your hands. Remove grass, stone, and debris, then crumble the soil finely.

2 Add indicator fluid from the test kit to the soil sample and shake it to mix well. Then let the entire mixture settle. Allow the color to develop for about one minute before you take a reading.

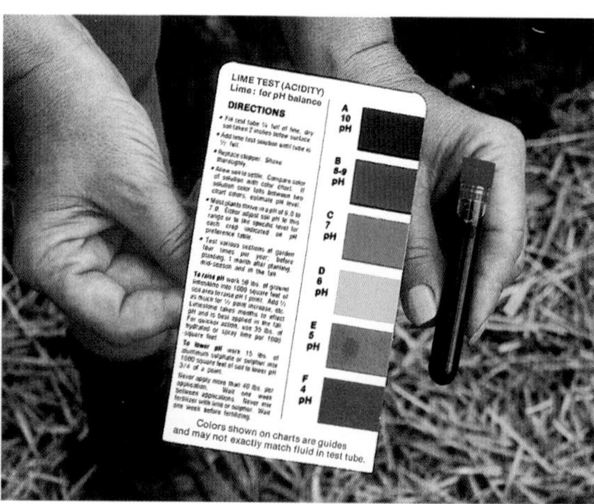

3 Complete the soil test by comparing the color of the solution in the tube with the color chart on the product packaging.

pH preferences of plants

alkaline soil

- Baby's breath
- Black locust
- Cactus
- Clematis
- Lilac
- Onion
- Peony

acid soil

- Blueberry
- Camellia
- Holly
- Hydrangea
- Rhododendron

neutral soil

- Lawn grass

choice of plants suitable for a particular area. For the lowest maintenance, choose plants that prefer a soil pH in the range that prevails in your area.

Sometimes conditions cause changes in soil pH. A soil test—done by you, a local nursery, or your county Cooperative Extension Service—will alert you to pH problems. You may have to adjust the soil pH slightly to accommodate certain plants. For instance, most lawn grasses prefer mildly acidic to neutral soil. In areas where more acidic soil is the norm, homeowners routinely sweeten the soil by spreading granular or dolomitic lime on it.

fertile soil

Fertile soil has earthworms, which thrive in the organic matter. Their presence indicates soil that also supports microorganisms that process soil nutrients. Earthworm castings add to soil fertility.

Good-grade loam has an ideal texture. It's rich and crumbly and has organic matter, which helps it retain moisture and drain well.

is a pH test necessary?

As useful as it is, a pH test isn't always necessary. The pH needs of most garden plants tend to fall into the mildly to moderately acid range. Because moderately acid soil predominates over large areas of North America, soil pH readings aren't necessary for selecting landscape plants. Trees, shrubs, and perennial plants that are native to an area are already adapted to the prevailing pH. This is one reason why native plants are so highly regarded. Throughout the country, local nurseries and garden centers carry plants that are appropriate to the soil conditions in their region. You also can find out which plants thrive in your area by noting successful gardens in the neighborhood.

There are times when being able to measure the soil's pH is helpful, such as when moving to a new property where there are few existing plants or when considering whether to grow a certain crop in the vegetable garden. Also, nearby construction may alter soil pH. Soil that you'd expect to be on the acid side might suddenly turn alkaline because of lime that leaches from masonry mortar. This happens in established beds along walls and foundations. Plants are the best indicator of pH consistency in soil. As long as they're healthy, the soil is fine. A sudden change in an established plant—for example, hydrangea flowers blooming pink instead of blue—signals pH problems. Sometimes plant leaves turn pale, their dark green veins etched in visible detail. This condition—chlorosis—indicates that the plants aren't getting enough iron, most likely because their soil is not acid enough. In these cases, testing the pH confirms that the problems are caused by altered soil acidity.

digging a garden bed

Planning your approach ahead of time helps ensure that your new bed will be successful. There are several issues to consider before you actually put shovel to soil. Location is critical. Beds intended to display colorful flowers must receive at least 6 to 8 hours of sun a day. As a result, this type of bed usually replaces lawn, which means you'll have to remove grass or sod first. Beds anchored by large trees or shrubs receive much less light and require shade-loving plants. Dig here with great care to avoid damaging the many roots in the top 12 inches of soil. Another issue is size. Even under the best circumstances, gardens are arduous to dig. Opt for a manageable project. The initial

YOU WILL NEED

- stakes
- string
- garden spade
- organic matter, such as compost, well-rotted manure, or leaf mold
- shovel
- granular fertilizer
- steel (garden) rake

1 Lay out the shape of the garden bed with stakes and string to establish a pleasing shape and size. Slide a spade under the existing lawn to free it from the soil.

2 Add organic matter to the exposed soil to improve its texture, drainage, and moisture retention. Dig it into the top 10 inches. This is a good time to add granular, slow-acting fertilizer, too.

3 Rake the soil smooth, removing small stones and breaking up lumps of soil. Make the bed as level as possible to ensure even distribution of rainwater.

designing the bed

Garden beds may be any shape or size. They are usually borders, backed by a fence, wall, walkway, or building foundation. These beds are viewed from the front, so locate the tallest plants near the back, where they won't block the view of smaller ones. Plants of medium height go in the middle, and the shortest ones are at the front. Island beds generally sit in the middle of an expanse of lawn, so you and everyone else can view them from all sides. Place the tallest plants at the center of an island bed. Put medium ones around them, and reserve the shortest for the perimeter of the bed.

width of a border bed might be double your arm's reach. Island beds can be twice that, because they're reachable from two sides. Remember that it's relatively easy to enlarge a bed later. Keep the bed in proportion to its surroundings. A bed along a wall should not be wider than the wall is tall. A bed under one or more trees or shrubs should be at least as wide as the height of the trees. Finally, consider the soil. Dig in organic matter to correct compaction and improve texture and fertility. In areas where clay soil can't easily be improved, raised beds can ensure good drainage.

weather

The cooler weather in fall is the best time to dig a new bed. It's also the best season to plant many perennials, shrubs, and trees. They have several months to establish strong roots before showtime in spring. After you dig and plant the bed, cover the exposed soil with a protective layer of chopped leaves or other mulch.

adding organic matter

The key to growing healthy, vital plants is healthy, vital soil. Yet because it's easy for us to take soil for granted, it's also easy to forget how fundamentally important it is. The result: Soils in most residential landscapes are neglected and in poor condition. An important lesson in gardening and yard care is that we must restore and maintain soil so it can provide essential air, moisture, and nutrition to lawns and gardens, trees, and shrubs. Almost half the volume of healthy soil is mineral particles from pulverized rock and flecks of organic material. The other half is equal amounts of air spaces and moisture between these particles. Most of the organic material is generally concentrated in the top 8 to 12 inches, especially in the top 3 inches. That's where the topsoil is dark and spongy and filled with teeming populations of organisms processing nutrients for plant roots and neutralizing potentially problematic fungal spores, bacteria, and viruses. Poor soil lacks rich topsoil. Builders often remove it from a site when they begin construction, then fail to replace it

YOU WILL NEED

- garden gloves
- well-rotted (aged) manure, leaf mold, peat moss, or other organic matter
- spading fork

1 Composted animal manure is a good source of organic material that you can add to soil. It supplies major nutrients, lively microorganisms, and helpful enzymes. Buy it in bags at garden centers.

2 Canadian sphagnum peat moss absorbs and holds moisture extremely well. Mildly acid, it has coarse organic fibers that condition all types of soil and improve its texture.

soil cover-up

Protect healthy soil from being compacted and depleted of organic material by covering it where it's exposed to weather. Spread an organic mulch or plant a groundcover on all bare soil to deflect heat, harsh sun, heavy rains, and weed seeds.

adequately when they finish the job. And their heavy equipment, followed by years of foot traffic and kids' play, compacts the remaining soil, forcing most of the air out of it. So, moisture can't penetrate it as well, the soil lacks life and fertility, and the only plants that can cope in it are weeds. Organic material can be your biggest problem solver. When you dig it into compacted soil, the fibrous material loosens the soil's texture and restores spaces to hold air and moisture. It also creates an environment that supports living organisms, from the tiniest microbe to the largest earthworm. As they eat and reproduce, they spur decomposition of the carbon and nitrogen in the organic material and break down rock particles into minerals. Add organic matter to the soil routinely to sustain this activity and build healthy topsoil that's capable of nurturing and protecting plants.

replenishing the soil

Plan to replenish the soil with organic matter every year. It constantly breaks down—especially quickly in hot regions—due to the activity of lively organisms. In established perennial beds where plants generally stay put, mulch between them with compost or leaf mold. Dig some into the soil every chance you get, particularly when you divide and transplant and when you plant annuals among the perennials.

3 Use a spading fork to dig organic matter into the soil. Distribute the matter throughout the entire area down to a level of 8 to 10 inches, where most of the plant roots grow.

amending the soil

Amending the soil means adding materials to improve its fertility, texture, or moisture-holding capacity. The prescription for deficient soil is usually a generous amount of organic material. However, some organic materials are more suitable for certain soil problems than others. Although all are derived from living sources—composed mainly of carbon and nitrogen—they vary in their specific contributions to soil. Some are more effective with sandy rather than clay soil. Others are better at providing nutrients to soil but only marginally improve its texture. Organic matter of any kind improves soil. Materials that are free and readily available obviously are always the most desirable. That's why compost is so touted: It's free and easy to make in your own backyard, no matter how large or small it is (see pages 70 through 73). Choose specific amendments to target particular problems. For instance, if the soil lacks humus—necessary to support microbial life and earthworms—dig in generous amounts of leaf mold. If the soil is

what amendments do for the soil

	adds volume	improves soil texture	aerates	improves drainage	holds water
ORGANIC					
Canadian sphagnum peat moss	■	■	■		■
commercial potting mix	■	■	■	■	■
compost	■	■	■	■	■
ground bark or sawdust	■	■	■		
humus	■	■	■	■	■
leaf mold	■	■	■	■	■
manure	■	■		■	
mushroom soil	■	■	■	■	■
seaweed (kelp)		■		■	
INORGANIC					
gypsum		■	■		
sand (builder's)			■	■	
vermiculite			■	■	■
water-absorbing polymer crystals (hydrogels)	■				■

compacted, is thin and sandy, or not acidic enough, dig Canadian sphagnum peat moss into the soil. It holds moisture and is slightly acidic. Although there has been a lot of talk over the past decade about the ecological implications of using peat moss in the garden, the bottom line is that the harvesting of peat in Canada does not impact the environment. The peat bogs are vast and the amount harvested is minimal—taken only from the top layer. At the same time as the harvest, the bog is reseeded. The greater issue is the transportation of the resource to various parts of the country. Look for local amendments that you can add to the soil. Inorganic amendments are derived from minerals or other nonliving materials. They, too, play a role in improving soil by supplying basic nutrients and increasing the soil's moisture and air-holding capacity.

adds nutrients	special considerations
	Acidifies soil.
■	"Soil-less" mixes have no nutrients.
■	May have antifungal properties.
	Don't use sawdust from pressure-treated wood.
■	Helps feed any soil.
■	The smaller the pieces, the faster the decomposition.
■	Choose aged manure to avoid burning the plants.
	Use only on lawns and ornamentals in case pesticide residues are present.
■	Wash off salt; don't use in clay soil.
■	Conditions clay soil.
	Use coarsest sand possible.
	Use with sandy or silty soil.
	Ideal for containers.

feed the soil

Nourish the soil with organic matter whenever the soil isn't frozen. Organic matter offers immediate benefits. Fall is a particularly good time to add both organic and inorganic amendments. Top-dress the lawn with topsoil, compost, or chopped leaves from a mulching mower. Dig organic material into beds, and mulch around shrubs and trees.

composting

When you make compost, you simply encourage the same decomposition process that takes place automatically in nature. Making compost is a very good way to recycle your yard debris and improve your soil. All you need is yard and garden waste—a collection of fallen leaves, weeds, prunings, or other healthy yard waste. Do not put plants that are diseased or infested with pests into the compost pile; throw them in the trash instead. In the presence of air and moisture, the teeming populations of microscopic fungi, bacteria, and other organisms that live on plant surfaces break down these collected materials. As they feed and reproduce in an elaborate food chain, they

building the pile

YOU WILL NEED

- cart or wheelbarrow
- composting fork
- brown/dry organic material (carbon)
- green organic material (nitrogen)
- water
- lime, fertilizer, topsoil, compost activator (optional)
- compost thermometer (optional)

1 Mix yard and kitchen waste (never meat) in a heap that is about 3 feet high, wide, and deep. The smaller the pieces of waste are, the faster the microbial activity will decompose them.

2 Be sure there's much more brown (carbon-based) than green (nitrogen-based) material to spur the decomposition process. Lime, fertilizer, topsoil, and activators are optional additives.

3 If the materials aren't already moist, dampen them before you build the pile. There's no need to cover the pile—it won't smell. And rain is good for it.

4 Give the microbes new food and oxygen by turning the pile when the temperature drops. Compost is ready when it's dark and crumbly.

gradually transform organic waste into dark, crumbly, black matter with a nearly neutral pH—"black gold" to gardeners. Decide how quickly you want compost. A passive system is slower but easier than an active system. If you are in no hurry to harvest compost, pile yard wastes in a heap in a back part of your property as they accumulate over the months. After a year, dig underneath the pile to harvest a few bushels of compost. This passive method takes very little effort. Keep adding to the pile and harvesting over time. Enclose the pile if it's an eyesore.

Add 2 inches of compost on a garden bed—especially a new one. It's key to strong, healthy plants. Mix the compost into the soil with a garden fork.

You rotate these drum-type bins to turn the pile and provide more air to fuel decomposition. Turn the drum opening downward to empty the compost into a garden cart placed under it.

Finished compost is called black gold; it's dark and rich, lightweight and crumbly, and has a pleasant, woodsy smell. A small twig is the only clue to its origin.

don't compost wood

Separate sticks, twigs, pinecones, and other thick, woody items from the other raw materials before you build a compost pile. Because wood takes a long time to decompose, these items will cause lumps in the finished compost. An alternative is to chop or chip them into smaller pieces, then toss them in with the other materials.

composting

On the other hand, if your goal is to make as much compost as possible as fast as you can, you will want to take an active approach to composting. In an active system—which results in finished compost much faster but is more physically demanding and takes more of your effort—you accelerate the microbial action. Shred, cut, or chop moist materials into small pieces, build the pile all at once, and turn it periodically. Many composters recommend adding equal parts of brown (dried, dead plant material, such as leaves) and green (including kitchen scraps (vegetables only—no oil, meat, fat, fish, or poultry), crushed eggshells, coffee grounds (and the paper filters), tea bags (remove the staple) and any healthy garden prunings and yard waste. Use grass clippings

making leaf mold

If the yard debris on your property consists mostly of leaves, you can make leaf mold, which is similar to compost. Collect the leaves in a pile, moisten them, and wait for them to decompose. If you shred them or go over them with a mulching mower first, they will break down more quickly.

kinds of compost containers

Enclose unsightly passive piles that take years to decompose. Use wattle fencing, wire circles, or other materials that allow airflow.

A pile of green and brown organic waste decomposes gradually if left undisturbed. Add fresh waste to the top; harvest compost from the bottom.

A triple bin is most convenient for a more active composting system. Turn the pile into the next bin when it reaches peak internal heat.

sparingly—less than 1-inch deep. Lightly moisten the pile and let it cook. Using a compost thermometer, check for heat in the core; that indicates strong microbial activity. When the pile cools somewhat, turn it to add air and reinvigorate the microbes. Protect the pile from heavy rains, and add composting worms (red wigglers available at bait shops) to speed the breakdown. Expect compost in six to 10 weeks. Use compost to improve the texture and moisture-holding capacity of the soil on your property. It loosens heavy clay and bulks up sandy soil. And it revitalizes microbes in the soil.

Use a triple-bin arrangement if you want to produce quantities of compost on a continuing basis. Removable front slats help you turn one pile into the next bin. Fill the first with new material.

An easy way to fence in your compost pile—while keeping it open so air and rain can get to it—is with turkey wire or chicken mesh framed in wood.

composting dos and don'ts

- Do clip, shred, or chop materials into smaller, roughly uniform-sized pieces for faster decomposition.
- Do put coarser materials—such as sticks, corncobs, and pinecones—in a pile of their own for more even decomposition.
- Do use peanut hulls, straw, shredded paper, and sawdust (from non-treated wood).
- Do make sure that brown (dry) materials are in far greater proportion than green (moist) materials to prevent your pile from smelling.
- Do take advantage of local materials beyond the yard, such as farm-animal bedding, wood chips, fruit and vegetable trimmings, nut hulls, grape skins, and seaweed.
- Don't put meat or meat products, salad dressings, butter, or other fats in the pile.
- Don't include diseased plants or weeds with seeds.
- Don't include human feces or used kitty litter.

making leaf mold

Leaves are a valuable natural resource. Rather than regard them as a nuisance, be grateful that the trees on your property drop a new supply of them every fall. It takes very little effort on your part to recycle them into a wonderful soil conditioner—leaf mold—for the yard and garden. Unlike compost, leaf mold is only partially decomposed, leaving bits and pieces of the leaves visible in the finished product. And, again unlike compost, leaf mold is derived only from leaves. You can make leaf mold the same way nature creates it on the forest floor. Just pile up moist leaves and wait for them to decompose. If you want to speed up the process, you can shred the leaves into smaller pieces before piling them up. If you want to improve its appearance, you can enclose the pile with snow fencing, chicken wire, or something similar. Make sure the container allows air to circulate, because oxygen fuels the decomposition process. Over the winter, the pile will shrink as decay reduces the volume of leaves—a sign that the process is well under way.

YOU WILL NEED

- turkey wire or hardware cloth
- tall stakes (optional)
- sledge hammer (optional)
- leaf rake
- mulching mower
- compost fork
- wheelbarrow or garden cart

1 Set up a wire cylinder or similar container to hold the accumulated leaves you'll be collecting. (It will help keep the wind from blowing the leaves around.) If necessary, add stakes for stability.

2 Rake up leaves as soon as possible after they fall. The job will be easier if you gather small amounts frequently, rather than rake a large accumulation all at once. It also prevents matting and lawn damage.

Leaf mold helps build healthy soil in several ways. When mixed into poor soil, it improves its texture. The coarse organic material creates air spaces in the soil, making it easier for roots to penetrate. Leaf mold also improves the soil's ability to absorb moisture and keep it available longer for plant roots. As the leaves continue to decompose, they improve the soil's fertility by creating a population of active microbes. Leaves are a favorite food of earthworms, which convert the leaves into nutrient-rich castings that are distributed throughout the soil. Spread leaf mold on top of bare soil as an organic mulch. It keeps the soil from being compacted by hard rains and drying sunshine. And it helps the soil retain moisture by decreasing evaporation, absorbing rain, and reducing wasteful runoff. Leaf mold gradually breaks down in the heat of summer, so renew the mulch layer whenever it becomes thin.

discouraging weeds

Leaf mold mulch effectively discourages weeds if you remove existing weeds from the area first. Spread a thick layer of leaf mold to block the sun from seeds that remain in the soil. The layer can be thinner in shaded areas where weeds are less bothersome. And it should be no deeper than 3 or 4 inches over tree roots.

3 The smaller the pieces of organic material, the faster they decompose. Shred leaves by mowing the lawn where they lie with a mulching mower, then raking. Or rake them into a pile and mow over it.

4 Load the shredded leaves into the cylinder. (Damp leaves will decompose faster.) Don't compress the leaves in the container; good airflow promotes decomposition.

5 When spring comes around, the leaves in the center of the pile will be fairly decomposed and those on the outside less so. When you transfer the leaves to a wheelbarrow or cart, be sure to mix the various layers together before you spread them.

mulching

The best way to protect the bare soil on your property is to mulch it. A layer of organic material several inches thick buffers the soil against compaction from the harsh effects of heavy rain and baking sun and helps the soil retain oxygen so it can support vigorous plant roots. It improves any soil by blending valuable organic material, or humus, into its top layer as the mulch gradually decomposes. In nature, soil is always protected by a covering of organic material. Layers of leaf litter in the woods and blankets of waving grasses on the plains prevent erosion and absorb rainfall, just as your lawn and groundcover beds do. A layer of organic mulch provides similar protection to soil

weather

During the winter, fluctuating temperatures alternately freeze and thaw the soil. This often disturbs plant roots and may heave bulbs or plants out of the soil. A winter mulch does not prevent soil from freezing, but it provides insulation to maintain more even low temperatures.

A good way to recycle fallen leaves is to use them to mulch bare soil all around the yard. Shred or chop them so they don't mat and block water from the soil.

Buckwheat or hulls from pecans, cocoa beans, and other nuts make a uniform, colorful mulch for small garden areas. They are particularly attractive under low, fine-textured plants.

Gravel is an appropriate mulch for arid landscapes and beds with plants that need good drainage, such as rock gardens.

Pine needles provide a handsome, brown covering for the soil. Use them around acid-loving plants such as conifers, rhododendrons, and hollies.

that *isn't* covered by plants. In your landscape, it forms an attractive cover that discourages weeds and masks imperfections. More importantly, it helps conserve water by absorbing rainfall and preventing runoff. Soil covered by a layer of organic mulch stays damp much longer between rains or waterings because the mulch blocks evaporation. Mulch protects nearby plants, too. A good layer of organic mulch between newly planted groundcover plants discourages weeds during the time the plants need to grow larger, knit together, and cover the soil on their own. Trees and shrubs

River rocks used as mulch suggest rocky shorelines or dry riverbeds in landscape settings. On sunny sites, they retain warmth, creating a microclimate around the plants. They also allow air access to the soil. On the minus side, they don't do a very good job of discouraging weeds.

thrive on mulch, too. Circles of organic material under them not only condition the soil and improve its fertility, but they also create a barrier to prevent injury to their trunks and stems from lawn mowers and string trimmers. A layer of organic mulch on the bare soil in your yard also contributes to the general health and vigor of the entire landscape because it shelters many kinds of beneficial organisms. For example, ground spiders and ants nest in rich organic material along the edges of lawns. From there, they prey on pest insect larvae and eggs in the soil under the lawn and garden beds. Avoid spreading mulch too thickly. Anything over

mulching trees and shrubs

A layer of organic mulch over the root zone of newly planted trees and shrubs helps them get off to a good start. Cover the entire area where the soil was disturbed and is bare. This will prevent weeds from sprouting and competing with newly developing plant roots for soil moisture and nutrients. It also helps keep soil moist during the critical early growth period.

Shredded paper makes a suitable mulch for protecting soil and discouraging weeds. If it becomes unsightly when rains wet it down, cover it with a thin layer of leaves or bark nuggets.

Leaf mold (partially decomposed leaves) contributes valuable organic matter to the soil as it continues to decompose (see pages 74– 75). Use it for plants in woodland settings and informal gardens.

Wood chips are long-lasting—and inexpensive, if you can persuade a landscaper to drop them off for free. Allow them to age for a few weeks, then spread them on paths and under trees and woody plants.

Cocoa bean shells offer a fine-textured, uniform covering, plus a wonderful smell—especially after a rain. Their rich brown color contrasts beautifully with turfgrasses and colorful groundcovers.

2 or 3 inches threatens to become a suffocating blanket that blocks air and moisture from the soil. This causes plant roots to gravitate toward the soil surface in search of these essentials. In cases where surface tree roots are a problem, mulch lightly to improve the appearance of the yard, but don't try to bury the roots. Organic mulch inevitably breaks down over time, and the mulch layer becomes thinner. Expect to add to it periodically, usually in the fall, to restore it to a 2- to 3-inch depth.

mulching a tree

1 When you mulch an established tree with grass growing beneath it, put a layer of cardboard over the lawn before spreading the mulch. This will keep the grass from penetrating the mulch.

2 Make the cardboard collar at least 2 or 3 feet wide. Moisten it so it softens and conforms to the contours of the ground and the root flare at the base of the trunk. Then cover it with wood chips.

3 Limit the mulch layer to 2 or 3 inches, so that the tree roots still can get enough air and moisture. Otherwise, the roots will migrate toward the soil surface. Be very careful not to pile mulch against the tree trunk. Unlike root bark, trunk bark can't handle constant moisture and will rot. If you feel so inclined, add a border of bricks, rocks, or other attractive material around the collar.

dividing perennials &

If you divide your perennials and bulbs, you'll keep them looking their best. By *not* doing so, you force them to spread into large clumps and crowd their space. As a result, flowers are smaller, leaves lack good access to light and air, and roots become tangled and massed. Then their overall health declines, because individual plants are less able to absorb nutrition from the soil. This makes them weaker and vulnerable to pests and disease. You can protect them from crowding: Every few years, cut large clumps into smaller pieces for replanting. This also gives you an opportunity to examine the roots and bulbs for rot or insect damage. Often the center of the plant mass grows woody; if this is the case, you can discard it after you cut away the younger, more vital parts of the plant. Division is

dividing and replanting daylilies

YOU WILL NEED

- shovel, spade, or trowel
- sharp knife
- water

1 Divide daylilies by digging and lifting a clump with its root ball. Cut back leaves for easier handling. Shake off excess soil to expose the roots.

2 Use a sharp knife to cut down through the roots and separate a chunk of plant. Be sure it has at least one "fan" of leaves, complete with good roots.

weather

Don't depend on fickle spring rainfall to water replanted divisions adequately. Like any transplant, they need regular moisture while their roots struggle to establish at a new site. Water them well at planting time and every day or two thereafter.

3 Set daylily divisions in the ground at the same depth at which they grew before. Spread the roots in the hole, fill the hole with soil, then water well.

bulbs

the best way to maintain plant health and optimum size for the garden, as well as increase the number of plants. It reliably produces plants that are exact replicas of the parent, and at no cost. A single large hosta or clump of daylilies will yield several small chunks of rooted plants. Place them elsewhere on the property or give them away. A bed of iris or daffodils can become crowded, because the mother bulb develops offshoots, or bulblets. Gently separate the bulblets from the mother bulbs, then replant the mother bulbs at the correct spacing. Now you can move the bulblets to new sites. You may have to wait another year or two for them to mature and produce flowers.

daylily care

The newer reblooming types of daylilies need frequent division. These hybrids are programmed to produce a great flush of blooming stems in spring. Then they send up several new stems and continue to bloom throughout the summer. For the best performance from 'Stella d'Oro', 'Happy Returns', and others, divide them every two to three years. To increase their blooms even more, pinch off dead flowers promptly.

dividing and replanting iris

1 Dig each crowded clump of iris rhizomes, then trim the leaves back to 5 inches. Separate healthy plants with good roots from woody, damaged ones.

2 Set the healthy rhizomes in a shallow trench, roots downward. Cover the roots and half of the rhizome with soil so the other half shows above the soil.

3 Plant small rhizomes about 3 to 4 inches apart in beds. Position them so that their fans of leaves are oriented in the same direction.

dividing perennials & bulbs

Divide most perennials as soon as they begin to show growth above the soil. Because their roots have been dormant all winter and are just starting to grow, they won't experience much shock during the process. Wait to divide spring bulbs until after they bloom and their leaves ripen and die back. Dig and divide plants that need rejuvenation after they bloom. (Read about dividing perennials in fall on pages 84 through 87.) Pay attention to the type of roots the divided plant has and how deep they grow. Make sure that each division from the main plant has sufficient roots to support it. Gently tease divisions apart from the mass, ensuring that

dividing in place

Another way to divide plants is to do it in place. Sometimes the clumps have gotten too large to dig easily out of the ground in order to gain access to the root ball. Ornamental grasses are a good example. Dig down with a sharp spade into the planted clump, cut pie-shaped chunks out of the root ball, and remove them. The main plant is undisturbed. Fill in the hole with soil, and water well.

dividing and replanting daffodils

1 Dig up crowded clumps of daffodils in spring. They are one of the few bulbs you can divide while their leaves are green. Gently tease the tangled roots apart to separate the bulbs.

2 Lay the bulbs on the soil as you want to plant them in the ground. Plant them in natural-looking drifts rather than in soldierly rows. Space bulbs 4 to 6 inches apart.

3 To plant lots of bulbs, use a long trowel especially designed for bulb planting. Insert the trowel 4 to 6 inches deep and rock it forward. Drop the bulb in the hole, pull out the trowel, and tamp down the soil.

each one has at least two buds from which the new growth will sprout. Replant them at exactly the same depth at which they were growing before. Peony buds should be just visible at the soil surface. If you plant them any deeper, the peonies won't bloom.

volunteer seedlings

1 On some plants, such as hellebores, flowers left to fade and set seed will self-sow. To prevent this, you can pinch or cut off spent flowers promptly. Or look at it as a way to get lots of new free plants.

2 Carefully dig up the seedlings and tease apart the roots. Replant them in another suitable area of the garden, or plant them in individual pots and give away to friends or share with other gardeners.

perennials to divide in spring

Always divide plants after they flower. For spring-blooming perennials and bulbs, this usually means early summer to early fall. For summer- and fall-blooming perennials, this usually means spring. After the plants die back in fall, their roots rest in dormancy over the winter. Then in spring the plants begin to send up new shoots. When they have only a few inches of growth, they're easy to handle. The replanted divisions are young and resilient and have plenty of time to recover and become established before it's time to bloom again.

good candidates

- Aster
- Astilbe
- Bee balm
- Black-eyed Susan
- Chrysanthemum
- Coreopsis
- Daylily
- Goldenrod
- Hosta
- Liatris
- Ornamental grass
- Phlox
- Purple coneflower
- Sedum 'Autumn Joy'
- Veronica
- Yarrow

dividing perennials & bulbs

There are at least four good reasons to divide perennial plants. One is to maintain their health and vigor, because overcrowding stresses plants. When crowded, their dense foliage doesn't dry out after morning dew or rainfall. This, in turn, invites fungal disease, which thrives on poor air circulation around the plants. Stressed plants also invite insect infestations, which only add to the problems. As some perennials age, the center of the clump may become woody and unproductive. And the soil around the plant may have been depleted of nutrients from years of inattention. A second reason to divide plants is to maintain their beauty and peak flower production. Aged and overcrowded plants

digging and dividing daylilies

YOU WILL NEED

- daylilies
- shovel
- water
- sharp knife or hatchet
- organic mulch

weather

In many parts of the country, fall is a somewhat rainy season when cool temperatures reduce a plant's need for moisture. However, if rainfall is sparse, be sure to water transplants regularly. Fall-divided plants need consistent water to spur root growth before the soil freezes.

1 Dig up the clump of daylilies to be divided by inserting the shovel deep into the soil around the perimeter to loosen roots and isolate the clump.

2 Force the shovel under the root ball and lever the ball up and down to loosen and position it on the shovel. Then lift the shovel and root ball.

4 Spray the soil off the root ball. Then identify individual plant crowns with one or more "fans" of leaves and lots of roots emerging from the base.

5 Pry or cut apart individual crowns. Roots of older clumps may be so tough and tangled that you'll need to chop them with a hatchet.

have small flowers and sparse, small leaves. They're root-bound so they don't take up nutrients efficiently from the soil. The result is faded flower and foliage color and often stunted stem growth. Third, when you divide and replant, you also control excessive spread. Enthusiastic growers, such as yarrow and artemisia, need dividing every year or two. Finally, by dividing plants, you make more plants. And most perennials, other than those with taproots, can be divided easily. When you cut off rooted sections from the root balls of existing plants, you not only have free new plants, but ones that are

3 Shake or brush the excess soil from the root ball. Don't worry if you break a few roots along the way. Daylilies are tough.

6 Replant the divisions promptly so the roots don't dry out. Plant at the same depth as before and water well. Cover the soil with mulch.

dividing perennials

plant name	when to divide	how often
Artemisia	spring or fall	1–2 years
Astilbe	spring	1–3 years
Baptisia	spring or fall	10 or more
Bee balm	spring or fall	2–3 years
Black-eyed Susan	spring or fall	4–5 years
Boltonia	spring or fall	4–5 years
Chrysanthemum	spring or fall	3–5 years
Coreopsis	spring or fall	1–3 years
Daylily	anytime	4–5 years
Daylily, rebloomer	spring or fall	2–3 years
Epimedium	early spring	6–10 years
Garden phlox	spring	1–3 years
Goldenrod	spring or fall	4–5 years
Hellebore	spring	10 or more
Hosta	spring or fall	10 or more
Hypericum	spring or fall	1–3 years
Lady's mantle	spring or fall	6–10 years
Ornamental grass	spring	3–4 years
Peony	late summer	10 or more
Sedum 'Autumn Joy'	early spring	6–10 years
Veronica, spike	spring or fall	1–3 years
Yarrow	spring or fall	1–2 years

dividing perennials & bulbs

rooted and ready to grow. They're exact replicas of the originals, sharing their desirable characteristics and growth habits. Divide your perennials either in spring or fall when heat or frozen ground isn't a factor. Wait until a plant clump is large, so the loss of chunks of its roots won't undermine its health. If your goal is to obtain more plants, do your dividing in early spring. Because they're just beginning to emerge from dormancy and send up small shoots, the plants won't be shocked much by the process. The roots have been resting all winter and aren't yet required to support major growth. The obvious exceptions are those plants that bloom in spring. Wait to divide bleeding heart, barrenwort, pulmonaria, and others until they've finished

digging and dividing hostas

YOU WILL NEED

- shovel
- trowel, sharp knife, or spade
- compost
- water
- organic mulch

weather

Divide plants late in the day or when the sky is overcast. If rain is expected, replant just before it's due. Protection from the sun will spare them additional stress during the process.

1 Spring is the best time to divide hostas, but you also can do it in fall after they bloom. Dig around and under the clump to loosen the roots.

2 Lift the root ball out of the ground. Use a trowel, sharp knife, or spade to cut between leaf stems and through the roots to separate chunks of plant.

4 Tuck hosta divisions into shady beds around the property or in their own bed. Enrich the soil with compost so it holds moisture and drains well.

5 Plant each division at the same depth as before. Firm the soil over the root zone. In fall, hosta foliage is mature and will soon die back with frost.

blooming. Spring division gives transplants plenty of time to become established. However, if your goal is to improve plant health or control spread, divide in fall—unless the plants are fall bloomers. Cut back their stems and dig them up. If the center of the plant is old and woody, cut rooted sections from healthier outer portions of the clump and discard the spent center part of the root ball. If plant roots are badly matted or have bulged toward the soil surface, make sure each division has roots by teasing them apart and cutting down through the plant crown.

3 Isolate individual plants or small groups of plants. To minimize stress, make sure that each section has some leaves and lots of roots.

6 Water newly planted hosta divisions well. Spread a 2- to 3-inch layer of organic mulch over the soil to insulate it for the winter.

digging and dividing chrysanthemums

1 Hardy mums bloom from late summer to mid-November in many parts of the country. Divide them after they bloom; some late bloomers can be divided in spring. Cut off dried flower stems back to the leaves.

2 You can divide mums in place simply by digging a section out of an existing planting and removing it, then refilling the hole with soil. The alternative, of course, is to dig up the entire clump, then divide it.

3 Shake the soil from the roots, then cut down through the stems and leaves into the woody crown to create separate plants. Be sure each division has plenty of roots.

4 Replant new divisions as soon as possible. Keep them well watered throughout autumn if rainfall is sparse. Mulch them with chopped leaves or other organic matter to insulate the soil.

lawns

selecting grasses

For the best-looking, easiest to maintain lawn, plant varieties of grasses that are well-suited to your climate and the intended use of the lawn. Recent research by seed companies and universities has led to the introduction of many improved varieties of lawn grasses. Some are more resistant to insects and diseases than older varieties, while others are more tolerant of shade, drought, or heavy wear. Check with your local Cooperative Extension Service or local nurseries to find out about varieties adapted to your area. Lawn grasses are classified as either cool season or warm season. Cool-season grasses are generally adapted to northern climates, where they grow vigorously in

Kentucky bluegrass is best suited to full sun in areas with cold winters. In fact, it is one of the most cold-hardy grasses, often used in public parks. It needs regular watering to make it through dry periods. Kentucky bluegrass is prized for its thick dense turf and fine texture. Some of the best of the new varieties include 'America', 'Blacksburg', 'Blue Star', 'Chateau', 'Eclipse', 'Julia', and 'Midnight'.

spring and fall and may turn brown in very hot summers. They are often sold as a blend of several varieties of the same species, such as several varieties of Kentucky bluegrass, or as a mixture of two or more different species such as Kentucky bluegrass and fine fescue. Growing blends or mixtures is a good idea. If one or more of the varieties doesn't grow well or is destroyed by disease, chances are that the others will take over and flourish. The most common cool-season grasses include fine fescue, Kentucky bluegrass, perennial ryegrass, and tall fescue. The new varieties

reading the labels

When you shop for grass seed, be aware of some of the descriptive terms used. Low maintenance means that it will grow with a minimum of watering and feeding. Disease resistant implies a grass that will grow and thrive even where disease-causing fungi abound. Many will be resistant to certain diseases, but not all. Greenup refers to the time (usually spring) when the grass breaks its dormant spell, which could even be from heat in summer. It then starts to grow quickly, turns lush green—and needs mowing.

selecting grasses

of Kentucky bluegrass, unlike the old standards, are quite disease-resistant. They keep their fine-textured looks without a lot of feeding and have some drought tolerance. Fine fescue includes several grasses—chewings fescue, hard fescue, and creeping red fescue—that are often mixed with Kentucky bluegrass as they thrive in shade and drought. Perennial ryegrass is one of the main components of cool-season grass mixes. It germinates quickly and wears well. Warm-season grasses are adapted to the South, growing best in hot weather, and going brown and dormant when temperatures dip to freezing. Zoysiagrass is the most winter hardy of the southern grasses and is sometimes grown to Zone 7. It stays brown all winter in cooler climes, however, and is slow to greenup in spring.

If you like the relaxed look of a longer lawn, grow tall fescue. The new varieties make a wonderful low-maintenance lawn—they are drought-tolerant and stay green all season in sun or shade without feeding. Don't mix tall fescue with other grasses. A warm-season grass that will perform equally well is buffalograss, which grows to just 4 inches without mowing. Although it doesn't require feeding or watering, it can turn brown in extremely hot or cold weather.

It's a dense grass that's somewhat tolerant of shade and grows best in the upper South. Bermudagrass is suited to Florida and the Gulf Coast and thrives when it gets abundant water. It wears well, staying green longer than other warm-season grasses. St. Augustinegrass is a coarse grass, adapted to the humid coastal areas of the South. It is not tolerant of freezing weather or much shade but stands up to sun and high traffic. Bermudagrass is common to the mild-winter West Coast and southern regions. Some varieties can be started from seed, while others are grown only from sod or sprigs.

Water the lawn in the daytime so the blades of grass can dry out in the warmth of the sun, thus preventing infection with fungus. In cold climates, a mix of fine fescues with Kentucky bluegrass is best in areas with dappled shade. In southern regions, Bahiagrass is the lawn of choice, growing even in poor, sandy soil. However, it is susceptible to dollar spot, brown patch, and mole crickets.

laying a sod lawn

Turfgrass sod is an attractive option when it's time to renovate a tired old lawn or put in a new one. It's an instant fix and, when properly installed, eliminates problems with soil erosion, mud, and weeds. And you can lay it almost any time during the growing season. Professionally raised grass in high-quality sod is sturdy and dense from the outset and is usually weed-free. You can find sod in several of the most common grasses for your area. Although the initial cost of sod is considerably more than grass seed—especially if you hire a contractor to lay it—seeding costs about the same in the long run since you have to overseed in spring and fall following the initial seeding to grow a dense lawn.

YOU WILL NEED

- shovel
- organic matter
- granular fertilizer
- rake
- fresh sod
- water
- wheelbarrow/cart
- kneeling board
- sturdy knife

1 Establish a bed an inch below grade so the new lawn will be even with walkways. Dig organic material and slow-acting, granular fertilizer into the soil, then rake the bed smooth and level.

2 Store the sod in the shade; keep it rolled and moist until you're ready to use it. Bring one or two rolls at a time to the site in a wheelbarrow or cart. Moisten the soil bed just before laying the sod.

weather

For best results, lay sod in the spring or fall when there's likely to be more rainfall to help the lawn become established. However, you can patch bare spots in existing lawns any time of the year that the ground isn't frozen. Be prepared to water often during the hot summer months.

4 Lay subsequent rows so the end seams are never flush with those of adjacent rows. Coax the edges as close together as possible, but don't stretch them.

5 Don't stand on newly planted sod; instead use a kneeling board to lay additional rows. Use a sturdy knife to cut sod to fit irregular spaces.

Laying a sod lawn is an expenditure of time and money. Think of your lawn as a garden of grass. Before planting, prepare the soil as you would any garden bed. Add plenty of organic matter so the soil will retain moisture, yet drain well. Aerate it to encourage microbial activity. Once the sod is planted, deep watering is essential—the water must penetrate 6 inches below the sod—to encourage roots to penetrate deeply as they knit the sod to the soil. Pay attention to the seams between pieces of sod and the edges along walks and drives and water them carefully because they dry out quickly.

3 Lay the first length of sod along a straight edge such as a sidewalk. Unroll the grass strip gently, placing it snugly against the walk. Start the second roll of sod so its end neatly abuts the first.

6 Tamp the sod, or gently use a roller to establish good root contact with the soil. Fill any gaps with loose soil. Generously water the entire lawn.

choosing sod

Fresh, healthy sod is the key to a successful sod lawn. Because the grass in commercial sod is professionally grown in top-quality soil that receives regular fertilizing and watering, it is sturdy, dense, and weed-free. Sod should be newly harvested—ideally within a day before it's laid. Arrange for it to be delivered as soon as you've finished preparing the soil. The sod will arrive piled on pallets in rolled or folded strips, with the soil side exposed. The strips of sod are generally 1 to 2 feet wide and 4 to 10 feet long. Unroll a strip to inspect it. The grass should be at least 2 inches long and of a uniform green color. The soil on the underside should be dark and moist, about 1 inch thick, and show a tight matrix of healthy roots. Store the pallets in the shade. Keep the pieces of sod moist, and cover them to avoid drying out in case there's an unexpected delay.

Sod is available in many types of grass. If you're doing a patching job, try to find a sod with grass that resembles the color and texture of the grass surrounding the patch. When in doubt, compromise by choosing a mixture of grass types. An advantage to sodding is that it gives you an opportunity to introduce a new grass blend or mixture that's appropriate for your site. If it's an area that gets a lot of foot traffic, use a mixture that features tall fescue, which stands up best to wear and tear. Or if the area is primarily for display, a blend of Kentucky bluegrasses may look elegant.

starting a lawn from seed

Sowing grass seed is the most common method of starting a new lawn of cool-weather grasses. Grass seed is relatively inexpensive and covers a large area of prepared soil quickly. Buy the best quality seed so you can benefit from all the latest technology in breeding sturdy, disease-resistant grasses. Seed mixtures combine several kinds of grasses such as Kentucky bluegrass, tall fescue, and perennial ryegrass in various proportions. Their respective weaknesses offset each other to assure a green lawn all season. Blends, on the other hand, combine several varieties of the same kind of grass, such as three types of Kentucky bluegrass, to provide a uniform look. Local nurseries and garden centers

YOU WILL NEED

- shovel
- organic matter
- rake
- granular, slow-acting fertilizer
- seed
- water
- polyspun garden fabric or straw

1 Careful preparation of the soil is critical to the success of a lawn grown from seed. Clear out all vegetation, then dig in some organic material to improve the soil's ability to hold moisture.

2 The grass seed must touch the soil, so remove any stones and debris that you find. Using a garden rake, smooth out the soil; be sure to eliminate any dips or bumps.

5 After about a week of weeding, it's time to sow the grass seed, following package instructions. Water lightly to moisten the seed and soil.

6 Mulch the newly seeded area to protect the seed. Polyspun garden fabric or straw helps maintain essential moisture in the seed bed.

carry formulations appropriate for your region. The keys to success in growing a lawn from seed are proper timing, good preparation, and aftercare. Fall is the best time to sow cool-weather grass seed. In zones 5 to 7, for example, sow seed around Labor Day to give the grass time to extend its roots deeply into the soil so it can endure the heat of summer. The healthier the soil, the better the lawn. Prepare the soil two weeks before you sow the seed to allow time to get rid of emerging weeds. Water faithfully and plan to add more seed the following year so your new lawn will be dense and plush.

3 Spread granular, slow-acting lawn fertilizer evenly over the soil. Be sure to follow package instructions for application. The fertilizer provides uniform, consistent nutrition over several months.

4 Rake the fertilizer into the soil to rough it up and make a good seed bed. Add water and wait for several days for any newly surfaced weed seeds to sprout and grow. Remove the weeds.

7 For optimum germination, keep new grass seed constantly moist. Seedlings will penetrate straw or push up the light garden fabric as they grow.

8 Keep watering, less frequently but more heavily, as roots continue to grow. When the seedlings are 3 inches tall, remove the fabric and lightly mow.

liming lawns

In certain regions, the soil is more acid than grass prefers. If you live in such an area, spread dolomitic or granular limestone on the lawn. It takes effect in about 3 to 6 months. Lime is alkaline, so it neutralizes excess acidity, sweetening the soil. Never fertilize and lime a lawn at the same time. The combination produces ammonia gas, releasing the fertilizer's valuable nitrogen into the air.

using plugs and sprigs

Warm-season grasses, such as Bermudagrass, zoysia, or St. Augustinegrass, are usually planted as sprigs or plugs because they don't set viable seed. Starting a lawn with these individual plants is much less expensive than using regular sod, although both sprigs and plugs are rooted pieces of sod. Sprigs are thin 3- to 6-inch pieces of grass stems or runners without soil. Plugs are 2- to-4-inch chunks of sod, either round or square, with soil around their roots. Spring is the best time to plant sprigs and plugs. Before planting, prepare the soil well. Till or dig in organic matter and add granular, slow-acting fertilizer. Smooth out the soil with a rake. The biggest

planting plugs

YOU WILL NEED

- plugs
- shovel
- organic matter
- fertilizer
- rake
- trowel
- water

1 Buy fresh plugs and keep them moist. Clear the site of weeds, stones, and debris. Dig in some organic matter and granular, slow-acting fertilizer, then use a rake to make the soil smooth and level.

2 Plant plugs as soon after purchase as possible. Set them on the soil equidistant from each other in a grid pattern. The closer together they are, the sooner the grass will spread to form turf.

3 Dig a hole for each plug, deep and wide enough to accommodate its root system. Set plug in hole and gently press soil over roots and against crown.

4 Water the plugs well and often. Eliminate weeds that sprout between them. Mow when the grass is 3 inches tall to stimulate it to spread.

problem you'll face will be weeds. Digging the soil brings weed seeds to the surface; they'll sprout wherever there is bare soil as soon as they're exposed to sun and moisture. Because there's a lot of bare soil between the sprigs or plugs of grass, it's worth the time and effort to deal with the weeds first. Water the prepared soil and allow a week or two for the weeds to sprout. Remove or kill the weeds, then plant the grass, disturbing the soil as little as possible. During the time it takes the grass to knit together into a solid lawn, dig up any other weeds you find.

planting sprigs

Sprigs are available by the bushel. Or you can make your own by separating grass plants from sod.

Keep sprigs moist until planted. Place longer ones in furrows in prepared soil about 6 inches apart. Poke shorter pieces into the soil with your finger.

Sprigging is the least expensive and fastest method of establishing or repairing a lawn of warm-season grass. However, sprigs require more initial and post-planting care than plugs and are less likely to survive adverse conditions. Whether you use plugs or sprigs, it is important to keep them from drying out before you plant them.

There are three different ways to sprig a lawn. The *broadcast* method is the fastest way to install sprigs. You simply toss shredded stems evenly over a prepared, moist soil bed, then cover them with a light layer of soil. Invariably some will be completely buried and fail to grow, but the roots of most of the sprigs will take hold. The *furrow* method is more time-consuming. Dig 3-inch-deep furrows in the soil 4 to 12 inches apart. Plant each sprig so that the roots are buried and the foliage is above soil level when the furrow is smoothed over. A third option is to plant sprigs individually in a *grid pattern*.

Whichever method you choose, aftercare is critical. Walk over the area or roll it with a lawn roller at half weight to firm the soil around the crowns of the newly planted sprigs. Water immediately after planting. Continue watering frequently so the young plants don't dry out before they become established. Keep the area free of weeds. It may be necessary to fill in between the sprigs with extra soil to bring the planting bed up to grade level. This helps the horizontal runners sent out by the sprigs establish themselves quickly. When the grass is 3 inches tall, mow, cutting less than ½ inch off the blades of grass.

plugging repairs

Plugging is an ideal way to repair small sections of lawn that have died. It's also an easy way to revitalize a lawn in stages as time and money allow. The day before planting, mow the surrounding lawn area very short and water the space heavily. Plant the individual plugs 3 to 10 inches apart in a pattern that suits the empty space.

repairing the lawn

Even the nicest lawn has occasional problems. The best defense is to keep it healthy by fertilizing and topdressing with organic material once a year. Mow your lawn correctly and aerate it periodically to discourage thatch buildup and soil compaction. Even with the best care, bare, thin, or weedy patches occasionally develop in certain areas. Deal with these problems as soon as possible so the damage doesn't spread. Weeds rapidly will fill in bare areas if you don't populate that space promptly with new grass. Repairing a lawn problem is a two-step process. First, try to determine the underlying cause. Sometimes an accident, such as a fertilizer spill, creates a bare spot

overseeding

YOU WILL NEED

- lawn mower
- rake
- grass seed
- seed spreader
- lawn roller (optional)
- topsoil or compost (optional)
- water

1 Mow the existing grass as closely as possible; be careful not to scrape the crowns of the plants. Remove the clippings to expose bare soil, so the seed will have direct contact with the soil.

2 Use a garden rake to rough up the soil between the grass plants. This and the stubble of the freshly mown grass will make a good seed bed for the new seed you'll be adding.

3 Sow seed at the rate recommended for new lawns. This compensates for reduced germination as some seed falls into existing grass, not on the soil.

4 Roll the area lightly. Topdress it with topsoil or compost (optional). Water frequently. Mow the new grass when it reaches 3 inches in height.

in the lawn. Or the cause might be chronic disease, destructive insects, or competition for light and moisture from overgrown neighboring plants. Correct these deficiencies first, or your repair efforts will be futile. Give a thin, tired lawn new vitality and disease resistance by overseeding it with new grass seed. In northern states, do this in the fall, so the cool-season grasses have time to develop strong roots before they have to face summer. In southern states, repair lawns of warm-weather grasses in the spring by sprigging or plugging; these grasses need warm weather to grow well.

seeding tip

Spread a thin layer of topsoil, straw, or polyspun garden fabric over the lawn area that you've just patched with seed. This protects the seed and, later, the sprouts. More importantly, by covering the soil, it reduces moisture loss. A constant supply of moisture is the key to good germination.

patching with seed

1 Delineate the spot you'll be repairing by digging all the way around its border. Remove and discard any poor grass and weeds within the area. Keep the remaining bare soil free of debris.

2 Invest as much time and effort in preparing the soil in this small repair area as you would for an entire lawn. Dig in organic matter and granular, slow-acting fertilizer. Rake the soil smooth and level.

3 Sow seed thickly. Use a variety that corresponds to the surrounding grass if possible. Otherwise use a mixture of grasses appropriate to the region.

patching with sod

Sod is the quickest and easiest way to patch a dead or damaged turf area. You can lay it any time during the season. Keep the sod moist until you plant it. Prepare the soil the same way you would for patching with seed. Keep the area an inch or so below grade so the new grass will be level with the lawn. Then cut a piece from the strip of sod to conform to the repair site. Firm it onto the soil, placing its edges snugly against the surrounding lawn. Walk on it to settle it into place. Water deeply and often.

mowing the lawn

Mowing the grass correctly improves the health and appearance of any lawn. Even older grass varieties growing in less than ideal soil respond to modern mowing practices. Your lawn will look greener, stay thicker, resist weeds more effectively, and hold up better in adverse weather with correct mowing practices that minimize the stress on grass. Mowing dramatically reduces the lawn's leaf surface,which means that the grass doesn't get as much energy from the sun to promote growth. As a result, each plant must struggle to replace its foliage as rapidly as possible so it can continue to build strong, deep roots. Constant cutting requires constant effort to

mowing height

Grass mowed with the cutting blade set high (3 to 4 inches) is healthier than grass mowed closer to the ground. Because the grass doesn't need to regrow as much leaf length, it can devote energy to growing deep roots. And the deeper the roots, the more self-reliant the grass becomes. Plants need less water and fertilizer because they get more from the soil. The resulting sturdiness helps them resist competition from nearby weeds.

Mulching mowers have specially designed blades that cut grass and leaves several times. The tiny pieces fall among the grass plants. They gradually decompose and help feed the lawn.

Riding mowers are most appropriate for large-scale, relatively flat properties and for people who are unable to walk a lot.

adjust mower height

During the growing season, you'll want to mow your lawn at different heights in response to changing weather. In spring and fall, when rainfall is most generous, most grasses do best at 2 or 2½ inches. When summer brings heat and drought, raise the mower to cut the grass at 3 inches. Longer grass suffers less stress and shades the soil, keeping it cooler and moister. The best mowers feature convenient adjustment mechanisms for raising and lowering the cutting blade. A hand-operated lever can usually be found near one or more of the wheels. On some mowers, one lever raises or lowers the four wheels at once.

replace the foliage. Therefore, it's best to mow your grass lightly, taking off about one-third of the length of the blades at a time, minimizing loss and stress. Moreover, your grass will look greener because more foliage remains. The roots grow deeper and the lawn is less vulnerable to pests and diseases. Best of all, the lawn grows more slowly. Don't cut the grass short—less than 2 inches tall. Tailor your mowing schedule to the type and condition of your grass. In spring and fall, when rainfall is more generous, you'll be mowing more frequently. And during the drier summers, you'll be doing so less frequently.

thatch myths debunked

Thatch isn't caused from leaving clippings on the lawn. Grass clippings are mostly water and typically break down within 10 days. Thatch is an accumulation of dead grass plant crowns and stolons that mat on the soil surface. It's usually caused by compacted soil and over-fertilization. A layer of thatch more than ¼ inch thick keeps water from reaching the soil, and it harbors pathogens. Remove it with a thatching rake or a power dethatcher.

mower heights in inches

grass	spring/fall height	summer height
cool-season grasses		
Fine fescue	2"	2½"
Tall fescue	2–2½"	3"
Kentucky bluegrass	2"	2½–3"
Perennial ryegrass	2"	2½–3"
warm-season grasses		
Bermudagrass	1½ "	2"
Buffalograss	2"	3"
Centipedegrass	1"	2"
St. Augustinegrass	1"	3"
Zoysiagrass	1–1½"	1½–2"

mowing tips

- **Sharpen the mower blade at least twice a season.** Dull blades increase plant stress by butchering the foliage rather than cleanly cutting it. The frayed tips turn brown, losing moisture and inviting disease.
- **Don't mow wet grass.** It doesn't cut evenly, and the clippings clump in the mower bell and on the turf. Walking on wet grass bruises it and spreads fungal disease to healthy grass.
- **Mow lightly and often.** Reduce stress on the grass plants by cutting only ⅓ of each blade with each mowing. Although this requires more frequent mowing, you're not forcing it to constantly regrow so much of its energy-collecting foliage.
- **Mow tall.** Tall grass shades and cools the soil, discourages weeds, and shelters beneficial ants and ground spiders that prey on pest insect eggs in the turf.
- **Leave the clippings.** A season's grass clippings slowly and consistently contribute as much nitrogen as a typical application of fertilizer.
- **Vary the mowing pattern.** Repeated walking over the same area promotes soil compaction. Prevent wear patterns by mowing horizontally one week, vertically the next, then diagonally.

feeding the lawn

Strictly speaking, fertilizer feeds the soil, so the soil can feed the lawn. In areas where the soil is poor, grass gets most of its nutrients from fertilizer. Grass plants are heavy feeders. They need lots of nitrogen to fuel the constant growth, necessary because the leaf blades are cut regularly during mowing. Ideally your soil will contain sufficient nitrogen (N), as well as the other essential nutrients—potassium (P) and phosphorus (K). But if it's like most soils in residential areas, it's compacted and deficient in organic matter. As a result, the soil doesn't have enough air and food to support the microbes that normally process nutrients for plants. Poor soil can't do much for the lawn besides holding the grass plants in place, so fertilizer bears most of the responsibility for grass nutrition. However, you can—over a period of years—reduce your lawn's dependency on fertilizer by periodically aerating and topdressing the soil with organic material.

Choosing a lawn fertilizer isn't as complicated as it may seem when walking down the aisle at the

weather

Fall is the best time to fertilize lawns of cool-weather grasses. Because grass plants are going dormant and no longer need to spend energy on foliage growth, they can devote their effort to developing strong, deep roots. For this reason, fall and winter fertilizers have a bit less nitrogen and more phosphorus.

To green up your lawn quickly, spray it with fast-acting, water-soluble fertilizers. The leaf tissues absorb nutrients directly, spurring rapid growth. You'll need to repeat the sprays periodically.

Slow-acting, granular fertilizer gives grass consistent, uniform nutrition for at least two to three months. It gradually releases nutrients in response to soil temperature and the activity of soil organisms.

garden center. Use a granular product to provide the annual main meal for the lawn. A complete fertilizer provides the essential nutrients (NPK) plus, in some cases, trace minerals. Although you usually can't go wrong if the bag has the words "lawn fertilizer" on it, you may prefer to determine the actual proportions of the big-three nutrients in each bag by referring to the three numbers on the label. The first number, the amount of nitrogen, is often the highest. However, giving grass a big burst of nitrogen in spring fuels the development of foliage and stems—which means you have to mow earlier and more often. Instead, look for a continuous-acting or timed-release fertilizer that will slowly feed the lawn over the growing season. The best time to fertilize is in the fall, stimulating root growth, rather than leaf growth. Use products labeled as fall or winterizer fertilizers.

spreader tips

Use a mechanical spreader to apply granular fertilizer evenly over the lawn. Rotary or broadcast spreaders are fast and scatter the fertilizer widely. Drop spreaders release fertilizer in broad strips. To avoid missed streaks or spots with a drop spreader, make your passes in a horizontal direction first, then follow up with verticals.

fertilizing the natural way

The essential nutrients in some commercial fertilizers are synthesized from chemicals. Those in other fertilizers are derived from natural sources such as animal manures and pulverized rocks. Both types of formulations are available for lawns. You also can make your own lawn fertilizer from natural sources of nitrogen (N), phosphorus (P), and potassium (K). Blend roughly one pound of N with ½ pound each of P and K. Vary the ingredients for the effect you require. Sift them for uniform consistency.

sources of nitrogen	**%N**
dried/shredded cow manure	2
dried/shredded poultry manure	3
fish meal	5
blood meal	14
cottonseed meal	7
sources of phosphorus	**%P**
bone meal	10
rock phosphate	30
sources of potassium	**%K**
wood ashes	5
granite dust	6
greensand	7

aerating the lawn

Aeration is the best way to correct compacted soil—the number 1 enemy of healthy lawns. The soil in a typical residential yard has had all of the air pressed out of it by children's play, foot traffic, mowing, parked cars, heavy rains, and possibly construction equipment. It can't support its own life, let alone the life of grass plants. The cure is to open up the soil so air can enter it. This enables the organisms that live on the organic matter in the soil to carry on their business of processing nutrients for plants. The best way to get air into the soil under a lawn is to make several passes with a power core-aerating machine that extracts soil cores, leaving holes that gradually fill

YOU WILL NEED

- cool day
- mower
- water
- core-aerator (power or hand model)
- rake (optional)

1 Choose a cool day to minimize stress on the grass. Cut the lawn shorter than usual, then moisten the soil. Rent a power core-aerator to do the job in one day, or use a hand model over several days.

2 Core aerators punch hollow tines into the soil and eject plugs of soil topped by turf. Holes should be about 4 inches apart and 3 to 4 inches deep for the most effective aeration.

compaction control

Choose one or more of the following options to control soil compaction under your lawn:

- *core aeration*
- *spiking*
- *humic acid*
- *organic topdressing*
- *bioactivators*
- *biostimulants*

3 Leave the cores on the grass to dissolve gradually in the rain, providing a topdressing. The air holes fill in with moisture and organic debris.

4 Optional: Rake the small soil plugs to break them apart, accelerate decomposition, and distribute the soil evenly over the lawn.

with air, organic debris, and moisture. Aerate in spring or fall for a year or two if the soil is badly compacted. And before you overseed or install a new lawn of seed or sod, aerate to create a good soil bed. Don't roll new sod with a full-weight roller, because it will compact the soil all over again.

aerating sandals

Special sandals with spikes allow some air to enter the soil. But they're not as effective as core aeration, because they don't remove entire cores and rarely penetrate deeply enough. However, you can use them as a stopgap measure between aerations. And if you routinely spike areas that get heavy foot traffic, you can prevent them from becoming bare.

core aerator

dethatching the lawn

Thatch is an accumulation of dead crowns and stems of grass plants on the soil surface that build up around the base of living grass in the lawn. Some thatch is normal and helpful because it blocks evaporation of soil moisture. But when a layer becomes more than ¼ inch thick, it prevents water and air from entering the soil and harbors pest insects and disease pathogens. Excessive thatch usually develops if the soil is too compact or if you use too much fertilizer and pesticides. Some grass varieties, such as zoysiagrass, are more prone than others to thatch buildup. Although grass clippings accumulate on the thatch layer, preventing it from breaking down rapidly, the clippings themselves don't cause thatch. You can promote some thatch decomposition by aerating the soil and dressing it with organic material, but the fastest and most effective control method is to remove the thatch. Either rake it out of the turf by hand or remove it with a power dethatcher or a dethatching attachment on a roto-tiller. Minimize damage to the grass by doing this in the cooler seasons of spring or fall.

small-lawn hint

Hand core aerators are extremely handy for treating small lawns. Also use them for turf areas between stepping stones, along walks, and near trees to avoid damaging shallow roots.

controlling lawn weeds

Lawn weeds are plants that aren't grass but that insist on growing in the lawn. Some may be desirable garden plants that migrate over the boundary of the flower bed. Others are unwelcome in the garden and lawn because they're coarse, ugly, and utterly lacking in charm. Whatever the case, they break up the consistent beauty of your lawn—and, worse, they overrun the grass, choking out newly emerging foliage. Weeds that produce rosettes of wide leaves close to the soil block the sun and moisture from young grass runners. The real nuisances are the weeds with deep taproots, such as dandelion and thistle, because they're so difficult to remove. Weeds are often

timely weeding

Attack weeds in spring while they're young. As soon as they're visible and identifiable, dig or pull them after rain moistens the soil. Fill bare spots with grass as soon as possible, or new weeds will return with a vengeance.

turn up the heat

Some weeds, especially those that only pop up in small clusters, can be effectively killed by heat. You can pour boiling water directly on the plants, or use a propane torch to kill them.

Broadleaf plantain has 3- to 6-inch leaves that grow close to the soil. Its narrow flowers sit atop thin stalks and produce seeds June through October.

Chickweed creeps to form mats of leaves and tiny white flowers in lawns from spring through fall in most areas of the country.

Creeping Charlie snakes across lawns, forcing its way among the grass blades. It bears tiny, purple flowers amid grape-like leaves in the spring.

Dandelion produces jaunty yellow flowers emerging from low-growing rosettes of coarse-toothed leaves. Puffy seedheads assure its spread.

indicators of problems, because they move in fastest where the lawn is thin and where grass is weak and easily intimidated. They rapidly take over where soil is bare. Certain weeds signal nutritional deficiencies, compaction, and depletion of organic material. For instance, the presence of sorrel or dock suggest that the soil is too acid. (Most grasses prefer the soil to be slightly alkaline.) Prostrate knotweed indicates compacted soil; yellow nutsedge signals waterlogged soil. Large colonies of weeds can be the result of overusing quick-acting, water-soluble fertilizers. An extra-large crop of

Crabgrass forms flat mats of grassy leaves in sunny lawns everywhere but Florida and the Southwest. It leaves behind copious seeds.

Purslane has succulent stems and tiny oval leaves sprawling over areas with thin, poor soil. A cousin of portulaca, it produces tiny, yellow flowers.

Realistically, zero tolerance for weeds in a lawn is impractical. It requires far more energy, time, and toxic herbicides than is justified or safe. Most lawns tolerate up to 20 percent to 30 percent weeds and appear green and lush. The one above has small colonies of clover, chickweed, and crabgrass that are undetectable even from a short distance.

controlling weeds by mowing

If you mow grass at taller heights, you can do an effective job of controlling annual weeds such as crabgrass. Tall grass shades the soil where the seeds of weeds fall. If the seeds don't get sun, they don't germinate. Regular mowing discourages those that do germinate, because the mower constantly cuts off the flowers, preventing the seeds from developing. Then, when frost comes, the weeds die.

controlling lawn weeds

weeds also may be a signal of incorrect mowing. If you mow the grass too short, you reduce its vigor and inhibit its ability to shade the soil and keep weed seeds from germinating. Crabgrass, clover, and chickweed thrive in short grass. It's neither necessary nor practical to eradicate all weeds in your lawn. Your goal should be to control their numbers so that the weeds don't detract from your lawn's appearance. The best way to control weeds over the long term is to correct any soil problems and adopt good maintenance practices to keep the lawn dense and healthy. Pulling out emerging weeds early in the season is the simplest immediate control. This keeps annual weeds from setting seed before they die. It's easier to pull out perennial weeds when they're

controlling annual weeds

Apply pre-emergents to control annual weeds before they sprout. An environmentally friendly treatment, made of corn gluten, is best applied in the fall. Most chemical pre-emergents, however, are best applied in early spring, before the forsythia are in full bloom. They form a chemical barrier on the grass that inhibits germination of all seeds. Don't aerate or overseed grass treated with conventional pre-emergents until fall.

Veronica forms tight mats of leaf-covered stems on the soil. The small, bright blue flowers of this self-sowing annual bloom from April to August.

Violets are perennial garden plants that tend to seed into lawns. Lavender or white flowers on thin stems poke above heart-shaped leaves in spring.

White clover features small balls of tiny, white flowers on thin stalks. They rise above three-petaled leaves that sprawl as a mat of rambling stems.

Wood sorrel, or oxalis, forms creeping mats or small upright plants bearing small, green or bronze clover-shaped leaves and tiny, yellow flowers.

young. If weeds become well established in your lawn, choose the least toxic herbicide. Spot-treat isolated patches of weeds with a spritz of herbicide. Spray or spread herbicide over your entire lawn only if weeds are extensively distributed throughout the turf. Because the weeds are growing among plants you don't want to kill—the grass—use a selective herbicide. You can buy one for *grassy* weeds, such as nutsedge, another for *broadleaf* weeds such as plantain. After the weeds die, clear out the remnants and immediately scatter grass seed or lay sod on the bare spots.

edible lawn weeds

plant	edible part	use/preparation
Burdock	root	pickled, boiled in soups and stews
Chickweed	leaves	chopped in salads
Cresses	leaves	young in salad; cooked in soup
Dandelion	leaves, flowers	young leaves in salads, steamed, wilted, or cooked in dandelion gravy (served over mashed potatoes); young flowers in wine; dipped in egg then cornmeal and fried
Lamb's quarter	leaves, shoots	young in salad; cook and use like spinach
Plantain	leaves	blanch and saute in butter and garlic
Purslane	leaves, stems	very young leaves chopped in salads, salty garnish; blanch and saute with olive oil, garlic, and chile
Red clover	flowers	chopped in salads, steeped in tea, cooked in soup
Shepherd's purse	leaves	blanch and saute with olive oil, garlic, and chile
Violet	leaves, flowers	young leaves in salad, add to marinara sauce; flowers in fruit salad, syrup, sorbet, candied

controlling lawn pests

Some pest insects are always present in a lawn. Usually they only use it for a time to shelter their eggs and feed their larvae. The adult beetles and moths are an integral part of the richly varied assortment of living organisms that inhabit residential ecosystems. In their various life stages, they remain inconspicuous most of the time while they play their role in maintaining balance, seldom causing visible damage. However, something unusual—such as a significant decline in the health of the lawn, extremes in temperature or rainfall, or the destruction of the pests' natural predators—occasionally takes place. The result is an explosion of the pest population—and visible lawn

using birds to control pests

Birds nesting in or around your property eat an enormous number of insects. Even those species that normally eat seeds and fruits will seek out insects for their insatiable young ones who can't yet digest seeds. Offer their mom and dad some water, shelter, and feeder snacks to keep them nearby.

army worm

description and trouble signs

These caterpillars cluster to feed on grass leaves at night and rest under dead or dying sod during the daytime. Their bodies are brown and hairy, and they have green, beige, or black stripes down their backs. In spring, adult moths deposit eggs on the grass, where the newly hatched larvae begin to feed. Army worms are most active in the spring and fall, and you usually can spot their handiwork in the form of irregular bare patches in the turf.

controls

- Spray *Bacillus thuringiensis* (Bt) on the affected grass during the period when the army worms are feeding. Repeat every 10 to 14 days until they're gone. Reapply if it rains.
- Spray beneficial (predatory) nematodes on affected lawn areas as directed on the product label.

billbug

description and trouble signs

Adult billbugs chew holes in grass stems to deposit eggs in them. The reddish-brown beetles are $\frac{3}{4}$ inch long and have long snouts. Newly hatched, legless larvae feed on grass stems and crowns, breaking them off at the soil line and creating patches of dead grass. Sometimes the white, pudgy larvae are visible on driveways in May or June. Damage appears mid-June through July. They work quickly and are particularly fond of Kentucky bluegrass.

controls

- Remove the thatch layer to expose the billbugs to their bird and insect predators.
- Drench the affected area of lawn with insecticidal soap and water as directed on the package label.
- Spray heavily infested lawns with a commercial broad-spectrum insecticide listed for billbugs.

damage. A good offense is the best defense, and prevention is the best way to deal with lawn pests. Head off potential problems by taking measures to maintain the natural balance in the yard and create a stable environment that will support and maintain a healthy lawn. Grow several kinds of plants in addition to grass to ensure the presence of a variety of beneficial insects. Avoid using broad-spectrum insecticides that are indiscriminate—killing good bugs as well as the bad ones. Put up feeders, birdbaths, and nesting boxes to encourage birds to stay nearby and patrol for pest insects. Plant varieties

chinch bug

description and trouble signs

Tiny, inconspicuous bugs damage grass in each of their life stages. Adults have black bodies marked with a dark, triangular pad separating their folded wings. Immature bugs are reddish-colored. They're happiest in hot, dry weather and create large, yellowish, spreading circular patches in lawns that are afflicted with thatch. Chinch bugs often begin near sidewalks and streets, congregating at the center of these areas as the grass there turns brown and dies.

controls

- Remove the thatch layer to expose the chinch bugs to their bird and insect predators.
- Drench the affected area of lawn with insecticidal soap and water as directed on the package label.
- Spray heavily infested lawns with a commercial broad-spectrum insecticide listed for chinch bugs.

spider mite

description and trouble signs

Various mites afflict lawn grasses (and weeds) by sucking juices from the undersides of the leaves, causing them to yellow, wilt, and die. Mites are most active during the hot months of summer, especially when there is little rain or irrigation. Although they're virtually impossible to see without magnification, their trademark fine webbing is often visible between leaves. Typical examples are clover mites, which are red, and Bermudagrass mites, which are greenish.

controls

- Water the lawn to eliminate the dry environment that mites prefer.
- Suspend fertilizing to limit the amount of succulent grass growth that attracts mites.
- Drench the affected area of lawn with insecticidal soap and water as directed on the package label.

Using Bt

Bt (Bacillus thuringiensis) *is the active ingredient in many caterpillar insecticides. This bacteria paralyzes the caterpillars' digestive tracts when they eat it, causing the caterpillars to die from starvation. Before applying Bt, mow the lawn. Then mix the powder with water as directed on the package. You can add a surfactant or sticker such as a couple of drops of liquid soap—the plainer the better—to help the solution adhere to grass leaves and penetrate thatch. Spray leaf surfaces until the blades are dripping. Bt breaks down faster in sunlight, so spray on a cloudy day.*

controlling lawn pests

of grass that are resistant to pests in your region. Mow the grass tall to shelter beneficial ants and spiders that reduce the number of pests by eating their eggs. Aerate and feed the lawn to help it develop deep roots so it can withstand the stress of minor insect damage. Be observant. Watch for trouble signs such as mole activity, flocks of starlings or other birds on the lawn, and moths flying low over the turf. In spite of your best efforts, however, extreme weather or other circumstances occasionally can upset the delicate balance, enabling pest insects to get an upper hand. At this point, you need to take action. But before you do so, determine how much damage you really have—and whether you can live with it—and reserve the most toxic and intrusive

routine timing of pests

The emergence of pest insects is amazingly predictable. Their arrival is usually within a day or two of the same date, year after year. This makes control much easier because you can begin your measures immediately, before populations expand. Prevent problems next year by picking as many beetles as possible off plants before they can lay their eggs. And write in your garden journal or calendar the date they emerge this year, and mark that date on next year's calendar so you can be alert for them.

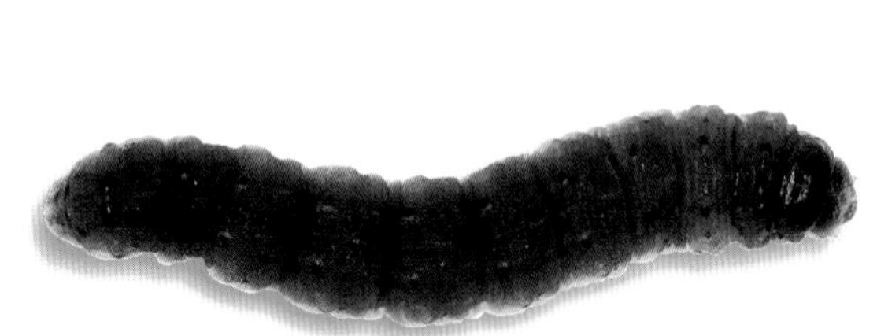

cutworm

description and trouble signs

Cutworm describes many kinds of moths whose larvae plague lawns. The caterpillars are fat, soft, and bristly, and their color depends on the adult moth species. Variegated cutworms are gray, mottled with dark brown and have a row of colorful spots running down their backs. They live at the soil surface and are most active from spring through late summer. Cutworms leave telltale dead spots where they have cut the grass stems at their base.

controls

- Drench (puddle) affected areas of the lawn with water to force the worms to the surface. Then you can handpick and collect them for the trash.
- Spray Bt on the grass when cutworms are feeding.
- Spray beneficial (predatory) nematodes on the affected parts of the lawn.

mole cricket

description and trouble signs

These brown, $1\frac{1}{2}$-inch-long insects chew the stems of warm-season grasses above and below the soil surface. They're partial to moist, warm weather in the South. Mole crickets work night and day, creating areas of the lawn that appear streaked or closely clipped. Underneath, their travels create tunnels 6 to 8 inches deep, damaging grass roots. The air spaces cause the roots to dry out and the turf above to feel spongy.

controls

- Remove the thatch layer to discourage crickets.
- Spray beneficial nematodes on the grass.
- Drench the affected area with insecticidal soap.
- Spray the lawn with an insecticide containing neem, as directed on its label.
- Sprinkle diatomaceous earth (DE) on affected areas.

measures for only the most dire situations. Several weapons are effective against common pests. You can control many soft-bodied pests by spraying the grass with insecticidal soap or drenching the soil where they are active. Or coat the blades of grass with the bacteria, *Bacillus thuringiensis* (Bt), which sickens and kills various caterpillars when they eat it. You can spray the lawn with microscopic predatory nematodes that burrow into the soil and seek out caterpillars as hosts for their eggs. The new larvae kill the caterpillars. Handpick or trap moths and beetles to reduce the egg population.

friendly ants

Though ants are absolute nuisances in the kitchen, they're allies in your yard. They range through the soil, preying on the eggs of numerous pest insects and, as a result, significantly reduce their populations. Normally they nest at the edges of lawns, in stone walls, or in crevices. Mounded nests all over the lawn indicate soil problems such as a deficiency of organic matter.

sod webworm

description and trouble signs

Various moths lay eggs that hatch into grass-eating caterpillars. They vary from greenish to beige to brown or gray and have shiny brown heads and four parallel rows of distinctive dark spots on their backs. They build silk-lined cocoons on thatch, where they lurk and feed on grass blades. Kentucky bluegrass and fine fescues are among their favorites. They cause small brown spots in a lawn in late spring, which become large dead patches by midsummer.

controls

- Remove the thatch layer to deny sod webworms a place to lay eggs.
- Spray beneficial nematodes on the grass.
- Drench the affected area with insecticidal soap.
- Spray Bt on the grass when the sod webworms are feeding.

white grub

description and trouble signs

These beetle larvae are thick, white worms with brown heads. They lie curled in the soil and, as the weather warms, migrate to the surface to feed on grass roots. They emerge in summer as Japanese beetles, June bugs, and others. Grubs typically do their damage by destroying grass roots, causing irregular brown patches of lawn. At this point, you can pull up the sod easily, revealing the perpetrators in the soil beneath.

controls

- Aerate or spike the lawn in late spring to kill the grubs that are near the soil surface.
- Spray beneficial nematodes on the grass.
- Mow grass tall in summer after the beetles emerge.
- Collect the adult beetles as they feed on favorite plants before they can lay eggs in the lawn.

controlling lawn diseases

Most lawn diseases are caused by fungus. Because of this, the methods of prevention and control are pretty much the same. Fungal spores continually exist in grass, thatch, and soil. Other organisms that share the same living quarters maintain the balance of these populations of fungus by preying on them. Occasionally, fungus outbreaks occur when weather or conditions in the lawn change, upsetting the balance. Then the fungi overrun their predators and overwhelm the nearby grass. Usually the first signs of trouble are discolored patches in the lawn. To verify that the problem is a disease—and not insect infestation—try to pull up a handful of grass plants. If the grass

weather

Fungal disease outbreaks are often caused by temporary weather extremes. Certain diseases become active when the weather suddenly gets very hot and dry; others respond to unusually cool and moist conditions. When this happens, the infection is usually temporary. The best response may be simply to wait until the extremes moderate. However, if a disease appears chronically, regardless of weather, you'll need to take control measures.

Brownspot causes sizable, brownish gray, irregular patches, sometimes ringing circular green spots, during hot, humid days of mid- to late summer. It likes grass stressed by overfertilization and thatch.

Dollar spot thrives in humid weather on dry, undernourished lawns. It appears as bleached beige spots of dead grass up to 5 inches in diameter that may be covered with cobwebs in early morning.

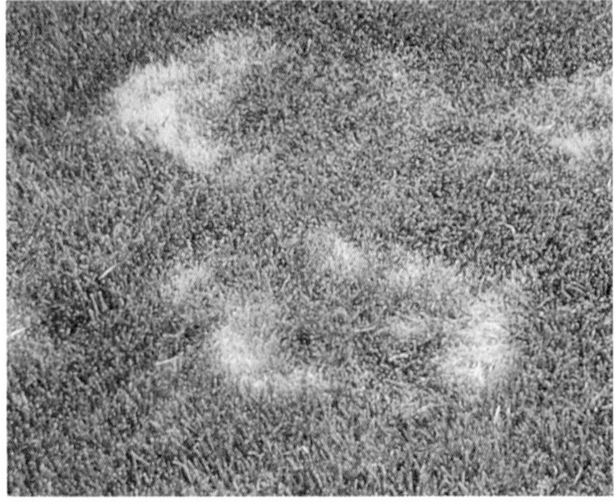

Fusarium blight thrives in hot, humid areas and starts as 2- to 6-inch reddish spots that turn tan then yellow. Roots and crowns show rot.

Leaf spot causes pale-centered, blackish purple oval spots on damp grass—mainly in early spring or late fall—on shady, closely mowed lawns.

doesn't come out easily, the problem probably is caused by disease. It is easy to prevent many diseases before they take hold. Choose modern, resistant varieties of grass. Plant a mixture of many kinds of grass so their vulnerabilities offset one another. Minimize stress: Mow the lawn high, use restraint with fertilizer, and water well—only when necessary—to encourage deep roots. Aerate the soil periodically and remove excessive thatch. Resort to control measures only if infection is serious or chronic. Protect nearby healthy turf from infection by spraying it with a fungicide formulated for grass.

Fairy ring infection causes bright-green, circular patches of fast-growing grass in the Pacific Northwest. Perimeters brown, the grass declines, and a cluster of mushrooms may appear at the edges.

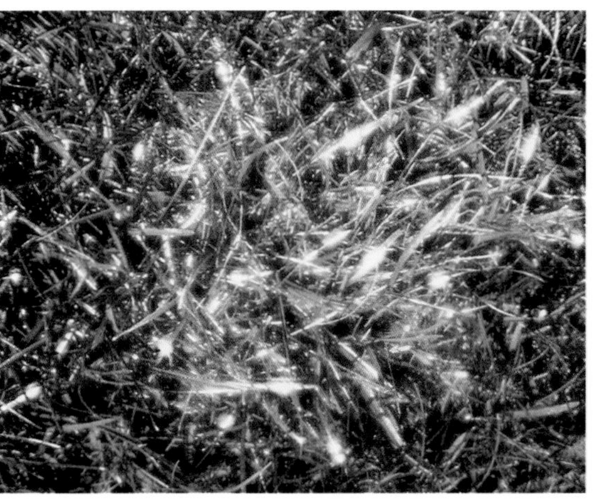

Pythium blight starts as blackened, water-soaked, 2-inch patches that eventually lie flat. In humid weather, a cottony growth may be visible. Foot traffic spreads the disease, but dry weather stops it.

Powdery mildew coats Kentucky bluegrass with a grayish film in cool, humid, shaded areas. Severe infection turns grass yellow and kills it.

Red thread, a problem in the Northeast and Pacific Northwest, creates rusty red lawn patches. Cool, humid weather and low nitrogen encourage it.

controlling stress

Grass that is stressed is most vulnerable to disease. Some stress, such as that caused by atypical weather, is uncontrollable. However, you can avoid stress caused by:

- *too much or too little fertilizer*
- *overly acidic soil*
- *insufficient sunlight*
- *excessively short grass*
- *heavy thatch*
- *lack of water*
- *compacted soil*

regional lawn care checklist

Cool Climates

Spring

- ❑ Sharpen the lawn mower blade if you didn't do so during the winter.
- ❑ Have the lawn mower serviced.
- ❑ Patch or overseed early with perennial ryegrass. Its rapid germination ensures sturdier seedlings going into summer.
- ❑ Aerate the lawn to treat compacted soil.
- ❑ Topdress the lawn with organic matter, if necessary.
- ❑ Spread granular, slow-acting fertilizer. (This is optional if you fertilized in the fall or winter.)

Summer

- ❑ When hot weather sets in, raise the mower to cut at 3 inches or higher.
- ❑ If the soil is good, water only when rainfall is delayed more than 10 to 14 days.
- ❑ If the soil is poor and rain is scarce, water weekly.
- ❑ Spot-treat weeds and patch bare spots.
- ❑ Halfway through the season, sharpen the lawn-mower blade.

Warm Climates

Spring

- ❑ Plug, sprig, or sod new lawns after you've carefully prepared the soil.
- ❑ Sharpen the lawn-mower blade.
- ❑ Fertilize lawns for spring greenup. If soil is acidic, do not lime until fall.
- ❑ Dethatch and aerate the lawn, if necessary.

Summer

- ❑ For summer mowing, adjust mower to correct height for the type of grass in your lawn.
- ❑ Water lawn as needed—frequently if the soil is poor, every 7 to 10 days if the soil is good.
- ❑ Use plugs or sprigs to patch any bare spots in the lawn where weeds once grew or insects caused damage.

Fall

- ❑ If soil is too acid, spread lime. (Wait at least two weeks to fertilize.)
- ❑ Aerate compacted soil under turf, if you didn't do so in the spring.
- ❑ Topdress with organic material or mow a layer of fallen leaves to mulch them into the lawn.
- ❑ Just after Labor Day, seed or sod new lawns, or overseed existing ones.
- ❑ Fertilize the lawn on or about Thanksgiving to promote strong root growth throughout the winter.
- ❑ Prevent the grass from matting under the snow by lowering the mower and cutting the grass a bit shorter just before winter.

Winter

- ❑ Put out markers to indicate lawn edges so you don't damage the lawn when you shovel snow.
- ❑ Avoid walking on frosted or snow-covered lawns.
- ❑ Drain gas from lawn mowers and weed trimmers.
- ❑ Purchase and use non-salt de-icer for sidewalks and drives.

- ❑ Overseed warm-weather grasses with annual rye to produce a green turf during the winter.
- ❑ Sharpen the lawn-mower blade again to help keep the grass healthy.
- ❑ Use plugs or sprigs to patch any bare spots in lawn where weeds once grew or insects caused damage.

- ❑ Mow lawn if you overseeded it with ryegrass.
- ❑ Install sprinkler system if turf is planted in sandy soil. (This is optional, depending on your watering habits.)
- ❑ Service power lawn mower and weed trimmer.

lawn alternatives

choosing a groundcover

All kinds of plants make good groundcovers. In spite of this, lawn grass continues to be what most Americans use to cover large expanses of the yard and to keep it from washing away. But there are lots of other groundcovers —shrubs, vines, annuals, perennials, conifers, and herbs—that do a better job of protecting soil and decorating yards. Almost all of them require less overall attention, including watering, fertilizing, mowing, and repairing. And almost all of them are more versatile and contribute more to a healthy environment than grass. The universal stereotype of plain-green, low-growing plants doesn't define a groundcover plant. Even though the familiar and

season hint

Many good groundcover plants are annuals or herbaceous (soft-stemmed) perennials which die back in the winter. The soil they protected all summer becomes bare and is exposed to harsh winter weather. To keep the soil in good condition, spread 3 to 4 inches of organic material over the area after the ground freezes.

Barrenwort is a perennial that blooms in spring. After its dainty yellow, pink, or white flowers fade, the wiry stems keep the heart-shaped leaves until fall. Grows in partial shade. Zones 5–9.

Bishop's weed, or goutweed, spreads readily. Its leaves are plain green or variegated, and they serve well in sun or shade, long after their white flowers fade in early summer. Zones 4–9.

Cotoneaster is a hardy shrub. This low-growing, tiny-leafed version bears small flowers in spring and red berries in fall. It handles dry slopes. Zones 5–7.

Heath and Heather are low-growing plants that accept sun or shade. They bear tiny flower spikes in spring (heath) or fall (heather). Zones 5–7.

reliable pachysandra and English ivy do an excellent job of protecting and beautifying areas—large and small—lots of other plants do just as well. Actually, any mass planting that grows together to form a canopy and effectively covers the soil with texture and color is a potential groundcover. There are no rules for height or type, though in some cases you may want something that remains low to the ground or, conversely, is tall enough to hide eyesores.

The site will be a major factor in your choices. For example, some plants thrive in shady areas, while others function better on slopes or in long borders.

Bugleweed, or ajuga, grows whorls of purple-tinged, green, or variegated leaves where its runners root. It bears spikes of blue, pink, or white flowers in spring. The plant is easy to control. Zones 3–9.

Cinnamon fern grows in shady areas. It has a cloud of soft green foliage and forms vase-shaped clumps of fronds, punctuated with cinnamon-brown reproductive stems. It spreads slowly. Zones 4–8.

Hosta foliage has varied colors, patterns, and shapes to brighten shady areas all season. In summer, it bears white or lavender flowers. Zones 3–8.

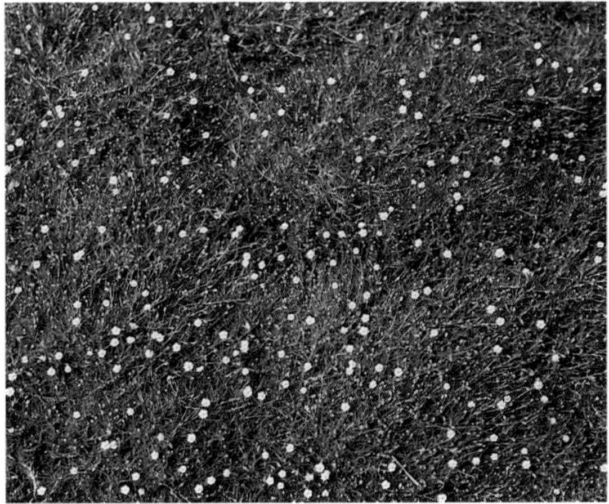

Irish moss, or baby tears, forms a tight mat of tiny, hairy, green leaves and blooms in summer. It grows in moist, shady areas in zones 10 and 11.

choosing a groundcover

You can use all kinds of garden standbys as groundcovers, or look to new plants at the nursery. Consider using culinary herbs, ornamental grasses, or the newer low-maintenance roses. Imagine patches of ferns, spring bulbs, or mosses. Groundcover plants shelter the soil and the living organisms that dwell in and around it. Groundcovers serve as a living mulch to reduce moisture evaporation, control erosion, and prevent harsh weather from compacting the soil. Use a variety of plants on different parts of your property. Diversity not only makes your outdoor environment more attractive, but it also creates a healthier ecosystem. A

mixing bulbs and evergreens

Hardy flowering bulbs cover the ground spectacularly in spring. However, after they bloom and their leaves mature and die back, the ground is bare. Take advantage of the beauty of these flowering bulbs—and maintain a year-round covering on the soil—by planting them among evergreen groundcover plants such as pachysandra, ivy, or even a ground-hugging juniper. The green foliage sets off the colorful bulbs, then it hides the ripening leaves.

Ivy, a classic groundcover, has tough, triangular, evergreen leaves on strong, running stems. Leaves may be 1 to 4 inches wide, variegated in cream, white, gray, and green. Zones 5–10.

Wild ginger clusters in neat, low patches of patterned leaves. Its heart-shape leaves hide inconspicuous flowers in spring. It spreads slowly in shady sites. Highly collectible. Zones 2–8.

Lungwort likes moist soil in partial shade. It's available in a host of variegated white and green leaf patterns and shapes. Tiny, funnel-shaped spring flowers begin pink and fade to purplish. Zones 4–8.

Maidenhair fern features dark, 2-foot stalks, branched into a curved, horizontal pattern covered with dainty, pale green leaflets. It spreads slowly in shady, cool, moist soil in zones 3–8.

broad selection of plants attracts a wider range of beneficial insects and other creatures to control pests and diseases. Include a few plants that are indigenous to your region, because they're particularly adapted to your climate and soil. They also serve wildlife better than others and are usually low-maintenance. Use groundcovers to solve landscape problems around the yard. They'll cover surface tree roots, brighten shady spots, and hide eyesores such as decaying stumps and utility boxes.

Lady's mantle spreads its beauty in sun or partial shade. In late spring, clusters of tiny chartreuse flowers atop long stems emerge from distinctive, gray-green, scalloped leaves. Zones 4–7.

Lily-of-the-valley spreads in shady areas by means of underground bulblets. Its legendary fragrant flowers bloom in spring. Like other hardy bulbs, its leaves die back by late summer. Zones 2–7.

Prickly pear cactus thrives in any soil. Waxy, yellow, cupped flowers appear at the top margins of its rounded, prickly, succulent leaves in summer, followed by edible fruit. Zones 6–8.

Periwinkle, also known as myrtle, is low-growing, with small, narrowly oval, glossy green leaves all year long. Small, blue flowers decorate the mass of foliage in the spring. Zones 6–8.

choosing a groundcover

Plants with thorns or stickers discourage trespassers from cutting across certain areas. In large yards, you'll get the best effect by planting smaller, finer-textured plants in the foreground and locating taller, coarser-textured ones toward the back. Use brightly colored varieties to draw attention to an area or divert it from another one. Switch from one plant to another to indicate boundary changes.

You can find potential groundcover plants for almost every landscape. Some prefer shady, moist conditions, while others can handle dry or sunny sites and poor soil. The virtue of most groundcover plants is that they're inclined to grow larger in

using shrubs as groundcovers

Shrubs make excellent groundcovers. Ground-hugging or dwarf versions of evergreens, such as juniper—or small, low-growers, such as wintercreeper or cotoneaster—are ideal for sunny slopes or other areas that are difficult or dangerous to mow or where erosion is a problem. You can even cover that sunny slope with roses. New, low-maintenance landscape roses, such as Flower Carpet®, Meidiland™, or 'The Fairy,' bloom all season with virtually no care.

Sedums have succulent leaves on straight, 2-foot stems. Rounded flowerheads mature over the season from pale green, to fuzzy pink, to red, to rust—then dry for winter beauty. Zones 4–9.

Snow-in-summer is very easy to grow and enthusiastically creeps over sunny sites with poor soil. In June and July, its silver-gray leaves are covered with small white flowers. Zones 3–7.

Sweet woodruff weaves a web of fine roots just under the soil. Whorls of leaves are topped by delicate, white spring flowers. Plants are tenacious, neat, and tidy. Zones 5–8.

Thyme offers a selection of low-growing, woody, evergreen plants. Most have small, dark green or variegated aromatic leaves. Tiny, lavender-pink flowers appear in late spring. Zones 4–9.

clumps or by running stems or roots. As a result, their areas are filled with vigorous spreaders. However, beware of those that are so aggressive that they need constant controlling. They endanger other plants and create more problems than they solve.

Spotted dead nettle sports crinkled, variegated leaves on 6-inch stems. It likes shade and produces tiny, lavender flowers intermittently over the summer if left unsheared. Zones 4–8.

Variegated lilyturf (liriope) forms neat clumps of 8- to 12-inch, straplike leaves, striped yellow and green. Tiny lavender flowers appear on spikes in late summer. It grows in sun or shade in zones 6–10.

planting a groundcover

1 Purchase flats of rooted cuttings or individual young plants, or use divisions from existing plants. Keep their roots moist. Dig organic matter and slow-acting fertilizer into the soil.

2 Set the small, rooted plants in a grid pattern, equidistant from one another. The closer together you plant them, the sooner they'll knit together to cover the soil and create a continuous mass.

3 Water the transplants well and mulch between them with organic material. This will keep the soil moist longer and discourage weeds until the transplants have enough time to grow together.

groundcover buying guide

You'll find that the most satisfactory groundcovers will have many of these qualities:

- *Spread fairly quickly to cover bare soil.*
- *Tolerate a range of soil types.*
- *Spread reliably, but not rampantly.*
- *Easy to pull up if they spread too far.*
- *Have winter interest such as evergreen leaves, berries, or seedheads.*
- *Have interesting shapes and colors.*
- *Need minimal pruning, mowing, or grooming.*
- *Hold up for many years with little or no fuss.*

ornamental grasses

Ornamental grasses are easy to grow. As a group, they're tough and self-reliant, needing very little care over the years. Although they are members of the same family as the lawn grasses, they couldn't be more different. In fact, they have a host of virtues that lawn grasses lack. For starters, ornamental grasses boast resistance to drought, pests, and disease. They offer seasonal color, variegated leaves, and showy flowers. These strong characteristics make them a truly low-maintenance, high-performance group of plants. They're also environmentally correct—requiring no fertilizers, pesticides, or additional watering. Furthermore, they continue to perform all

weather

Although ornamental grasses tend to be stiff and sturdy, some of the tall ones are vulnerable to heavy winds and rainstorms. They're more likely to get matted down if they're not getting as much sun as they would like. Use unobtrusive stakes and string supports to keep the stems from flopping.

Blue fescue grows as 12-inch-wide clumps, 6 to 12 inches tall. It flowers in the summer in response to the heat. Its distinctive gray blue leaf blades are a standout in the winter. Zones 4–8.

Maiden grass (miscanthus) has many popular varieties, developing clumps of widely arching, 1-inch-wide, pointed leaves, reaching up to 12 feet tall in various colorations. Zones 5–9.

Hakone grass can handle shade. It forms low, arching clumps of bamboolike, variegated leaves. This grass also does well in containers. Zones 5–9.

Pampas grass has tall, plumed stems that are often used in dried floral crafts. It grows best where summers are hot and dry. Zones 7–10.

winter, creating light and movement with their handsome, vertical, straw-colored leaves and fluffy seedheads. Perhaps part of their appeal lies in the ancestral relationship we have with them. From the grassy savannas of Africa to the Great Prairie of North America, people lived among tall grasses. They built their homes with them and fed their livestock with them. Like lawn grasses, some ornamentals adapt to cool weather, others to warm conditions. Some spread by widening clumps, while others send runners or horizontal roots under the soil. And, like their cousins, they come in annual and perennial

dividing grasses

Divide overlarge clumps of ornamental grass in spring before the new shoots start to appear. Cut back the dried, bleached stems and then dig up the rootball. Use a sharp spade, saw, or ax to hack rooted chunks from the rootball, then replant each one. If the rootball is too large to dig up, cut out pie-shaped wedges while it's in the ground. Remove them to replant elsewhere, and fill in their spots with soil.

Eulalia grass is beautiful in winter. Its September flowers release seeds and dry atop bleached, dried, grass fronds. Use it to shelter and feed birds and screen out noise or neighbors. Zones 5-9.

Purple maiden grass flowers earlier than most, its pink tint evolving to outstanding red-orange fall foliage. Water in drought. Zones 5–9.

other great grasses

There are many wonderful grasses suitable for residential yards and gardens. In addition to the ones individually pictured and described here, many others have similar virtues. Some are annual, others perennial. They offer a variety of sizes and colors, as well as interesting flowers.

name	height
Big bluestem/Andropogon	5–8 feet
Feathertop	1½–2½ feet
Feather reed grass	Up to 5 feet
Giant reed	14–18 feet
Japanese blood grass	1–1½ feet
Little bluestem	2–3 feet
Meadow foxtail	2–3 feet
Northern sea grass (oat grass)	3–4 feet
Ravenna grass	7–15 feet
Switch grass	Up to 7 feet

varieties. But the similarity ends there. Ornamental grasses have enormous versatility. They not only make good groundcovers, but they also can play lots of other roles in your yard. Include them in flower beds and borders as vertical accents and color contrasts. Use low-growers to cascade over walls, and substitute taller versions for shrubs. Grow grasses in containers. Use them as accents. Plant them along boundaries as a living fence, or use them to screen a view and buffer traffic noise. Bring them indoors, too, and use their wonderful seedheads in dried and fresh flower arrangements or floral crafts. Although most ornamental grasses thrive in

using grasses as groundcovers

Ornamental grasses make excellent, long-lasting groundcovers. Because they generally require very little maintenance, they're a good choice for sunny sites. Choose those that develop as clumps that gradually enlarge each year to fill in and cover bare ground. Avoid those that spread by underground roots, because they're often hard to control.

Ribbon grass features creamy stripes on its spiky-green leaves. Because it spreads vigorously by underground runners, it eventually becomes difficult to control. Try planting it in a container. Zones 4–9.

Purple fountain grass is known for its upright, purplish red foliage and soft, fuzzy flowers atop 2- to 3-foot stems in summer. Drought-tolerant and hardy in Zone 9, it's often grown as an annual.

Fescue 'Elijah Blue' is a popular form of blue fescue with a strong, silvery blue color that grows to 8 inches tall. It has a tough constitution. Plant it in a sunny site that has well-drained soil. Zones 4–8.

Zebra grass is a form of maiden grass that grows in narrow clumps and is more floppy than upright. Its trademark foliage features horizontal yellow stripes against a green background. Zones 4–9.

hot sun and ordinary soil, some tolerate partial shade and moist soil. Choose grasses that suit the site. Plant in the spring at the exact depth as they were in their pots. Water well until they get established and send up new shoots. Don't fertilize or add any amendments, such as peat moss, to the soil. The only attention they require is cutting back in spring to make way for new shoots. After a few years, the clump may outgrow its allotted space. Move it or dig it up and divide it in the spring.

A garden full of ornamental grasses is a special place of color and movement all year long. First, the various grasses display their uniquely colored and patterned leaves. Then their flowers bloom, release seeds, and become puffy and delicate, as the grasses bleach and dry to a golden, winter beige.

A planting of five types of maiden grasses by a pool adds to the color, quiet, and privacy of the scene. The tall, softly arching leaves soften the effect of the adjoining masonry by suggesting falling water. The grasses also absorb sound and screen the view to enclose the pool area.

planting a slope

Slopes or inclines on your property can be problem areas. Sometimes they're so steep that you have trouble keeping your footing while working there. And they tend to erode unless they are planted to stabilize and hold the soil. Although your first thought might be to plant grass, the same grasses that make a great lawn aren't suitable for most slopes. Gentle inclines are difficult to mow and maintain. Steep ones are so dangerous that lawn mower manufacturers warn against mowing them. The best solution in either case is to plant low-maintenance plants as a groundcover. Soil on slopes tends to be dry because water runs downward before it has a chance to soak in. South-facing slopes are the toughest, because they receive intense sun during a good portion of the day—in summer and winter. As

YOU WILL NEED

- gloves
- weeding tools
- boards, stakes, hammer
- shovel and trowel
- organic material
- slow-acting fertilizer
- garden rake
- plants
- mulch or netting

1 Clear the area of weeds, stones, and any other debris. Wear a thick pair of gloves to protect your hands from glass or other sharp objects.

2 Save extra work later by taking the time now to pull or kill roots of perennial weeds. They'll be harder to deal with after the groundcover is established.

5 Plant as close together as the supply of plants allows, so they'll grow together faster. Stagger the rows so the plants can hold the soil better.

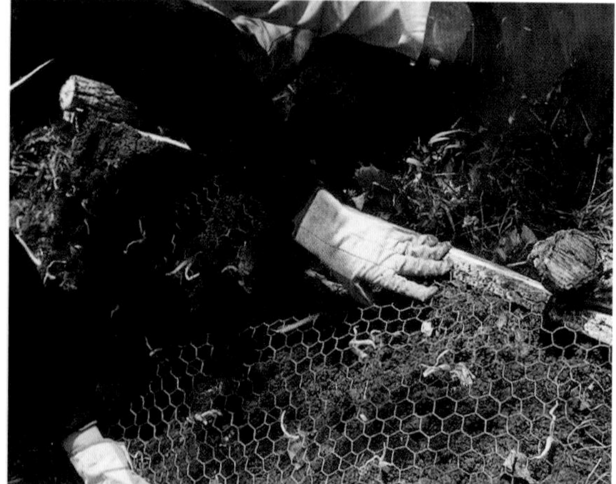

6 Cover the planting with polyspun garden fabric, landscape fabric, bark nuggets, or straw to hold the soil when it rains. Netting also works well.

a result, plants on these slopes are subject to scorching and desiccation. Fortunately, several alternatives, such as ornamental grasses, artemisias, juniper, and rosemary, can stand up to these pressures and stay attractive year-round. Prepare, water, and mulch the soil on a slope just as you would anywhere else you'd be planting groundcovers. However, you'll want to cover the soil on a grade as fast as possible, because once you've cleaned it off for planting, it's vulnerable to erosion. So spend the money it takes to get larger plants with well-developed root systems that will spread quickly. Then plant them as closely as possible so they will blend together rapidly and anchor the soil.

planting shrubs as groundcovers

Before you plant shrubs as groundcovers, kill the weeds in the area with a natural herbicide. Then dig individual holes, exactly as deep as each plant rootball is tall. Set each plant in a hole upright, then fill in and firm the soil over the roots. Water, then mulch the entire area with some coarse organic material to hold the soil until the plants spread to cover it.

3 Prepare for possible erosion after the slope is exposed by setting up a temporary barrier to retain the soil while you're planting.

4 If the soil is compacted and infertile, dig in some organic matter (to improve drainage and water retention) and some granular, slow-acting fertilizer.

regional lawn alternatives

Cool Climates

Spring

- [ ] As temperatures rise, remove winter mulch from beds.
- [ ] Cut back ornamental grasses to make way for new shoots.
- [ ] Divide overlarge clumps of ornamental grasses into smaller chunks to plant elsewhere.
- [ ] Mow or burn (if legal) meadows and prairies.
- [ ] Fertilize perennial groundcovers with a granular, slow-acting product.
- [ ] Renovate longtime groundcover plantings by cutting them back or mowing them at the highest mower setting. Topdress the area with organic matter to improve the soil.
- [ ] Plant new groundcovers and meadows.

Summer

- [ ] If rainfall is scarce, water grasses and groundcovers.
- [ ] Edge groundcover beds to control any exuberant new growth.
- [ ] Optional: Clip pieces of stem from groundcovers to root in water or damp vermiculite.

Warm Climates

Spring

- [ ] Cut back dried fronds of ornamental grasses and divide them into smaller plants, if necessary.
- [ ] Plant new groundcover beds or extend and renovate established ones.
- [ ] Rake, weed, and trim groundcover plantings as growth proceeds.

Summer

- [ ] If rainfall is scarce, water grasses and groundcovers.
- [ ] Trim groundcovers that overgrow their boundaries.
- [ ] Optional: Clip pieces of stem from groundcovers to root in water or damp vermiculite.

checklist

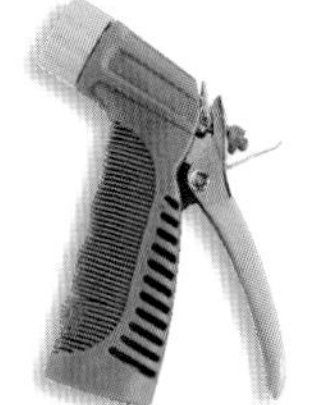

Fall

- ❑ Continue to water groundcovers in dry periods.
- ❑ Continue to edge and clip groundcover beds.
- ❑ After hard frost, mulch beds of non-evergreen groundcovers.

Winter

- ❑ Record information on the selections, care, and performance of groundcover plantings—especially new ones—over the past season.
- ❑ Drain gasoline and oil from power equipment and check spark plugs.
- ❑ Clean and sharpen garden tools to guard against rust.
- ❑ Order seeds and seedlings from mail-order nurseries and suppliers.

- ❑ Plant groundcovers when weather cools.
- ❑ Plant or overseed meadows and prairies.
- ❑ Divide overlarge clumps of groundcover plants into several smaller plants to locate elsewhere or give away.
- ❑ Shape up planted areas by trimming plants, clearing debris, and spreading fresh mulch.

- ❑ In warmest zones, continue to plant and tend groundcovers. Weed and mulch as necessary.
- ❑ Record information on the selections, care, and performance of groundcover plantings—especially new ones—over the past season.
- ❑ Drain gasoline and oil from power equipment and check spark plugs.
- ❑ Clean and sharpen garden tools to guard against rust.
- ❑ Order seeds and seedlings from mail-order nurseries and suppliers.

flowers in the garden

starting seeds indoors

Getting a jumpstart on the season is only one of the reasons for starting your own flowers and vegetables from seed. It also lets you try unusual varieties of favorite plants that are available only from seed. Also, seeds are less expensive than commercial seedlings. And having seedlings ready to transplant as soon as the weather permits gives you an instant garden. Finally, if you have seeds, you can plant a fall crop of certain vegetables when no commercial seedlings are available. Chase winter away by getting organized early. To ensure the widest choice, send your seed orders to mail-order suppliers shortly after the new year. Most annuals need six to eight weeks to grow—once they've germinated—before you can plant them outdoors; some require even more time. Estimate the best time to plant seeds indoors by checking the calendar and counting back from the date you expect the last frost in your area—adding the two weeks it usually takes for seeds to germinate. For the sturdiest seedlings possible, buy commercial seed-starting kits or individual

YOU WILL NEED

- peat pots, cell packs, or flats
- soil-less seed-starting mix, premoistened
- seeds
- indelible marker or pencil
- wooden sticks or plastic plant markers
- plastic cover
- fluorescent lights
- water

1 Fill peat pots, cell packs, or flats with the moistened mix to ¼ inch from their tops. Firm the mix slightly but do not pack it tightly.

2 Sow seeds either by scattering them over the mix or by dropping them individually in rows. Cover lightly with more mix.

seeds to start indoors

plant name	days to germination	time from seeding to planting outdoors
Basil	10	2–3 weeks
Coleus	10	6–8 weeks
Marigold	5	2–3 weeks
Petunia	10	6–8 weeks
Salvia	15	6–8 weeks
Snapdragon	10	6–8 weeks
Sweet alyssum	5	6–8 weeks
Zinnia	5	2–3 weeks

containers made of peat. Water the planted seeds from beneath, to prevent disease. (You can plant peat pots directly into the garden, which minimizes damage to the tender new seedling roots.) A soil-less seed-starting mix is best; it's sterile (which prevents disease) and drains well, yet retains necessary moisture. Some of the best seed-starting kits come with plastic covers and a heat mat, which provides bottom warmth that encourages seeds to germinate and grow well. Seedlings require 12 to 14 hours of daylight —hard to come by in February or March—so you should use fluorescent lights to ensure straight, sturdy stems. Gently brush the seedlings every so often to help encourage healthier growth. Acclimate new seedlings to the outdoors gradually; harden them off. Do this by setting them outside for a few hours—then increasingly longer each day for a week—before planting them in the garden.

moistening the potting mix

Adding moisture to soil-less potting mixes containing peat moss can be a challenge. The trick is to use very warm water. Always add the water to the mix, not vice versa. To moisten an entire bag of mix, put it under a running faucet for a few seconds or pour warm water into it. Let the mix sit for a while to absorb the water. Moisten smaller amounts by pouring the mix into a pan or pail; add water and blend it by hand.

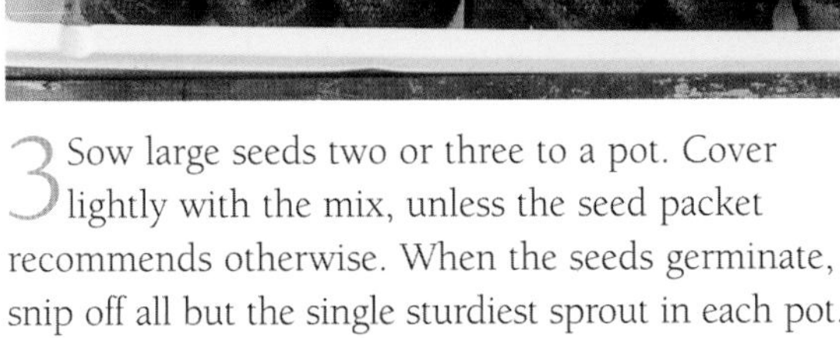

3 Sow large seeds two or three to a pot. Cover lightly with the mix, unless the seed packet recommends otherwise. When the seeds germinate, snip off all but the single sturdiest sprout in each pot.

4 Use an indelible marker and wooden sticks to label plants in each flat and pot. Include the name of the plant and the date started. Later add the date they germinate and the date planted in the garden.

5 Cover the containers with plastic to hold in humidity until the seeds germinate. Keep the containers out of direct sun and open the cover each day to let in fresh air. Once the sprouts appear, remove the plastic. Position the containers so the plants are about 6 inches from fluorescent lights. Water as needed.

starting seeds outdoors

Sometimes you'll have better luck sowing seeds directly into a prepared garden bed later in spring rather than starting them indoors ahead of time. That's because some plants simply don't transplant well, and others germinate so quickly that there's little to be gained by starting seedlings in advance. And, of course, direct sowing eliminates the need for seed-starting equipment, pots, and the actual transplant process. Oftentimes the hardest part about sowing seeds outdoors is being patient while the soil dries out and warms up. Squeeze a handful of soil to test it. If it sticks together in a ball, it's too wet; if it crumbles a bit, it's fine for planting. Certain plants—such as pansies, sweet peas, lettuce, spinach, and garden peas—grow best in cool weather. Plant their seeds in early spring, two to three weeks before you expect the last frost. Be sure to wait until there is no danger of frost before planting most other flower and vegetable seeds. They need warm soil to germinate and long days of sunshine to thrive. Direct seeding into the garden

YOU WILL NEED

- lime, sand, or sturdy string
- seeds
- pencil or indelible marker
- wooden sticks or plastic plant markers
- water

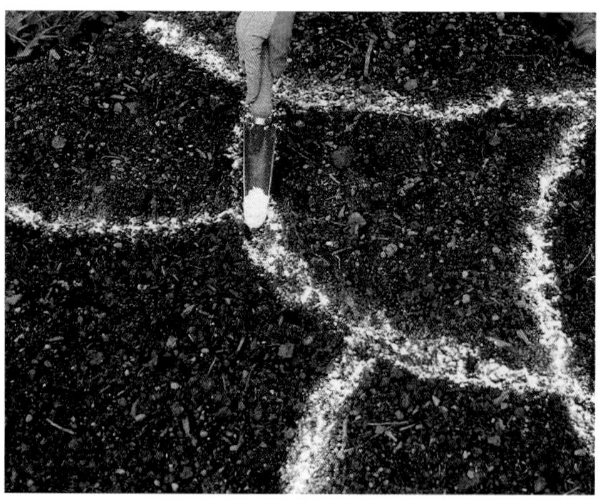

1 After preparing the soil, mark off the planting area with lime, sand, or sturdy string. These markings can be removed later.

2 Scatter seeds on top of the soil or trace straight furrows at the depth specified on the seed packet. Dribble seeds held between thumb and forefinger.

getting seeds to sprout

Some seeds require some help to germinate. They are usually seeds that are large or that have a thick seed coat. Seeds that need pretreatment include parsley, moonflower, and morning glory. Do this by soaking the seeds overnight in tepid water. The other method is to place the soaked seeds between two sheets of moistened paper or toweling, roll up the paper, and put it in a plastic bag overnight. Check the seeds every morning and evening until they've sprouted *(left)*, then plant as usual.

is a snap. However, the new seedlings face natural hazards such as birds, soil pathogens, and rain-compacted or sun-baked soil. A well-prepared seedbed—one with loose and crumbly soil that drains well—compensates for some of these difficulties. To duplicate these conditions, loosen the soil (using the appropriate tool—trowel, shovel, or power tiller)—remove stones, and mix in organic matter such as compost, peat moss, or chopped leaves. Then add granular, slow-acting fertilizer to provide season-long, consistent nutrition to the plants. Rake the soil smooth. Seeds usually sprout too close together. When they have developed two or three sets of leaves, thin the plants. Remove as many as necessary to establish the spacing recommended on the seed packet. When the plants are several inches tall, mulch the soil between them to discourage weeds.

3 Label areas or rows as a reminder of what's been planted. Weeds sometimes germinate along with the plants you're growing, so labels help to identify the new seedlings.

4 Cover seeds with a thin layer of soil to a depth specified on the seed packet. Firm the soil gently for good contact with the seeds. Some seeds need light to germinate and should not be covered.

5 Moisten the soil if rain is not expected. Use a gentle, fine spray to avoid disturbing the seeds. Make sure the soil doesn't dry out. Keep the young seedlings moist after they sprout, too.

planting seeds

- *Tiny seeds are more manageable for sowing when mixed with sand.*
- *Large seeds or those with hard seed coats germinate faster if soaked overnight in tepid water prior to planting.*
- *Seeds embedded in tapes facilitate uniform spacing.*
- *Seeds of some so-called hardy annuals, such as calendula, nigella, pansy, poppy, and snapdragon, can be sown in fall, because they can handle winter cold and dampness.*

transplanting seedlings

After a period of gradually acclimating to the wind and sun outdoors, young plants are ready to go into the garden. This process can be traumatic for the plants, so try to choose an overcast day or wait until late in the day to plant. This spares the seedlings extra stress from bright sun while they cope with the inevitable transplant shock. They also adjust much better if their new soil is loosened, moist, and reasonably warm. Dig a hole for each seedling about the size of its pot. Tip each plant from its container, tapping the bottom to dislodge it if necessary. If its roots are encircling the root ball (because of confinement in the pot too long) loosen them by hand or cut vertical slits in the root ball. Set each plant in a hole at the same depth that it grew in its pot. Gently but firmly press the loose soil around the plant to seat it in the ground and force out any air pockets, then sprinkle with tepid water. After a week, water the new transplants with water-soluble plant food mixed at half the strength recommended on the label.

spacing plants

One way to avoid problems as seedlings mature into full-sized plants is to allow enough space between them when planting. Although the garden may seem bare at first, giving plants the room to grow without being crowded ensures good air circulation, which deters diseases. Mulch the bare soil between small plants to discourage weeds from filling the space while the seedlings grow.

Set small plants in rows to edge beds. Screen an undesirable view with a row of tall plants. Plant flowers in rows for convenient cutting.

Ornamental plants make an impact when grouped. Odd-numbered clusters work best—three large plants or up to nine small ones per group.

aftercare

- Water newly transplanted flowers and vegetables every day or two in warm weather until their roots grow deeper in the soil. When they show new stem and foliage growth, you'll know that their roots are established properly.
- Spread a 2-inch layer of organic material on the bare soil between the young plants. This mulch will discourage weeds and help keep the soil moist.
- Pull any weeds that appear in the planting area. They compete for water and soil nutrients.
- Early in the season, watch for unexpected temperature drops. Have polyspun garden fabric handy to cover the transplants if frost threatens.
- Insert stakes into the soil or erect trellises for plants that will need support.
- Inspect plant foliage regularly for insects or disease. Pinch off tender plant tips, if necessary, to eliminate clusters of aphids.
- As transplants mature, pinch off stem tips to increase side branching and compactness.

Tuck young transplants into existing beds among flowers that require the same amount of light and water. Do not crowd them.

choosing nursery-grown plants

- Go to a reputable nursery or garden center, where they're likely to receive the best care.
- Buy early when the plants are fresh and young.
- Check for moist soil and perky foliage to determine that the plants have been properly cared for.
- Choose plants that are compact and stocky, with firm stems. This means they've received good light.
- Look for leaves that are a rich green and free from discolored spots or signs of insects.
- Examine the plant's roots by slipping it from its pot. The roots should be well developed throughout the potting mix but not tightly tangled or trailing out of the bottom hole of the pot.
- Select plants that are in bud but not fully flowering. Younger plants transplant more successfully than older ones.
- Check to be sure that all the plants in a market pack or flat are healthy.

planting flowers

Flowering plants may bloom annually or perennially. *Annuals* are genetically programmed to live their entire life cycle in one season. They sprout from seed in spring, then mature, flower, set new seed, and die (when frost arrives). Although some may tolerate light frost, they're unable to withstand temperatures below freezing. Annuals are remarkable for their flower production—virtually nonstop over the season. Many leave behind their seeds to grow and bloom the next season. *Perennials* are more permanent plants. They live for many years, their roots developing gradually to support increasing top growth over several seasons. The majority are able to withstand winter weather in most regions, although some are "tender" perennials and do not survive in far-northern winter climates. Perennials bloom for only

planting bare-root perennials

YOU WILL NEED

- bare-root plants
- shovel or trowel
- water

1 Unpack mail-order plants immediately and check them carefully. Look for damaged roots and, if leaves are present, signs of insects or disease.

2 Plant bare-root perennials promptly. Dig a hole in prepared soil and form a hill or cone of packed soil at the bottom to support the roots.

3 Spread the roots on the cone and cover them with soil so the crown—where the roots join the stems—is level with surrounding soil. Water well.

a limited time each year. The remainder of the season their foliage collects energy from the sun to build strong roots for next year. Annuals and perennials are sold by mail order and at garden centers. Young plants are sold in flats or cell packs that hold four to twelve or more. Older plants are usually in individual pots. Plant them as soon as possible after you buy them. Be sure to keep the soil moist if there's a delay. Trim off any broken stems or damaged leaves. If the plants come in plastic pots, knock them out of the pots before you put them in the ground. Make sure you keep the soil and roots intact as the plants go into their holes. Plant ones that come in peat or coconut-fiber pots directly into

special handling for taprooted perennials

Some bare-root perennials, such as this Siberian aster, have a long taproot. Plant them deeply.

Move a spade back and forth to make the hole. Then position the taproot and press the hole closed.

Plants may have either taproots or fibrous roots. Both depend on the root hairs to take up water and nutrients from the soil and pass them to the main root system. Carrots are a good example of a taprooted plant. So are dandelions, butterfly weed, and balloon flower. In taprooted plants, root functions are concentrated in one main root. This tapered, thick structure grows and elongates as it penetrates deep into the soil. The root hairs are concentrated on this structure, so don't break off a part of it or you might doom the plant. This makes taprooted plants a challenge to transplant. That's why they're usually sold as young transplants. It's too risky to dig and package them for sale when they're mature and the taproot is large because the root is so brittle that it's easily damaged when handled.

Handle young plants with taproots very gently. Carefully choose a place for these plants; they won't tolerate being moved once they are established and grow larger. All taprooted seedlings are fragile. If they've been field-grown, their roots might have been damaged when they were dug up. Plants that are raised and sold in peat pots—which can go directly into the ground, pot and all—are best because the plant is least disturbed by the planting process. Keep transplants moist until planting time. Place taprooted plants in soil that has been deeply cultivated so the root grows downward freely. Soil that's compacted, has heavy clay, or contains large stones impedes root growth and causes stress. Before planting, add organic matter—such as peat moss or compost—to improve soil texture.

benefits of flowers

Adding flowers to a landscape improves the health of all plants. A variety of bright and colorful blossoms attracts many beneficial insects, most of which especially like open, daisylike blooms. These predatory insects, which are virtually invisible, attack and kill other insects that not only threaten plants but carry diseases that can cause even more damage.

planting flowers

the prepared bed. Follow the same procedure outlined on pages 142 and 143 for transplanting seedlings. Mail-order perennials usually arrive dormant—still in their winter rest cycle and without any leaves. Some are shipped bare-root rather than in pots with soil. Their roots are wrapped in moist sphagnum moss, wood shavings, or similar material. The absence of soil eliminates the chance that soil-borne diseases will be passed across state lines. These plants also weigh less, reducing the cost of shipping. They probably were grown outdoors in real soil, so their roots are well-prepared for transplanting into your own soil.

planting container-grown plants

YOU WILL NEED

- container-grown plants
- garden shovel
- trowel
- knife
- water
- organic mulch

1 Before planting, set container-grown plants on the bed to determine the best placement. Odd-numbered groupings look most natural. Allow space for perennials to mature and spread each year.

2 Dig a hole large enough to accommodate the root ball when it's removed from the container. Set the plant in the hole so that the top of the root ball is level with the surrounding soil.

3 Gently tip the plant out of the pot. If necessary, tap the bottom of the pot with a trowel handle to free the plant. Loosen tangled roots and make vertical cuts in any that are circling the root ball.

4 Set the plant in the hole and fill in around the roots with soil. Firm the soil, then water well. Mulch the bare soil around the plant with chopped leaves, compost, or other organic material.

Site the transplants—both annuals and perennials—where the available light suits their needs. Water them as you plant them, then continue watering on a regular basis, particularly if rainfall is limited in your area. Sufficient moisture will help them cope with the stress of having been shipped. Don't fertilize them until you see their ready signal: new leaf or stem growth. Some plants will grow tall and need support. Set stakes near them in the soil while the plants are young to avoid root damage.

easy-to-grow perennials

The plants listed below are widely available at retail outlets across the country. They're also recognized as reliable and sturdy within the perennial plant industry as well as by gardeners across America.

- **'Sprite' astilbe –** a diminutive hybrid astilbe with glossy dark green foliage; produces sprays of shell-pink flowers in midsummer shade gardens
- **'Moonbeam' coreopsis –** small, eight-petaled pale yellow flowers grace the tips of thin stems covered with narrow leaves; blooms all summer in full sun
- **'Palace Purple' heuchera –** boasts handsome deep purple foliage all summer in partial shade; bears tiny, pale bluish-white flowers clustered at the ends of wiry stems in spring
- **Creeping phlox –** neat, deep green foliage on creeping stems mats to cover the ground in woodland settings; produces clusters of small florets in white, blue, or pink in spring
- **'Sunny Border Blue' veronica –** offers a strong, vertical accent for the garden and bears spikes of rich, violet-blue flowers in summer; does best in a sunny site
- **'Magnus' purple coneflower –** jaunty, daisy-like flowers with droopy purple petals bloom in midsummer when many other perennials are idle; thrives in full sun
- **'Goldsturm' black-eyed Susan –** provides billows of late-summer daisy-like golden blossoms with dark centers on coarse, hairy stems

diagnosing plant symptoms

Plants give clear signs when they aren't healthy. Inspect them for symptoms at the nursery before you purchase them. Examine their foliage, stems, and roots. Choose only plants that appear to be sturdy and vigorous. Beware of bargain plants that might have been neglected or kept too long on the shelves at the garden center.

- **Yellow or wilted leaves –** neglect; lack of water, light, or fertilizer
- **Spotted or discolored leaves –** possible fungal disease
- **Lower leaves fallen onto soil in pot –** irregular watering; temperature stress
- **Dark marks or blotches on the stem –** injury or disease
- **Specks on undersides of leaves –** possible insect infestation
- **Spindly stem –** insufficient light
- **Lots of flowers, few buds –** overfertilization and/or advanced age of plant
- **Weeds in the container –** nutrients not getting to plant due to weed competition; infertile soil
- **Roots emerging from container –** plant outgrowing its pot

supporting flowers

Flowering plants are ornamental and add wonderful color and texture to your landscape. Although some yards are informal—with flowers spilling willy-nilly out of beds and over fences—many plants in this setting look best if they are supported. Such plants will benefit from more sunlight and better air circulation, and their flowers are less likely to be splashed with mud or their stems broken in rainstorms. Take advantage of the enormous number of commercial staking devices, or make your own. Choose a support appropriate to each plant's habit and shape. Train climbing stems while they're tender and flexible. To prevent root damage, insert stakes near plants when

keeping vines in line

Some vines, such as moonflower, can grow up to a foot a day, so make sure it's growing where you want it. Check often for stems or tendrils that wander off-limits.

twining vines

Some vines twine around a support in either a clockwise or counterclockwise direction. If you're training such a vine (morning glory, pole bean, or moonflower, for example) and it falls off the support after you've wrapped it in one direction, wind it the other way.

Support branching plants, such as these purple coneflowers, by inserting sturdy stakes around the perimeter of the clump. Zigzag string from one stake to another to form a support matrix for the stems.

Metal ring supports, commonly used with peonies, also discipline clusters of supple stems that tend to flop. Use the supports temporarily around clumps of daffodils and freesias.

Reinforce tall plants in beds with individual stakes or a string matrix attached to stakes located around the entire perimeter of the bed.

A row or two of string fastened to stakes around the outside of a plant clump, such as these black-eyed Susans, sometimes does the job.

they are young. Set matrix or ring-type supports for clumping plants early in the season so the burgeoning stems can grow through easily. Inspect and repair permanent devices before plants begin their climb. Above all, make sure all supports are extremely sturdy.

Secure tall plants, such as lilies or delphiniums, to stakes with loose twist ties or soft yarn in figure-eight loops. Avoid root damage by inserting stakes into the soil near each stem when the plant is young.

You can purchase single-stem metal supports with easy-open loops to hold an individual flower stem, such as a lily, loosely and inconspicuously.

supporting vines

Fasten simple wooden "rungs" to a wall as a permanent ladder-type support for this mandevilla and other vines. Weave the stems along the support before they become woody.

Some vines will grab onto any object without encouragement. For an informal look, let sweet peas, clematis, and morning glory wrap their tendrils or stems around whatever is handy.

A few vines will obligingly climb horizontally, too. Train a clematis, such as this, to attach to rails or picket fences. Roses cannot cling so fasten their canes with twist ties.

Arbors and pergolas look best covered with vines. Guide young stems toward the base of the structure. Annuals, such as morning glory and lablab, bloom most of the summer.

Vines thickly established on a trellis create privacy and screen out unwanted views. Perennial vines will provide a mantle of leaves after their bloom period is over.

encouraging blooms

Pruning is not normally associated with flowers. Most people think of pruning shrubs and trees when this subject comes up. However, the judicious cutting away of part of a plant is just as important to the health and performance of annual and perennial flowering plants as it is to their woody cousins. Techniques called *deadheading* and *cutting back* are really just types of pruning, and both are key to maintaining flowering plants in a garden setting. They're also the best ways to encourage plants to deliver the most and best flowers for the longest possible time. There are lots of ways that pruning can encourage plants to bloom. If you cut back entire stems when they become leggy, you will stimulate the plants to replace them with new, vigorous growth that will eventually produce more flowers. Because you're eliminating worn and possibly damaged parts of the plant, you're also doing away with potential sites for disease or insect attack. This ensures that the plant will live out its natural life span and produce a maximum number of

attracting birds

Leave some flowers to dry into seeds for the birds to eat in fall and winter. They especially like black-eyed Susan, purple coneflower, bee balm, amaranth, thistle, and other plants with large seed heads. Of course, sunflowers are the all-time favorites, keeping birds fed well into the snowy months.

Disbudding—or removing certain buds as they form on plants such as peonies—directs energy to the remaining ones, producing larger flowers.

Delay cutting back faded blooms and bare stems of plants and you'll be rewarded with interesting seedpods. The seeds of money plant are perfect for dried arrangements.

self-sowing flowers

You usually can count on these flowers to reproduce themselves:

- Anise hyssop
- Blanket flower
- Calendula
- California poppy
- Chamomile
- Cleome
- Columbine
- Four-o'clock
- Foxglove
- Garlic chives
- Hollyhock
- Johnny-jump-up
- Marigold
- Morning glory
- Nicotiana
- Nigella
- Scilla
- Sweet alyssum
- Tall verbena
- Tiger lily

flowers. You can extend the life span of some biennial plants well beyond the normal two years by cutting their flower stems immediately after they bloom. Use sharp pruners and cut the stems cleanly to promote healing. Cutting stems partway is less drastic than removing them completely. It also forces plants to send out side branches. Cut them back just far enough to remove a cluster of faded flowers and bare stem down to the next leaves. New growth will obscure the cut, make the plant bushier, and provide more lateral stems to flower. The flowers may be smaller, but they will be more numerous.

Deadheading—pinching off individual blooms that are dead or dying—extends the bloom period by promoting repeat blooms. Because plants are intended to set seed, removing the flowers before they can accomplish that causes the plant to produce more flowers and try again to complete its life cycle.

pruning tools

Sharp pruners and garden shears make clean cuts. This is important because clean cuts heal faster, making plants less vulnerable to disease. They undergo minimum stress and look neater. Choose pruners with bypass blades rather than anvil-type blades, which tend to crush stems as they cut.

Deadheading flowers—promptly pinching or cutting off those flowers that have faded—stimulates a plant to produce replacement buds and more blooms. It improves the plant's appearance, too.

Deadheading flowers and stems—a practice that makes sense when you encounter long, bare stems—is appropriate for this black-eyed Susan. Cut back to where leaves emerge from the stem.

Cutting back means cutting major stems back to the foliage at soil level. This removes all the spent flowers and old stems, stimulating the plant to send up new stems with fresh buds.

encouraging blooms

Annuals respond to deadheading enthusiastically by diverting the energy that they would have devoted to making seeds into making new flowers. Deadheading also prompts certain perennials to complete the development of buds lower on the stem that might otherwise never bloom. To remove faded flowers on tender stems, simply pinch their stems between your thumb and forefinger and pull sharply. Sometimes it helps to press with your fingernail. If the stem is too tough, as are many perennials, use scissors or pruners. You can apply the same pruning techniques to foliage plants as well. Pinching off flowers, cutting back to the next leaves, or trimming to the ground stimulates the plant to produce new stems and fresh, young leaves. In the case of coleus, where the flowers detract from

disbudding

You can manipulate a plant's bloom size or bloom pattern by disbudding. It involves the selective removal of flower buds from a plant. For example, if you remove the terminal bud, you will induce the plant to produce more—but smaller—flowers than normal on side shoots. If you remove side buds, you'll encourage the plant to create a larger single terminal flower.

Deadhead plants to eliminate unwanted blooms. Pinch off flower heads from coleus to encourage desirable foliage and stall the plant's aging process.

Encourage branching by pinching off flower heads. The plant responds by producing new stems from the main stalk, giving it a bushier look.

Deadhead drifts of low-growing groundcovers, such as sweet alyssum, by shearing spent blossoms all at once. This revitalizes the entire planting.

Stimulate new flowering within weeks in a patch of damaged plants by cutting back affected plants to healthy stems with foliage.

the effect of the varied and colorful foliage, deadheading maintains leaf production. In plants where foliage is edible—such as basil, lettuce, or parsley—pinching and cutting back to eliminate flowers prevents the foliage from becoming bitter. Although these techniques benefit plants, they also cause temporary stress. Plants must rally to heal wounds and start to develop replacements for the lost foliage and flowers. Give them a light dose of fertilizer and plenty of moisture to help them rebuild tissues and maintain or increase blooming for the remainder of the season.

Some roses put on a spectacular show in June, then spend the rest of the season soaking up sunshine to prepare for next year. Prune off their spent blooms to improve their appearance and prevent disease. Other types, such as low-maintenance landscape and rugosa roses, keep flowering even with spent blooms on the plant. Hybrid tea, grandiflora, and floribunda rose varieties require regular deadheading for best summer-long production. Clip off spent flowers to a junction of five or more leaflets along the stem.

no deadheading needed

Some annuals deadhead themselves. They're sometimes described as self-cleaning plants. Their faded blossoms, often small to begin with, shrivel, dry, and drop off of their own accord. The next rain washes off any that have temporarily stuck to the foliage on their way to the soil. These plants, including wax begonia, impatiens, cleome, morning glory, and nicotiana, quickly generate lots of replacement flowers.

planning a cutting garden

A cutting garden is more practical than it is ornamental. Its gorgeous, colorful flowers certainly look beautiful, but they're only there temporarily. This type of garden is grown to be cut down. It's a production facility, where flowers are a crop you'll be using for indoor arrangements, gifts, floral crafts, and sometimes even cooking. Often tucked behind the house or inside a fence of its own, a cutting garden never has to be in display condition. In fact, it's often planted in space-saving rows or beds designed for regular harvesting. Many kinds of flowering plants are suitable for a cutting garden. For fresh-cut bouquets, choose ones with sturdy stems and a long vase life such as lilies, zinnias, and snapdragons. For dried-flower crafts and arrangements, plant flowers that easily air-dry and hold their color. As you plan your layout, be sure to site the plants so that the taller ones do not shade the smaller ones. And try to place similar flowers in groups, for easier harvest. After you cut them all, clear up the area and put in a new crop.

flowers for cutting

These flowers are traditional favorites for cutting gardens:

- *Aster*
- *Baby's breath*
- *Blue salvia*
- *Celosia*
- *Chrysanthemum*
- *Cleome*
- *Cosmos*
- *Daffodil*
- *Dahlia*
- *Delphinium*
- *Goldenrod*
- *Larkspur*
- *Lily*
- *Nicotiana*
- *Snapdragon*
- *Statice*
- *Sunflower*
- *Tulip*
- *Zinnia*

Long-stemmed flowers, whether perennial or annual, are the most popular and useful for cutting gardens. All types of daisies are big favorites and combine well with lots of other flowers. Silver-leafed artemisia and herbs, such as lavender and sage, have silver foliage that is handsome and aromatic.

Include all kinds of flowers in a cutting garden—early-season bulbs, spring annuals, summer bulbs and flowers, and fall-flowering plants. To ensure a steady supply of gladiolus, plant bulbs every few weeks. Don't forget plants with interesting foliage, pods, and seed heads.

Plant annuals in succession for maximum yield. As soon as you cut one stand of blossoms, pull the plants, cultivate the bed, and add seedlings for the next cutting. Or devote one bed to mature plants, a second to those on the brink of maturity, and a third to young plants—ensuring a steady supply over the entire growing season.

drying flowers

Dried flowers evoke memories of sunny days long after summer is gone. They keep the garden vibrant and real in your memory during the bleak winter months ahead. You can begin picking and drying flowers as soon as the plants start blossoming. By fall, many of the blooms you've picked will be thoroughly dried and ready for arranging. Those still growing in the garden will have wonderful seedheads and pods, which make lovely additions to arrangements. Flower drying is as much an art as a science. All kinds of garden and wild plants are good candidates for one or another of the common drying methods. Trial and error will reveal which flowers dry well and hold their color

preserving dried flowers

Spray flowers dried in silica gel with floral spray so they don't reabsorb humidity and droop. Treat air-dried flowers with floral spray or hair spray to prevent them from shattering. Be sure to coat all sides of petals and leaves thoroughly.

To show off maximum color and texture of dried flowers, display them in harvest baskets. Freshen and decorate your rooms by mixing lots of different blooms with aromatic dried foliage or scented oils.

Dried floral arrangements may be formal or informal. Because dried flowers have less density than their fresh counterparts, you'll need more dried flowers and foliage to fill a display container.

Wreaths of dried materials have an ancient history as symbols of friendship and good luck. Use sturdy flowers if you want to mount them on a door.

All varieties of rosebuds air-dry well. Wire their stems for support and hang them for at least four weeks. All roses darken in color when dried.

longest. Harvest flowers on a low-humidity day after the dew has dried. Choose those that are nearing their peak and are in perfect condition; discard any that show blemishes and insect damage. Collect enough flowers to allow for losses. Be sure to include as much stem as possible with each one.

Try all kinds of flowers, and don't forget wild ones such as Queen-Anne's-lace. Vegetable and herb gardens are treasure troves of possibilities. Flowering trees and shrubs are others. Harvest the blossoms of peegee and oak-leaved hydrangea in stages as they dry on the plants and gradually change color.

the best flowers to dry

Each of these flowers is an excellent candidate for drying. Of course, you'll want to find out which ones grow best in your part of the country.

- Astilbe
- Baby's breath
- Bells of Ireland
- Blazing star
- Celosia (crested or plumed)
- Cosmos
- Feverfew
- Globe amaranth
- Globe thistle
- Goldenrod
- Hydrangea
- Lavender
- Miniature rose
- Ornamental grasses
- Ornamental onion
- Scotch broom
- Statice
- Strawflower
- Thrift
- Yarrow
- Zinnia

flower-drying techniques

You can air-dry many flowers outdoors in shade and low humidity or indoors in a dry, warm attic. Hang bunched stems upside down or stand them upright in empty vases.

Bury multipetaled flowers such as these marigolds in a box of silica gel or other desiccant powder such as borax. Cover tightly. Check dryness in three weeks. To create a stem, insert florist wire into flower and wrap with florist's tape.

planting fall perennials

Fall is a wonderful time for planting. Though it's not the traditional planting season, it should be. In fact, it's an ideal time for lots of plants, including many trees and shrubs, to be moved from one place to another. Divide and replant perennials, set out hardy bulbs that will bloom in spring, and introduce new plants into your yard. Fall-planted perennials benefit from the increasingly cooler temperatures as they adjust to their new surroundings. Their roots don't have to support burgeoning leaf growth and cope with hot, possibly dry weather while they're trying to get established. About the only plants that don't do well are fall bloomers. Theoretically, you can plant

planting oriental poppies

YOU WILL NEED

- trowel
- organic matter
- slow-acting fertilizer
- Oriental poppy roots
- water

weather

Alternating freezes and thaws during the winter disturb soil and can cause it to heave newly planted bulbs and rooted plant crowns to the soil surface. Always mulch planting beds with 3 to 4 inches of organic material.

1 Dig planting holes slightly larger than each poppy root and 2 to 3 inches deep. Space holes a foot or more apart. Mix organic matter and granular, slow-acting fertilizer into the soil.

2 Plant dormant Oriental poppy roots in late summer to early fall. Divide established plantings to thin clumps or to increase the supply of plants. Oriental poppies like well-drained soil.

3 Spread the roots at the bottom of the hole, the knobby crown facing upward so that any foliage is above soil level. Fill the hole with soil; water well.

4 Firm the soil around the plant crown by hand and water again to rinse off any foliage. Mulch the bed with chopped leaves or evergreen boughs.

most container-grown items anytime during the season. However, goldenrod, chrysanthemums, and asters do best if planted in spring so their roots are well established by the time they produce their flowers. Unfortunately, you won't be able to find as wide a choice of perennials in garden centers in fall as you will in spring. The plants you do find may be severely root-bound after being confined in a pot all summer long. However, if properly handled, they should do just fine—and they might be on sale. If you live in an area where the ground doesn't freeze hard until November, perennials that

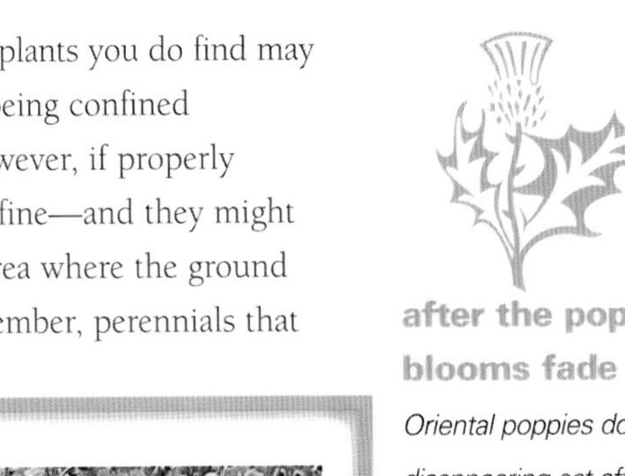

after the poppy blooms fade

Oriental poppies do a disappearing act after they bloom in late spring and early summer. Their leaves melt away as the plants go dormant to escape the heat. Plant annuals —or place planted containers—in the vacated area. Remove them in early fall when fresh, new poppy foliage reappears in anticipation of next year's bloom.

planting fall perennials

you plant just after Labor Day will have plenty of time to make themselves at home. Whatever the time of year, thorough soil preparation and the proper planting techniques are the keys to healthy perennials. Dig the soil to aerate it, and remove weeds, stones, and other debris. Take this opportunity to improve the soil's texture and water-holding capacity by digging in some organic matter such as peat moss, compost, leaf mold, or similar material. This also will improve drainage. Delay fertilizing until next spring if the soil is decent. When new growth starts in spring, sprinkle some granular, slow-acting fertilizer on the soil so the spring rains can soak it in. The food will provide consistent, uniform nutrition for several weeks while the

safety first

When working with stone, always wear protective clothing—gloves, sturdy boots, and long sleeves and pants. When you do any lifting, be sure to bend your knees to protect your back.

rodent alert

Rodents, such as mice and chipmunks, often nest in and around stone walls. Their activities disturb the soil behind the wall and might dislodge plants. Inspect plants often to be sure they're secure in the wall and are getting enough moisture.

planting perennials along a path

1 Be sure the plants you place in or near paths are low-growing and sturdy so they'll withstand wayward footsteps. The gravel base under stone walks provides good drainage for herbs and minor bulbs.

2 Create planting pockets by leaving generous spaces between stones or by removing existing stones or bricks from an established walkway. Dig holes deep enough to accommodate the root balls.

3 Set the root ball in the hole at or slightly above the surface of neighboring stones. Fill the hole with soil, and water the plant well.

4 Prune all stems that intrude onto the walking area. Water again to rinse the stones and thoroughly moisten the soil.

plants experience rapid new growth. Plant perennials at exactly the depth they were in their pots—never deeper. As you remove each plant from its pot, check the roots. If the roots are wrapped in circles, pry them loose or make vertical cuts through them to encourage growth to the sides. Set each plant in its hole, firm the soil over its root ball and around its stem, then add water. Water the plants every five to eight days, particularly when the soil feels dry. Mulch with 2 to 3 inches of chopped leaves, wood chips, pine needles, or compost to insulate the soil during the long winter.

planting a stone wall

1 Insert plants on the face of a dry stone wall—one with no mortar between the stones—by creating planting pockets. Temporarily remove a stone or eliminate a portion of it to open up a space.

2 Scoop out soil to make a hole, if possible. If not, pack soil into an empty crevice between stones. Most rock-garden plants have shallow, fine root systems and don't need much soil.

3 Position the plant and fill in around its roots with soil. Pack soil tightly around plants inserted into wall crevices. Wedge in small stones if necessary.

4 Snugly fit a stone against the new plant to hold it in place. Water thoroughly. The plant will receive moisture through spaces between stones.

plants for tough spaces

These plants are especially appropriate for planting in walls or paths:

- *Ajuga*
- *Corsican mint*
- *Creeping sedum*
- *Dianthus (pinks)*
- *Golden moneywort*
- *Johnny-jump-ups*
- *Lamb's ears*
- *Portulaca*
- *Serbian bellflower*
- *Soapwort*
- *Sweet alyssum*
- *Thyme (creeping and woolly)*

planting bulbs

Spring-flowering (or hardy) bulbs are the ultimate low-maintenance flowers. Because their roots can withstand winter cold and frozen soil, they bloom year after year. And they emerge on schedule every spring without any attention, long before you've begun your traditional gardening chores. A little fertilizer once a year and mulch over the soil keeps them happy. All plants in the bulb category have an interesting component—modified structures that store starch, which provides the energy to fuel their growth and flowering. Whether these structures are called bulbs, corms, tuberous roots, or rhizomes, they work the same way. After the plants flower, their leaves continue to soak up sunshine for several

mass planting

YOU WILL NEED

- spading fork
- organic material
- bulb fertilizer
- garden rake
- bulbs
- trowel or bulb planter
- water
- mulch

1 Good soil preparation provides the drainage that hardy bulbs require. Use a spading fork to dig down at least 12 inches in the soil to loosen and aerate it, so the bulb roots will grow deep.

2 Mix in organic material, such as compost, leaf mold, or peat moss, to enrich the soil and improve its ability to hold moisture. If your soil is heavy clay, consider building a raised bed.

selecting bulbs

Buy only top-quality bulbs for the best performance. Look for large, firm bulbs with smooth, unblemished surfaces. They're well worth the slightly greater cost.

4 To create an informal, natural-looking planting area, scatter the bulbs randomly. If necessary, adjust them slightly to maintain reasonable spacing.

5 Use a trowel or bulb planter to dig individual holes roughly twice as deep as the height of the bulb. Set each bulb in the hole, pointed tip upward.

weeks. This builds energy reserves from nutrients that are taken up by the roots and stored in the bulb. Their job completed, the leaves ripen, yellow, and collapse. Hardy bulbs rest beneath the soil, escaping summer heat until next season. The best time to plant bulbs is in early fall, when cool weather

3 Mix in granular, slow-acting fertilizer that's specifically formulated for bulbs. Then rake the area smooth, removing any stones, weeds, and other debris you find.

6 Fill each hole with soil and firm it gently over the bulb. If rain isn't expected soon, water the bed to settle the soil. Cover the area with mulch.

bulb-planting tools and tips

A hand trowel is an ideal tool for planting bulbs in clusters. Excavate flat-bottomed holes that are large enough for several bulbs. Odd-numbered clusters look best.

Use a bulb planter or an auger attached to a power drill to dig lots of individual holes in a large area. This makes it easier to plant bulbs in natural drift patterns.

A minishovel or a long-handled trowel works well for planting small bulbs. Insert it into the soil to the desired depth. Press it forward to open a crevice, then drop in the bulb.

Although narcissus are poisonous to animals, many other bulbs are tasty. Plant them in wire cages to protect them. Their roots can grow easily through the wire into the soil below.

planting bulbs

prompts them to come out of their dormancy. There are many kinds of hardy, spring-blooming bulbs. Some of the earliest bloomers are snowdrops, crocus, squill, and winter aconite, which brave the winter cold to carpet the ground with color as early as February in some regions. Tuck them into the soil at the front of the garden, under trees and shrubs, along walks, or even in the lawn. They multiply and spread by forming tiny bulblets. Use them to form large patches or clusters so they're very visible. Tulips, daffodils, and wonderfully fragrant hyacinths are favorites for spring. Different varieties of each bloom early, midseason, or late to provide a steady parade of color. You also can use them for cut flowers, so plant lots of them. Because daffodils are poisonous

tender bulbs

Gladiolus, canna, dahlia, caladium, tuberous begonia, and other summer-blooming bulbs are called tender bulbs. Their roots can't tolerate frozen ground, so plant them in spring for summer bloom if you live where winters are cold. In Zone 8 and warmer, you don't have to dig up tender bulbs in fall—they can stay in the ground year-round.

planting tulip beds

1 Plant beds of tulips or other hardy bulbs all at once rather than one bulb at a time. Create your layout by placing the bulbs on top of the soil, then moving them around to make the pattern you want.

2 Dig one large hole about 6 inches deep in the designated planting area and mix in organic matter to create good texture and drainage. Then sprinkle some bulb fertilizer on the soil.

5 Firm the soil over the entire area to ensure good contact with the bulbs. Add more soil if the level of the bed sinks below the surrounding ground.

6 Add water if you expect no rain. Use a gentle, deep-soaking spray, which won't disturb the bulbs. The moisture signals them to begin growing roots.

to animals, plantings in wooded areas survive for years. They still get the necessary sun, because they bloom and die back before most trees leaf out. Unfortunately, deer love tulips, so be sure to plant them where they're protected. Although spring bulbs are relatively carefree, they do need some attention. After they bloom, pinch off the faded flowers. This concentrates the plants' energy toward revitalizing the bulb. Allow the leaves to persist—fully exposed to the sun—until they yellow. Then clean them up to make way for more plants that might be coming up nearby.

3 Position individual bulbs at the bottom of the hole. Set them in small clusters or randomly (rows look like soldiers). Be sure the flat bottoms contact the soil and the pointed tips face upward.

4 Fill in the hole, covering the bulbs so that they're buried under 4 to 5 inches of soil. In colder climates, tulips are more likely to come back year after year if planted as deep as 8 to 10 inches.

7 Cover the beds with winter mulch by spreading 3 to 4 inches of chopped leaves, shredded bark, or other organic material to insulate the soil.

bulb-planting time

For the best root growth, plant hardy bulbs in early fall. The smaller the bulb, the sooner you should plant it, because small bulbs tend to dry out easily. However, if you anticipate a delay, store the bulbs temporarily in a dark, cool place. If you suddenly remember—in the middle of winter—that they're still in the cellar or garage, plant them whenever and wherever the ground isn't frozen, then water and mulch them well.

forcing bulbs indoors

You can bring spring indoors early by forcing bulbs to bloom ahead of schedule. Pot up daffodils, tiny iris, tulips, and crocuses at the same time that you plant them outside in fall (or even later, with leftover bulbs). Choose varieties recommended for forcing, and select only the largest, firmest bulbs. Set them in a refrigerator or other cool, dark place (ideally just above freezing) for several months, then enjoy their beauty all winter long. The chill time in the refrigerator simulates the onset of spring so the bulbs develop roots. Plant bulbs in any type of pot with a drainage hole. Broad, shallow containers, called bulb pans, are best because they don't tip over when

forcing tulips

YOU WILL NEED

- pot
- soil-less potting mix
- bulbs
- decorative mulch (optional)
- water
- cool, dark storage place

paperwhite narcissus

Paperwhites don't need a chill period, so they can be forced easily. Set bulbs snugly on a layer of gravel in a flat, shallow bowl without a drainage hole. Add water to cover the gravel, and maintain that level at all times. Keep in a sunny window.

1 Choose a pot that is at least twice as deep as the bulbs to allow for proper root growth. Be sure it has a drainage hole. Fill it about half full of soil-less potting mix.

2 Set bulbs barely touching, with their growing tips even with or just below the pot rim. A 6-inch pot will hold up to six tulips, three daffodils, or 15 minor bulbs such as crocus or grape hyacinths.

4 Water the pot well, then place it in a refrigerator or in a cool, dark room where the temperature remains between 33 degrees and 50 degrees Fahrenheit.

5 Check the moisture level every few weeks. When shoots begin to show, take the pot out into a bright, warm room so the bulbs will grow and bloom.

plants become top-heavy with bloom. Space potted bulbs closer together than those in the garden. For a lush, thick show, try growing two layers of different bulbs in a deep container. Plant one type of bulb, cover it with soil, then position the other bulbs between the growing points of those already buried.

3 Cover the bulbs with potting mix so the tips are just showing. You might want to add a thin mulch of attractive gravel or moss, though this optional step is strictly cosmetic.

bulbs you can force easily indoors

plant name	weeks chilled
Crocus	10–14 weeks
Daffodil	16–22 weeks
Grape hyacinth	12-16 weeks
Hyacinth	10–14 weeks
Paperwhite narcissus	no chill
Snowdrop	10–14 weeks
Tulip	14–20 weeks

amaryllis & paperwhites

The sight of blooming bulbs in winter, even if indoors, is indeed a promise of spring. On pages 166 and 167, you learned how to force hardy bulbs to bloom indoors out of season. That is a rather long-term project because of the chill period needed to get the bulbs growing. Other bulbs, such as amaryllis and paperwhite narcissus, are native to warmer parts of the world and don't require the chill of winter to begin growing and blooming. Both types of bulbs are sold from mid-September until the end of December. Often they're preplanted in pots and available as kits, which make good gifts. Both amaryllis and paperwhites take only six to eight weeks to bloom, compared to a

growing amaryllis

good lighting

Stems of amaryllis and other bulbs tend to lean toward the source of their light. If they're on a sunny windowsill, turn them a bit every day to encourage them to develop straight stems. If the light source is above them, as with fluorescent units, the stems will be straighter. Continue to adjust the fluorescent light so it remains within 6 to 8 inches of the buds at the stem tips as they grow. This will keep the plants shorter and more compact.

Soak amaryllis bulbs in water just before you plant them. Set each dormant bulb in a snug pot that has a drainage hole and is filled with potting mix. Bury the bulb in the mix, leaving its top one-third exposed. Keep the mix moist but not soggy, and set the pot in a sunny spot until the buds open. As the rapidly growing stalk elongates and bears four or five blooms, it might need support.

minimum of 12 to 14 weeks typical of forced bulbs such as crocus, tulips, and hyacinths. Buy and start amaryllis and paperwhites in fall so they'll bloom for the year-end holidays. The bulbs you buy at holiday time will flower for Valentine's Day. Store the bulbs dry at room temperature until you're ready to plant them. Don't wait too long before you pot them up, because they may start sprouting in their packages. Once they're planted, watered, and blooming, keep them in a cool room to prolong their beauty. They don't need direct sun once their buds are open, but give them lots of bright light.

growing paperwhites

Fill a 3- to 4-inch-deep container without drainage holes two-thirds full of pebbles. Position the bulbs on them, shoulders touching, with points up. Surround the bulbs with pebbles and add water just to their bottoms. Set the container in a cool, dark room for three weeks while the roots grow. Move it to a sunny, cool room to develop green shoots and buds. Expect flowers in about 10 days.

common forcing mistakes

There are at least five good reasons why forced-bulb projects can fail:

- **Improper storage of bulbs awaiting planting can cause irreparable harm.** Temperatures that are too high will kill the flower buds, although the vegetative buds that produce leaves may not die. If you delay the planting process for some reason, the bulbs may dry out.
- **Temperatures during the chill stage can be too low for too long.** Prolonged exposure to subzero temperatures will kill even tough crocuses and tulips. Ideally, temperatures should gradually drop as they would outdoors, settling at 33 to 45 degrees Fahrenheit. A refrigerator does just fine.
- **Bulbs can receive too little or too much water.** Potted bulbs need to be damp but not soggy. If you allow them to get too dry, they'll abort their flowers. Cover them with plastic, or water them periodically, especially if you're chilling them in a frost-free refrigerator, which removes moisture.
- **The transition from winter storage to the hot, dry indoors (winter to spring) can be too abrupt.** Sudden exposure to bright sun after many weeks in the dark may stunt their growth or shrivel new buds. Gradually move potted bulbs toward a sunny window.
- **Too little light can cause pale, limp leaves and stems**. At their normal bloom time outdoors, the daylight hours are increasing. Indoors in winter, bulbs need a sunny window and possibly the help of a fluorescent light.

regional flower checklist

Cool Climates

Spring

- ❑ Remove mulch from bulb beds to encourage the soil to warm up when temperatures during the nighttime hours are above freezing.
- ❑ Divide overlarge clumps of summer- or fall-blooming perennials and spring bulbs when they have finished flowering.
- ❑ Pinch faded blooms from flowering bulb plants, but allow the leaves to die back naturally to nourish the bulb.
- ❑ Set stakes and supports for early-summer perennials before the plants get too tall.
- ❑ Start summer-blooming bulbs indoors in pots for planting outdoors when the weather warms.
- ❑ Start seeds for warm-season annuals indoors under fluorescent lights.
- ❑ When all danger of frost is past, direct-sow seeds for annual flowers into prepared beds.

Summer

- ❑ Routinely inspect plants for pest problems. Knock Japanese beetles off foliage into a jar of soapy water. Keep the hose handy to spray off aphids and mites.
- ❑ Plant seeds for late-summer annuals.
- ❑ Deadhead faded flowers to keep plants compact and neat and to stimulate continuous bloom. Allow self-sowers to remain.
- ❑ Spread a 2- to 3-inch layer of organic mulch over bare soil between plants to discourage weeds and keep the soil moist and enriched.
- ❑ Promptly pull any plants that show viral or bacterial disease such as crown rot. Remove the nearby soil. Then disinfect the tools with a mixture of hot water and household bleach.
- ❑ Begin to harvest flowers for drying.

Warm Climates

Spring

- ❑ Spread organic material to mulch new areas or replace mulch that has decomposed. Dried grass clippings work well.
- ❑ Install a soaker hose or drip-irrigation system around perennials that need regular watering.
- ❑ Dig new beds or expand existing ones.
- ❑ Examine plants for insect infestation. Use a strong spray of water from the garden hose to knock off any aphids and mites you find.
- ❑ Pinch stems of annuals to encourage branching and compactness.
- ❑ Water hanging baskets and other containers of annuals daily if it's sunny.

Summer

- ❑ Deadhead faded flowers to groom plants and stimulate rebloom later in the season. Allow self-sowers to retain their last blooms.
- ❑ Check soil moisture if rainfall is sparse. Regularly water newly planted perennials.
- ❑ Spread a 2- to 3-inch layer of organic mulch, such as chopped leaves or pine needles, over bare soil between plants.
- ❑ Fill in bare spots with annuals to provide continuous color.
- ❑ As flowers bloom, pick them for drying. Pick herb foliage to dry before plants form flowers.
- ❑ Routinely inspect plants for pest problems. Knock Japanese beetles off foliage into a jar of soapy water. Keep the hose handy to spray off aphids and mites from foliage.

Fall

- ❑ Divide spring- and summer-blooming plants.
- ❑ Plant new spring-blooming perennials.
- ❑ Take cuttings of geraniums, coleus, impatiens, and begonias to root for houseplants.
- ❑ Dig up tender bulbs such as dahlia, canna, and gladiolus. Wrap or cover them with moist material and store in a cool, dark space.
- ❑ Keep polyspun garden fabric handy to cover annuals when light frost threatens.
- ❑ After a killing frost, cut back dead plants and put them on the compost pile. (Discard in the trash any that have fungal disease.) Also clean up perennial bed and borders.
- ❑ After the ground freezes, spread a winter mulch over any bare soil in the garden. Spread evergreen boughs over bulb beds.

Winter

- ❑ Spread winter mulch over perennial beds after the ground freezes hard.
- ❑ If the ground hasn't frozen yet, finish planting any bulbs that were overlooked during the fall.
- ❑ Take a soil test if the ground is still workable.
- ❑ Make a list of perennials that will need dividing in spring.
- ❑ Have the lawn mower blade sharpened.
- ❑ Catch up on unread issues of gardening books and magazines that have been lying around.
- ❑ Look through mail-order catalogs to select annual seeds you can start indoors during late winter. Try something new.
- ❑ Get out seed-starting equipment and order peat pots and other supplies.

- ❑ Clean up perennial beds and borders. Cut down dead flower stems. Dig up and remove diseased plants. Weed areas that weren't mulched.
- ❑ Divide overlarge clumps of spring- and summer-blooming plants to control their size and renew their blooming.
- ❑ Dig new beds and renovate existing ones. Plant new perennials and transplant others.
- ❑ Plant cool-weather annuals such as pansies.
- ❑ Keep polyspun garden fabric handy to cover annuals if light frost threatens.
- ❑ Renew organic mulch in areas where it has decomposed and thinned in the heat of summer.

- ❑ Protect perennials from heavy frost by covering them with a bedsheet, polyspun garden fabric, or a makeshift tent of plastic (with ventilation holes).
- ❑ Mulch bulb and perennial beds to insulate the soil from temperature fluctuations.
- ❑ Catch up on unread issues of gardening books and magazines that have been lying around.
- ❑ Get out seed-starting equipment and order peat pots and other supplies.
- ❑ Deadhead and maintain the area around cool-season annuals such as pansies.

edibles

planting vegetables

Production is the name of the game in growing vegetables. The current trend is toward smaller yards—and, therefore, less space to grow food crops—so planting patterns greatly influence the size of the harvest. A wide-row layout is the most efficient way to take advantage of available growing space, because it uses areas formerly devoted to paths between narrow rows of plants. This wider planting area becomes, essentially, a bed. Make a bed of any length, but limit its width to 3 to 4 feet across so you can reach the center of the bed from either side. Although it's not necessary to box in the bed, this is a good idea. When you enclose a bed with vertical boards, it's not only neater, but the soil

YOU WILL NEED

- string
- small sticks or dowels
- trowel or dibble
- seedlings
- water

1 Before planting, run lines of string to establish a grid. The grid will help you position young plants at the proper distance from one another.

2 Use a trowel or dibble to dig holes. Gently remove the seedling from its container. Grasp the leaves to guide it while supporting the root ball.

3 Set the plant in the hole at the same depth at which it was growing in its container. Firm the soil gently over the roots around the stem. Water well.

4 As this layout demonstrates, any given plot will accommodate many more plants when arranged in a grid pattern rather than in narrow rows.

won't collapse onto the paths. It also will be much easier for you to install row covers or erect supports for vertical growing. Prepared soil that's protected in beds works well because it's never compacted by foot traffic. Before planting the bed, prepare the soil by digging down at least 12 inches (18 is even better) and turning over shovelsful to loosen and aerate it. Mix in organic matter, such as compost or manure, and granular, slow-acting fertilizer. Remove stones and debris, then rake the area smooth. This creates a raised mound of loose, rich, crumbly soil for wide-row planting.

rotating crops

Crop rotation helps control disease and insect problems. Plant crops in different places each year to thwart pathogens and pests that overwinter near their host plants in the soil. For instance, plant this year's tomatoes in a different bed from last year and put green beans where the tomatoes were. In small gardens, even moving plants just a few feet away from last year's location helps.

5 Save space in the garden by helping crops to grow upright. Various structures can support peas, pole beans, melons, cucumbers, and tomatoes.

planting vegetables

Good soil is the key to good production, regardless of what you're growing in your backyard vegetable garden. A rich soil supports intensive plantings of various crops and sustains successive plantings. If soil is rich in organic matter and is never compacted by foot traffic, plant roots grow deeply and vigorously. In the superior soil of a raised bed, it's possible to plant more intensively than normally recommended. Set plants closer together so that at maturity their leaves will just touch those of neighboring plants. This helps shade the soil as well. Although each head of broccoli may not be as large, there will be more of them. You can further

weather

Although the last spring frost is usually around the same time every year, there are always surprises. Cool-weather crops such as broccoli and lettuce can handle a frosty morning. Protect young warm-season plants with clear-plastic tunnels, cloches, or polyspun garden fabric.

Lengths of black plastic sheeting laid over prepared planting beds in early spring will warm up the soil. Most warm-season vegetables require soil to be at least 55°F.

Cut slits in the plastic to dig individual planting holes and allow water to reach the soil. Set each plant in a hole, then firm the soil around its stem by pressing gently on the surrounding plastic.

Either direct-sow seeds or transplant seedlings into rows in a prepared garden bed. Temporarily mark straight rows with sprinkled lime or string fastened to stakes.

When the plants are a few inches tall, thin them to the correct spacing as indicated on their seed packet. They need good air circulation and enough space to grow well.

increase the yield if you interplant a variety of crops. Plant beets with broccoli. Beets grow rapidly in spring while broccoli is getting established, and they are ready to harvest about the time the maturing broccoli plants shade the soil and need more space.

Intensive planting uses every cubic inch efficiently—both on the surface and in the air. Choose climbing varieties, such as pole rather than bush beans. Vertically grown plants thrive because they're exposed to abundant sunshine and good air circulation.

Randomly broadcasting seeds of some crops, such as lettuce mixes or mesclun, over a section of prepared bed works well. Try it with carrots or spinach. Thin sprouts regularly as they mature.

Different crops require different spacing. Intensive planting in raised beds allows closer growing than specified on the seed packet. Thin young plants or plant seedlings with that in mind.

mulch for low maintenance

Mulching the soil is an important gardening technique.

- Mulch helps control soil temperature. When summer heat raises the soil temperature too high, plant growth stalls. A layer of organic material will cool the soil several degrees.
- Mulch also discourages weeds, which compete with seedlings for soil moisture and nutrients. By covering the soil, mulch prevents weed seeds from germinating and protects the soil from compaction by rain and hot sun.
- Mulch helps retain moisture by blocking evaporation from the soil surface. The spongy humus in organic mulch also absorbs rain, reducing waste through runoff. At the same time, it prevents splashing of soil-borne disease pathogens from the soil surface onto plant leaves.
- Decomposing organic mulch helps keep the soil alive. As the mulch breaks down, it contributes humus, which is teaming with microscopic life. These organisms—along with earthworms—process soil nutrients.

succession planting

Plant crops in prompt succession by using wide-row planting in beds to produce more food. Dig up the plants as soon as their main production is over and replace them with seedlings for a different crop. As the weather warms, cool-season crops, such as peas, are completing their production. Have young squash or cucumber plants ready to take their place on the trellis. As soon as the broccoli is finished, have tomato plants ready to take its place in the bed. A planting area that's never idle produces a surprising amount of food. Another type of succession planting is repeating the same crop over a period of time to stagger the harvest. You can avoid being inundated by an entire crop all at once by planting only a few beans, then waiting two to three weeks before planting more, then more even later. Unless you intend to freeze the crop, your harvest will be more manageable if you spread it over many weeks. Plant lettuce, carrots, and other favorites this way, too. Soil that produces a steady flow of produce over several months needs help, because a succession of

thinning

YOU WILL NEED

- sharp scissors
- trowel
- young transplants
- slow-acting fertilizer
- water

After seedlings have developed two or three sets of leaves, they'll be crowded and need thinning. Remove extra plants to achieve the correct spacing and allow the remaining plants room to grow.

Thin a crop of young plants by snipping off the stems at the soil surface. For larger plants, this is preferable to pulling them, when you might damage the roots of neighboring plants.

spacing plants

plant name	spacing between plants/seeds	thin young plants to
Beets	1 inch	5 inches
Carrots	1/4 inch	2–3 inches
Corn	3–4 inches	6–10 inches
Lettuce	1/2 inch	10–12 inches
Peas	1 inch	don't thin
Peppers	12–18 inches	don't thin
Summer squash	in hills	3–4 feet
Tomatoes	18–24 inches	don't thin

your own gourmet vegetables at home

The baby vegetables that are popular in restaurants are easy to have fresh from your garden. You can harvest many vegetables (with the exception of tomatoes and eggplants, for example) when they're small.

- When planting the garden, look for varieties that tend to stay small.
- To spur production, pick often. At season's peak, this may mean daily trips to the garden.
- Harvest peas, beans, and cucumbers regularly to keep them coming.

crops inevitably depletes the soil of nutrients. They must be replaced to maintain production over the entire season—plus an extended season. Mix a granular, slow-acting fertilizer into the soil when you first prepare the bed. This food provides a large portion of the nutrients needed for plant growth over several weeks. Depending on the product, it may last for 12 or even 16 weeks. Its continuous action releases essential nutrients consistently and uniformly. Plants get a steady, balanced diet. You may want to add fertilizer again midway through the season. Vegetable plants may be annuals, such as peppers or potatoes, or perennials, such as rhubarb or asparagus. Because perennial vegetable plants stay put year after year, they aren't involved in succession planting. They can't benefit from rotation, either, so be sure to fertilize and mulch their beds to ensure continued good health.

foliar feeding

Plants that produce heavily over a long period, such as tomatoes, benefit from a snack to augment their main meal of slow-acting fertilizer. Periodically over the season, spray a dilute liquid fertilizer or kelp product on their leaves to give the plants an energy boost.

continuous planting

Immediately replace exhausted early-season crops with seedlings for the next crop. This follow-up procedure, called succession planting, achieves maximum production from the garden space.

Between succession plantings, cultivate the soil to aerate and level it. Clean up old plant debris before replanting. Add granular fertilizer if previous crops, such as tomatoes, were heavy feeders.

cool-season crops

Cool-season vegetables can handle the chill of early spring and late fall. They fade rapidly when the warmth arrives in early summer and eventually succumb to freezing in winter. They're ideal for extended-season growing. Vegetables that don't mind being chilly, such as peas, broccoli, and spinach, make it possible for you to have two crops a year—one in spring, another in fall. Often the second crop, at the onset of winter, is the one that you're happy to put into the freezer.

try these cool-season vegetables

- Broccoli
- Brussels sprouts
- Cabbage
- Cauliflower
- Collards
- Garlic
- Kale
- Leeks
- Lettuce
- Onions
- Peas
- Spinach
- Swiss chard

supporting vegetables

There are several advantages to supporting and training vegetables to grow upright, away from the soil surface. They take up less space in the bed, making room for you to intensively plant other crops. The taller plants are healthier, too, because their stems and leaves get better air circulation, which reduces the chances of fungal disease. Moisture from rain or overhead watering dries off more quickly. Their fruits receive more sunshine so they ripen sooner and more evenly, and they're cleaner and more shapely. Certainly they are less likely to contract rot diseases or injury by soil-dwelling insects. And, finally, they're easier to harvest. Some vegetables are born to climb. Peas

weather

The winds and heavy rain that accompany summer storms are a threat to plants. Make trellises and other supports sturdy enough to withstand these conditions. Supports holding plants laden with fruit at the peak of the season are especially vulnerable because they carry so much weight.

Vining crops such as peas and pole beans grow nicely on wire-covered A-frame structures. When the produce is ready for harvest, it will be within comfortable reach from either side.

Support individual tomatoes or other tall plants by driving 8-foot stakes at least 12 inches into the ground. Plant a young transplant near each stake and loosely fasten its stem with soft strips of fabric.

Firmly insert wire cages into the soil to give tomatoes good support as well as access to air and light. Wide openings make it easy to pick the fruits.

Not all support structures need to be tall, such as this cucumber netting. Check seed packets and plant labels for information on the mature height.

and cucumbers have tendrils that take to a trellis with gusto. Tomatoes have flexible stems that can be tied to or woven through wide mesh. Pole beans naturally wind around stakes or any other vertical structure. In the case of melons and squashes, a double support works best. Encourage the vines to climb a sturdy trellis, then cradle each large dangling fruit—as it reaches maturity—in an individual sling. Do this by cupping a length of polyspun garden fabric, netting, or even old panty hose under the melon or squash, then fastening each end to the trellis netting.

Wooden lattice panels, their base deeply embedded in the soil for solid footing, provide an attractive support. Small pea tendrils cannot wrap around it, so place netting in front of the trellis.

Wire or nylon mesh with 4-inch openings allows for easy picking of peas, which in this garden are followed by tomatoes.

Build a freestanding tepee sturdy enough to hold several vines. Anchor it firmly in the ground to stand up to strong winds. It should be 8 to 10 feet tall.

tomato types

*There are two types of tomato plants. **Determinate** types grow only about 4 feet tall and stop. They don't need a tall trellis. A sturdy wire cage suits them fine. They also do well in containers with attached supports. **Indeterminate** types will grow as high as 20 feet if you let them. Make a 6- to 8-foot support for them—whatever is within maximum reach—and clip off the tips of the main stems when they reach that height. This promotes subsidiary branching and more production.*

trellis placement

Orient trellis panels on a north-south axis so that tall vines don't shade other shorter plants.

harvesting vegetables

Most food crops reach their peak flavor and nutritional value when they're still young and tender. As they approach maturity, these qualities begin to deteriorate. The seeds inside fruits and vegetables develop and ripen, causing the skins to become thicker—and their stems tougher—to protect the seeds inside. The optimum harvest time is just before that happens. Because different vegetables mature at different rates, the trick is to be ready to pick each crop at its prime. This might mean picking asparagus and tomatoes daily, and eggplant and lettuce every five days or so. You'll want to harvest ripening peas and pole beans every couple of days to ensure continuous

harvesting bell peppers

Harvest time makes a big difference with bell peppers. When they mature to full size, they are green but still have a bitter flavor because they're not fully ripe. Allow them to remain on the plant and ripen further for several more weeks. When they become red, yellow, or orange, they're sweeter. Because the peppers take so long to change color, individual plants don't produce as many peppers over the season. You may want to increase the number of plants to maintain production levels.

Green beans planted in mid to late spring continue to set beans through most of the summer if you keep picking the ripe beans. For best flavor, pick them when they are thinner than a pencil.

Chili peppers are as easy to grow as any other pepper. Let them ripen to their full color on the plant. Wear gloves when handling them and avoid touching your face—the oils are very pungent.

Greens can be grown as cut-and-come-again vegetables. As they get 4 to 6 inches tall, cut the tops, leaving the crown intact so they will regrow.

Zucchini are ready for harvest when they are 5 to 8 inches long. You'll find them at their peak flavor and tenderness at this young age.

production over the season. The time of day when you pick the garden's bounty is important. For most fruits and vegetables, early morning is best, because that's the time they have maximum starch (for sweetness) and crispness from the cooler, overnight temperatures. Pick them right after the dew dries.

Eat or store freshly picked produce promptly. If you allow vegetables to sit on a counter for hours, they lose moisture and vitamin content. To prevent their continued ripening, put them in a plastic bag in a cool, dark cellar or refrigerator. Never wash them before storing, because the moisture encourages rot.

avoiding fungal contamination

As a general rule, avoid picking crops when plants are wet from dew or recent rain. This is when fungal diseases, various mildews, and rots flourish and are most likely to spread. Avoid brushing against infected fruit or foliage, then moving from plant to plant while picking. This will transmit fungal spores onto healthy plants. Dampness makes them vulnerable to infection.

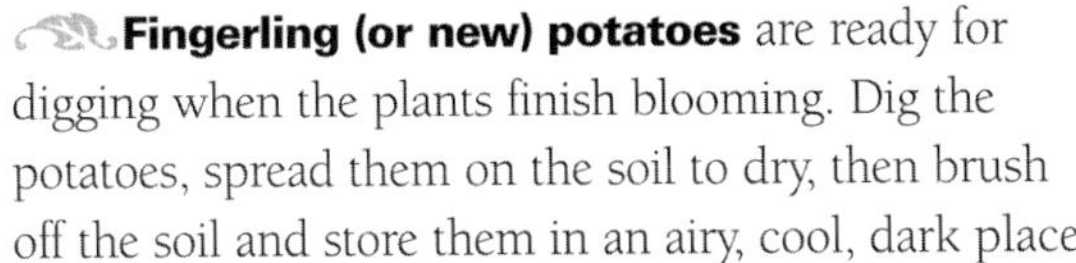

Fingerling (or new) potatoes are ready for digging when the plants finish blooming. Dig the potatoes, spread them on the soil to dry, then brush off the soil and store them in an airy, cool, dark place.

harvesting tomatoes

The ultimate harvest moment is when the first tomato of the season is ripe. Depending on the variety and when the plants were put into the garden or an outdoor container, this might be in early July. Although determinate tomato varieties are genetically programmed to grow and produce for only a certain period of time, indeterminate ones continue producing fruits until frost. Tomato stems are tough, so harvest the tomatoes with garden scissors or pruners rather than just yanking them off the vine. For best flavor, pick ripe tomatoes just before you're going to eat them. If you're picking a few days' worth of tomatoes, store them out of direct light at room temperature. Green (unripe) tomatoes will ripen on the kitchen counter.

herbs in the garden

Herbs are utilitarian plants. For thousands of years, herbs have been enjoyed for their benefits—as medicinal, culinary, dye plants, and as insect repellents. Today, many herbs are planted for their beauty as the popularity of culinary herbs increases. Traditional herb gardens are formal. The classic knot garden, popular since Colonial days, is grown for the form and structure of the plants, although it's possible to take small snippets without destroying the design. An herb garden in which only the border—often germander or boxwood—is shaped, and the other plants grow freely within bounds, is more practical for some people. Intersperse herbs in a mixed or perennial garden, where both their beauty and

growing conditions

Many herbs, including thyme, rosemary, lavender, and sage, are native to the Mediterranean. They grow best in very well-drained, lean soil—no extra organic matter in the soil. They thrive in full sun and will not perform well if the weather is cloudy or too humid.

Thyme is a Mediterranean herb that thrives in poor soil. Here, five types, including the variegated lemon thyme, are growing together. Using pebbles as mulch keeps the crown from rotting.

Calendula is also known as pot marigold or poor man's saffron. The flower petals, when chopped and added to rice or potatoes, add a bright yellow color and a flavor reminiscent of costly saffron.

Lavender *(right of the nasturtium)* is cherished for the clean scent of its flowers and leaves. The evergreen grayish leaves are attractive any time of year.

Sage, long believed to imbue wisdom, is essential seasoning for turkey stuffing. Semievergreen with gray-green leaves. Yellow 'Icterina' is pictured above.

utility can be appreciated. Certain herbs are indispensible for gardening cooks—parsley, sage, basil, thyme, oregano, chives, and rosemary. It's most convenient to grow them in large pots—even a big strawberry pot—right by the kitchen door so they are readily accessible anytime to add flavor to the cooking.

In a large, non-porous container, such as a whiskey barrel, hardy herbs will happily overwinter. Porous or unglazed containers, such as terra-cotta pots, can crack in below-freezing weather. Grow some herbs on the windowsill to enjoy in winter. For example, chives, parsley, and dwarf basil do well indoors in lots of light.

Herb vinegars are easy to make. Place culinary herb leaves (or edible flowers) in a clean bottle. Fill with a good quality, white wine vinegar. Let it infuse for several weeks. Sunlight will fade its color.

Window boxes are perfect for growing a variety of culinary herbs—close to the kitchen. Plant herbs with similar soil preferences together in one box.

Containers of freshly cut herbs make lovely centerpieces or aromatic table arrangements. Let rosemary and lavender dry naturally, put others in water.

growing herbs

When planning a garden, it is helpful to know which herbs are perennial and which are annual.

Annual herbs

Basil
**Borage*
**Calendula*
**Cilantro*
Dill
Parsley

Perennial herbs

Beebalm
Chives
**Fennel*
Hyssop
Lavender
Lemon balm
Marjoram
Mints
Oregano
Rosemary
Sage
Savory (summer & winter)
Tarragon
Thyme

** Reseeds readily*

edible flowers

Edible flowers do double duty: They are pretty as can be in the garden, and they add both flavor and color to any dish served up in the kitchen. From roses, lilacs and anise hyssop to beebalm, nasturtium, and chives, edible flowers span every color of the rainbow and flavors from sweet, perfumed, and licorice to spicily sweet, peppery, and garlicky. Although edible flowers have become common garnishes in restaurants, it's important to know what you're putting into your mouth. Not all flowers are edible, and not all food purveyors are aware of the potential toxicity of some. The most common (and safest edible flowers) are nasturtium, pansy, violet, Johnny-jump-up,

weather

Edible flower flavors vary with the weather. When it is sunny and dry, the flavors are most intense. For several days after a heavy rain, the flavor is weaker as if it were diluted by all the water.

Harvest edible flowers early in the day—after the dew has dried but before the sun becomes intense. Do not wash them until just before you are ready to use them. Don't soak the petals in water.

Nasturtiums may be vivid yellow, orange, or red as well as muted tones and bicolors. Both the leaves and the flowers have a peppery flavor and are best eaten uncooked. Toss petals into salads.

Pansies span every color of the rainbow, so you can have fun decorating food. Plan a party months ahead and grow pansies to match your decor, best outfit, or favorite color. Their flavor is slightly minty.

Borage's star-shape blossoms practically fall off the plant when they are ready to eat. They have a mild cucumber flavor that is delicious in lemonade. .

Roses may be tasteless, sweet, perfumed, or slightly spicy. Chop the petals and mix with sugar. Let it infuse for a week and use for baking and desserts.

calendula, chives, and sage. These flowers are easily grown without the use of chemicals or pesticides. Many roses are delicious, but you need to be sure they are grown organically. A good rule of thumb is: If you cannot positively identify a flower as edible, don't eat it. Edible flowers are fun; the addition of a few flowers can turn ordinary family fare into food fit for company. For example, chop a few tulip petals into tuna fish salad and serve individually in a whole tulip flower. Most people won't eat the whole flower, yet they enjoy the flavor it adds to the tuna.

Tulips have a wonderful crunch—especially at the base of the petals. The flavor ranges from pea- to beanlike. Use tulip petals as a low-calorie substitute for chips with dip. Another flower of many colors.

Pinks and other dianthus have a sweet clovelike taste. Do not eat whole—remove individual petals. Infuse petals in water for tea, or top a cracker and cheese with several petals. Makes a delectable sorbet.

'Tangerine Gem' marigold and the other Gem hybrids are the only good tasting marigolds, with a citrusy tarragon flavor. Use petals in devilled eggs.

Lilacs are another variable flower, with a grassy taste or a delightful perfumed flavor. Use in chicken dishes and fruit salads. Candy individual florets.

guidelines

- *If you have asthma, hayfever, or other allergies, do not eat flowers.*
- *Remove the pistils, anthers, and stamens before eating any flowers.*
- *Never eat flowers from a nursery, garden center, or florist; they are likely to have chemical residues that concentrate in the flowers.*
- *Flower flavors vary with variety (20 different roses will all taste somewhat different) and with the growing conditions. As with any herb or spice, you may not like the flavor of all flowers—that's okay.*

edible flowers

Apple
Anise hyssop
Beebalm
Broccoli
Chamomile
Chives
Dandelion
Daylilies
Hollyhock
Honeysuckle
Mustard
Pineapple guava
Pineapple sage
Rosemary
Sage
Scented geraniums
Sweet woodruff
Thyme
Tuberous begonias
Violets
Yucca

storing the harvest

A bountiful harvest is a joy that more than repays you for the time and energy invested in your garden. For optimal freshness and nutrition, harvest each crop at its peak of ripeness, then promptly use, process, or store it. Some vegetables are fragile or have ephemeral flavor and are best eaten straight out of the garden. Sometimes different varieties of the same vegetable are better keepers, so you'll want to plant those varieties as the fall crop. This information is listed in seed catalogs and on individual seed packets. Store only healthy produce that has been picked when it's fresh and newly ripened. Overripe, damaged, or diseased crops deteriorate rapidly, even if correctly stored. Store

weather

Fall vegetable crops maturing into cooler weather grow more slowly than spring-planted ones that mature into increasingly warm weather. This provides a larger window of opportunity for you to harvest them before they bolt, go to seed, toughen or become woody. Many cool-weather crops withstand—and even benefit—from frost. Some can remain in the garden under mulch almost all winter long.

Pumpkins are best picked after the first frost. Once they are cut from the vine—leave several inches of stem, let them cure in the dry sun for a few days. Pumpkins can stay in a cool, dry place for months.

Chili peppers can be strung on heavy twine to air dry. Be careful; use gloves. Once completely dry, remove chilis from twine and store in airtight container.

storing garden vegetables

vegetable name	cool place	in the garden	room temperature
Broccoli	■		
Brussels sprouts	■	■	
Carrots	■	■	
Chile (hot) peppers	■	■	■ (short term, dried)
Collards	■		
Corn	■	■	
Kale	■		
Kohlrabi	■	■	
Leeks	■	■	
Lettuce	■ (dry)		
Onions	■		
Peas	■ (dry)	■	
Potatoes	■	■	
Radishes	■		■ (short term)
Spinach	■	■	
Turnip	■		
Winter squash	■ (dry)		

vegetables properly. Don't wash them until ready to use. For short periods, keep them moist and cool in the refrigerator, dry and cool in a cold room or cellar, or at room temperature. For the long term (several months), process them for freezing, drying, or canning as soon as possible after you've picked them.

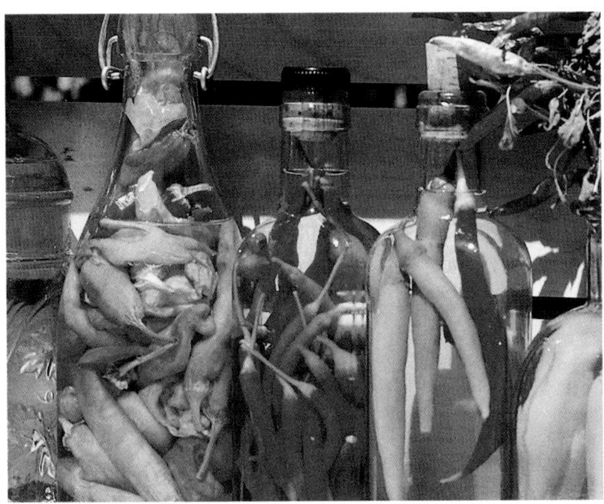

Flavored vinegars can be made from any number of herbs and vegetables—dill, rosemary, onion, garlic. Chili pepper vinegar in a handsome bottle makes a lovely holiday gift from the garden.

Edible wreaths are gorgeous ways to store herb, garlic, and pepper harvests once the individual plants have dried. Try making swags and other shapes.

making a braid of garlic

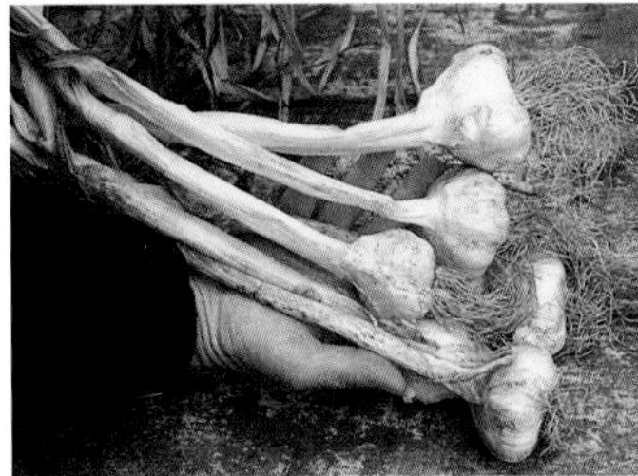

1 Harvest garlic bulbs within three weeks after their foliage ripens and collapses. Dig them up—with the foliage still attached—and clip off any overlong roots.

2 Allow the bulbs to air-cure in a dry shady place for a week or two until their skins are crisp and the foliage is dry yet pliable. Starting with the four largest plants, begin to braid the stems.

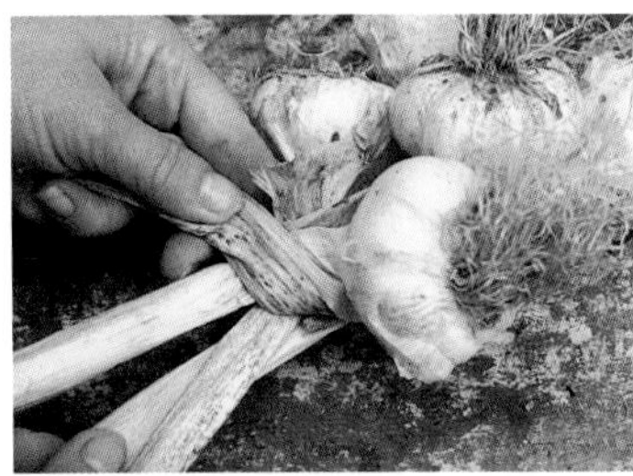

3 Wrap and weave the garlic stems, incorporating additional stems intermittently. As you proceed, try to graduate from larger bulbs to smaller ones for good proportion.

4 Add new stems so that the garlic bulbs lie progressively along the length of woven braid and don't bunch up at the base. Plan on a medium-length braid, rather than an overlong one.

5 Fasten the top of the braid securely with florist wire or a rubber band. Tie a bow or knot of decorative string that also can serve as a loop for hanging the braid. Although the kitchen is the logical place for display, garlic stores best in somewhat dry, cool conditions away from direct sun. Softneck garlic braids better than the hardneck variety and can keep for four to six months.

regional edibles checklist

Cool Climates

Spring

- [ ] Start seeds for warm-season vegetables indoors under fluorescent lights about 8 to 10 weeks prior to the date you expect the last frost.
- [ ] Build raised beds for intensive and succession planting. Cover the beds with black plastic sheeting to warm up the soil.
- [ ] Set up a soaker-hose irrigation system for beds to supply low-maintenance watering.
- [ ] Plant seedlings outdoors for cool-weather crops such as broccoli, cabbage, and lettuce.
- [ ] Do necessary maintenance on permanent trellises used for growing crops vertically.
- [ ] Harden off warm-season seedlings raised indoors to prepare them for transplanting into the garden.

Summer

- [ ] Harvest cool-weather crops such as peas. Pull out the vines and plant a summer crop.
- [ ] Cover berries and peas with netting to protect the crops from birds or animal pests.
- [ ] Plan to extend the gardening season into fall. Start seeds for cool-weather crops indoors or in a nursery bed outside about three months prior to the expected first frost.
- [ ] Water when rainfall is sparse. Most plants need about 1 inch of water a week.
- [ ] Remove black plastic mulch or cover it with organic mulch. Cover soil with organic material to moderate temperature and retain moisture.
- [ ] Monitor plants for insect problems and begin controls immediately.
- [ ] Stimulate production of squash, beans, eggplants, and others by picking them when they're young.

Warm Climates

Spring

- [ ] When danger of frost is past, set out warm-weather plants such as tomatoes and peppers. Sow seeds for squash, beans, corn, and melons.
- [ ] Mulch beds with organic matter to discourage weeds and keep the soil from warming too much and too soon.
- [ ] Use shade cloth or polyspun garden fabric to protect young transplants from strong sun.
- [ ] Harvest cool-weather crops, such as lettuce and broccoli, before hot weather causes them to bolt and set seed.

Summer

- [ ] Water when rainfall is sparse. Most plants need about 1 inch of water a week. Tomatoes like even more moisture.
- [ ] Mulch all bare soil in the garden to prevent evaporation of moisture and discourage weeds. Renew the layer when it decomposes.
- [ ] Monitor plants for insect problems and begin controls immediately.
- [ ] Plant succession crops of beans, carrots, and corn to stagger the harvest.
- [ ] Erect shade cloth over plants to shield them from the afternoon sun, even if they're sun-loving varieties. (They still need some shade in the hottest months.)

Fall

- Keep polyspun garden fabric handy to cover summer crops such as beans and peppers if an early light frost threatens.
- Harvest crops such as pumpkins, potatoes, sweet potatoes, and onions. Brussels sprouts, carrots, and other root crops can stay in the ground through light frosts.
- Clean up plant debris in harvested beds. Mulch or sow cover crops on empty beds to protect the soil over the winter.
- Mulch beds where root crops will be stored in the ground over the winter with thick layers of straw or chopped leaves.
- Tend fall crops such as broccoli, cabbage, spinach, and onions until they're mature and ready for harvest.
- Harvest green tomatoes and store them indoors.
- Build more boxed raised beds. Repair trellises. Clean out cold frames.

Winter

- After a hard frost, clean up dead, dried plant debris. Cover beds with several inches of straw or chopped leaves, or plant a cover crop to protect the soil.
- Mulch beds where root crops such as carrots and parsnips remain to protect them until they're all harvested.
- Look through mail-order seed catalogs and order seeds in time to start cool-weather crops indoors.
- In late winter, prepare one bed for planting cool-weather crops.
- Get out seed-starting equipment and order peat pots and other supplies.
- Build new compost bins or repair old ones. Turn and consolidate compost piles to prepare for the new season.

- Renew beds for fall planting by adding more organic matter such as compost and fertilizer.
- Sow carrots, beets, and other root crops as well as lettuce for fall harvest.
- Set out cole crop transplants such as cauliflower, Chinese greens, cabbage, broccoli, and mustard. Shade them if the days are still warm.
- Clean up plant debris in harvested beds. Mulch or sow cover crops on empty beds to protect the soil over the winter.
- Build more boxed raised beds. Repair trellises.

- Look through mail-order and seed catalogs in time to start cool-weather crops indoors.
- Continue to enjoy lettuce and Chinese greens by protecting them in a cold frame or with polyspun garden fabric, or a plastic tunnel.
- Get out seed-starting equipment and order peat pots and other supplies.
- Plant peas.
- Build new compost bins or repair old ones. Turn and consolidate compost piles to prepare for the new season.

vines

choosing a vine

By their nature, vines are upwardly mobile. They insist on vertical progress, even though they're firmly rooted in the soil. This virtue makes them enormously useful in residential yards. Their lush leaves and, more often than not, appealing flowers decorate the landscape with pillars, arches, and swags of color and texture. Many provide late-season bonuses of decorative seedpods, edible or ornamental fruit, and colorful fall foliage. And there's fragrance from moonflowers, autumn clematis, and others. Some vines, such as morning glory and hyacinth bean, are annuals. They die at the first hard frost in fall, so you'll have to plant them anew each spring—although some self-seed

weather

Vines moderate temperature. When their leaves cover a masonry wall in the summer, they block the glare of the sun and its reflected heat, cooling the area. Then when deciduous vines drop their leaves in the fall, the exposed wall absorbs heat and reflects light to create a warmer microclimate during the winter.

Boston ivy is a clinger that drapes walls with shiny, three-lobed leaves in summer. In fall, they turn deep red, and the reddish stems sport dark berries that birds love. Zones 4–8.

Bougainvillea flowers are tiny and white, upstaged by the brightly colored papery bracts that surround them. It's a southern staple along fences and on arbors and is hardy only in Zone 10.

Climbing hydrangea takes a few years to establish. Early each summer, its 6- to 8-inch-wide, lacy white blooms are worth the wait. Zones 4–8.

Dutchman's pipe is named for the unusually shaped flowers that nestle among drapes of foot-long green leaves. It's hardy to Zone 4 and grows in shade.

and save you the trouble. The woody vines are perennials. Kiwi, wisteria, climbing hydrangea, and wintercreeper are basically vertically inclined shrubs. They grow more substantial each year, the stems thickening with age, and require the same type of care as earthbound shrubs. Vines are ideal for small properties. Because they occupy a very small area of soil, spreading upward instead of outward, they use planting space efficiently.

Vines provide a link between the earth and the sky. They're especially useful in areas where trees are scarce, serving as substitutes by creating their own

Clematis flowers are summer standouts in purple, white, and shades of pink. This perennial's seedheads are composed of curved filaments that beautify through fall. Clematis is hardy to Zone 5.

Hardy kiwi produces 2- to 3-inch green leaves that shelter inconspicuous flowers. They give way to edible, inch-long, greenish fruits. Hardy to Zone 4.

dangerous vine

Certain vines are not welcome in home landscapes. Some are health hazards. For instance, every part of the poison ivy vine contains a toxic resin that causes severe contact dermatitis. Others are simply too aggressive. While you may be able to use constant pruning to control vines, such as Oriental bittersweet, porcelainberry, wild grape, and kudzu (above), it's impossible to prevent their escape into the wild; birds carry their seeds into parks, roadsides, woodlands, and fields. There the vines run rampant, choking out natural vegetation and smothering trees.

choosing a vine

kind of shade and balance in the landscape. Place vines strategically along boundaries or over walls and fences to define a space. Drape them on arbors or along railings to line passageways and guide foot traffic. Create a special rest and contemplation space around a vine-covered garden seat. Plant vines with drop-dead gorgeous flowers, such as clematis or mandevilla, to climb the mailbox post out front. Or use others to anchor large garden beds and balance their proportions. Vines also link the hardscape and the softscape. They tastefully soften architectural lines of buildings—expanses of wall, sharp corners, and rooflines. Exploit the

showing off stems

The twisted, ropy stems of mature, woody vines winding up posts of an arbor or pergola are ornamental in and of themselves. Prune new shoots along the lower parts of wisteria, honeysuckle, or kiwi vines to expose the bark at eye level. This also makes it easier to see and enjoy plantings in beds beneath the structure.

Hops features bristly stems that bear three- to five-lobed leaves. Female vines bear flowers that produce clusters of cone-like fruits used in beer-making. Hops vines are hardy to Zone 3.

English ivy, especially the large- or small-leafed, variegated varieties, covers vertical surfaces with masses of leathery, heart-shaped leaves year-round to Zone 5. Mature leaves are more rounded.

Mandevilla reveals tropical origins in its narrow leaves and funnel-shaped pink flowers. Twine it around lamp posts and arbors for summer bloom. Hardy in Zone 10, but grown elsewhere as an annual.

Moonflowers wait until hot weather to produce 5-inch-wide, iridescent white flowers that last until frost. A night-blooming relative of morning glory, grown as an annual, its fragrant flowers attract moths.

versatility of those vines that also are willing to do groundcover duty, such as English ivy and wintercreeper, to create a seamless transition between horizontal and vertical planes on your property. The changing color of the leaves of many deciduous vines, such as Boston ivy and Virginia creeper, creates a colorful, living mural. Vines also help set a tone. Who doesn't immediately sense the mood of a home described as a vine-covered cottage? To reinforce an informal look, allow your

Tropical kiwi thrives in zones 8 to 10 of the South and West and produces the familiar fuzzy fruits found in grocery stores around the country. Use both female and male plants to produce fruits.

Kolomitka vine is actually a hardy kiwi with wonderful ornamental foliage. Mature leaves, marked with blotches of pink and white, turn an ordinary wall into a mural of color. It's hardy to Zone 4.

Morning glory evokes memories of old-time gardens. Its funnel-shaped flowers—from white to reds and blues—casually scramble over fence posts and walls. It's a fast-growing annual.

Passion flower looks as exotic as it sounds. Its 4-inch flowers are blue to white, with intricate centers. It's cold-hardy only to Zone 7 but is often grown as an annual in the northern states.

choosing a vine

vines to roam at will by using permissive pruning. Annual vines and rambling types of roses (not vines, but very long-stemmed shrubs), both of which tend to be quite rambunctious, are great choices for an informal look. To add formality, choose more substantial, decorous perennial vines. Prune them strictly to maintain a dignified shape. Vines are an important element in a backyard wildlife habitat. They shelter birds, which like to have cover where they can perch in view of the bird feeder and check for predators before visiting it. Also, the stiff stems of woody perennial vines provide solid support for nests. Many vines, such as kiwis and grapes, bear

using vines as camouflage

Temporarily cover landscape eyesores with annual vines. Because they grow so rapidly, they effectively mask rotting stumps, new utility boxes, compost piles, and construction fencing. Let them climb dying trees and shrubs that you'd rather not remove right away. When the vines die back in fall, the weather will be cool enough to deal with those problems.

Purple passion flower, called purple granadilla, bears 3-inch-long, purple edible fruit. This variety, hardy in Zone 10 only, has three-lobed leaves, each 4 to 6 inches long with wavy edges.

Sweet autumn clematis billows over walls, pergolas, and arbors all summer long. In mid-August it produces clouds of small, fragrant, white flowers. This vine is cold-hardy to Zone 5.

Wintercreeper has evergreen leaves, either green or variegated with cream or yellow. Its thin, shrubby stems creep overland or climb a variety of vertical surfaces. It's hardy as far north as Zone 5.

Wisteria takes time out from twining around any handy—but strong—support to bear cascades of fragrant, lavender or white, pea-shaped flowers in May. It's cold-hardy to Zone 5.

fruit and are rich sources of food. Many flowers, such as climbing hydrangea, moonflower, and sweet autumn clematis, attract beneficial insects, bees, and butterflies. And hummingbirds enjoy the nectar from honeysuckle, trumpet vine, and mandevilla.

Virginia creeper, hardy to Zone 3, decorates walls with leaves divided into five leaflets, each 2 to 5 inches long. In the fall, they turn scarlet, setting off the blue berries that appear at the same time.

Yellow (golden) clematis has two things going for it—beautiful, 3- to 4-inch-wide flowers that bloom in late summer and attractive seedheads that develop after its blooms fade. It's hardy to Zone 5.

growing grapes

Grapevines are ornamental as well as edible. Display them attractively in a formal espalier design that looks elegant, yet provides desirable light and air to promote fruiting.

Encourage grapevines to cover a decorative arbor. It provides a sturdy base and is open to lots of light and air above and below it. The grapes are easy to harvest at the peak of ripeness.

Train grapes to grow on a chain link enclosure to obscure the fence's utilitarian appearance. Its crisscross design provides lots of places for the grapevines to attach securely.

Grapevines cling easily to a stair railing or other architectural features. When you prune them to promote maximum fruiting, you simultaneously control their growth.

A pergola gives grapevines plenty of area to expand. The fruit dangles attractively between the many horizontal supports—and is within reach when you're ready to pick it.

supporting vines

The constantly growing stems of vining plants need something to hold onto, or they will sprawl on the ground. You need to provide an appropriate support system for them. The strength of your structure will vary by type of vine. Some require extremely sturdy materials that will hold them up for many years. Wisteria, grape, and kiwi, which live for decades, grow increasingly bulky and heavy over time. Others, like annual vines, are relative lightweights. Because they live only for a season and die when frost arrives, their stems are relatively slim, and their mass—mostly leaves—doesn't strain most supports. The design of the support is a key factor, too, because vines attach

weather

Free-standing tepees and structures such as arbors and pergolas are vulnerable to harsh winds and rain, especially if they're supporting mature vines. Make sure the structure you're using is sturdy enough to support the combined weight of heavy, wet leaves and flowers or fruits against the strong winds and heavy rains of summer storms.

Tepees (or the more-formal tuteurs) support vines in vegetable and ornamental gardens. Tie string between the poles to help nasturtiums, scarlet runner beans, morning glory, and others twine as they climb.

You can buy special vine clamps that wedge into a masonry wall and support vines that can't hold on by themselves. Push the clamps into the mortar, then guide and fasten vine stems to them.

English ivy develops tiny aerial roots along its stems, called holdfasts, that enable it to grip surfaces without support, but that penetrate cracks and holes.

The stems of some vines, such as garden peas, produce dainty yet strong tendrils that curl around a narrow support and allow them to climb upward.

themselves in a variety of ways. Choose a support to accommodate each vine's growing style and future size. Some vines are *clingers*. English ivy, for example, forms sticky, hairy rootlets, called holdfasts, along its stems that attach directly to the surface on which it's growing. Clingers don't need special support and get along quite well on walls and other handy surfaces such as tree trunks. However, their rootlets can damage old or loose mortar in brick or stone walls, so check the mortar carefully before you plant clingers. Lots of vines—wisteria, morning glory, honeysuckle, and kiwi,

strangler warning

Never use a living tree as a support for a woody perennial twining vine. The vine will wrap around the trunk or branches and then, as the tree and vine stems grow wider, the vine girdles the tree, strangling it. Over the years, the pressure of the vine cuts off the tree's circulation, and it dies. Wisteria is a common offender.

It's easy to train twiners (vines that encircle supports with their main stems) to climb a support. This morning glory, after some gentle encouragement, will attach to the fence and cover it rapidly.

A trellis makes a lot of sense for young vines with flexible stems. Thread the tips of vines, such as this clematis, through the spaces and around the crosspieces while they still bend easily.

A support for a twiner, such as morning glory, needs vertical members. If it doesn't, string lengths of twine or wire vertically to create twining paths for it.

contrasting colors

Before you paint a support, consider the color of the leaves and flowers of the vine. Go for contrast. Here, you don't get the full impact of the lovely white wisteria blooms against a white trellis, but you do appreciate them against the green wall.

supporting vines

among others—are *twiners.* They climb by winding their stems around supports. Because they can't fasten themselves to anything as they're attempting to curl their way up a vertical element, wrap a wire or string around the new, young plants to help them get started. Then when they reach a horizontal member, they can hitch onto it and be on their way. Still other vines are *grabbers.* They develop special tendrils—sort of modified leaf stems—that grasp a nearby support as they ascend. Grabbers such as passion flower, cross vine, and sweet pea have tendrils that are thin and tender, so they do best on narrow materials such as wire,

combining vines

Create a special effect by combining annual and perennial vines on the same support. Or pair one that produces gorgeous flowers with one that has exceptional leaves. For example, encourage a free-flowering vine, such as morning glory, to weave among and through the stems of one with special leaves, such as Kolomitka vine. Or let clematis twine around a fence laden with Dutchman's pipe. Grow morning glory and moonflower together for flowers day and night.

Pergolas are ideal for heavy-duty vines, such as grape, wisteria, and trumpet creeper. The many large, open spaces offer good light and air circulation. Be sure to sink the posts in concrete.

This giant bean tepee is substantial enough to support a ladder and several vines laden with beans. When the vines mature and the beans are ready for harvest, the ladder comes in mighty handy.

Lattice is an extremely versatile and useful vine support. You can fashion it into a free-standing structure or mount it on a wall as a trellis. And it provides attractive screening after annual vines die.

Give your gazebo summertime privacy—and a beautiful, though temporary, facade—by enclosing it with latticed walls covered with flowering vines, such as this thriving honeysuckle.

chain link fencing, netting, or narrow trellis bars. Some plants called vines aren't vines at all. Climbing roses don't climb by themselves; they are shrubs with very long stems (canes) that you can coax to grow upward. Because they have no attachment mechanisms, they're basically *leaners*, and their canes lie against any vertical support that's handy. You can train them by loosely tying the canes to a structure, such as an arbor or pillar, that can bear their weight and guide them vertically.

A hand-hewn trellis like this one is especially appropriate for an informal setting. The honeysuckle effectively joins forces with its rustic support to contribute old-fashioned beauty to the scene.

Regardless of the design you choose, never fasten a support structure tightly to a wall. Leave about 6 inches between wall and trellis to permit air circulation and simplify the pruning process.

Accommodate small vines by adding lightweight trellises made of vinyl, bamboo, or wood lath to your walls. Clematis, cardinal flower, morning glory, or sweet peas create a lacy pattern like this one.

A matrix of wire fastened to the garage wall supports a honeysuckle, Kolomitka vine, and a nearby clematis. Thread heavy wire back and forth between screw eyes to make the support network.

planting and training vines

Plant vines and other climbers as you would any plant. Choose a location to fit its requirements for light and moisture. Perennial vines, such as wisteria and kiwi, are likely to be in place for many years, so select a site accordingly. Remember that flowering and fruiting vines need at least six hours of sun daily. Whether the roots of the plants you buy are bare, in container soil, or wrapped in burlap, be sure to keep them moist while you prepare the soil. Newly planted vines start slowly. Annuals wait for warm weather for their big growth spurt. Perennials, which will be around for years, spend several weeks growing roots and leafing out and grow very little. Many take their

planting a vine

YOU WILL NEED

for planting:

- gloves
- trellis
- shovel or spade
- vine
- compost
- water

for training:

- gloves
- twine or other soft tie
- hand pruners

1 Place a trellis a few inches away from a wall to protect the wall and encourage air circulation. Set the trellis securely in the soil and brace it so it is stable enough to withstand the weight of a vine.

2 Dig the planting hole several inches in front of the trellis to allow room for the roots to spread and to avoid crowding the growing stems. Make the hole only as deep as its rootball.

3 Center the plant in the hole so the growing stems can fan out on both sides. Make sure the longest stems are against the trellis.

4 Add compost around the rootball, then fill in the hole with soil. Firm the soil over the roots, then water well.

entire first season to do so. Climbing hydrangea is notorious for its dawdling. The old saying, "The first year they sleep, the second year they creep, the third year they leap," aptly describes many perennial vines. Nevertheless, you need to guide a vine's growth from the outset. Don't let stems flop on the ground. Instead, lead them to the base of their support, even if it means using a temporary stake until they can reach the bottom of the trellis. In some cases, you may need to prune them early to guide their growth. Cut off all but the sturdiest stems of twiners to start them winding around a post.

training on a trellis

1 Train the longest branches to begin climbing the support. Tie each one—as shown with this barberry stem—loosely against the frame. The slack provides leeway for the branch to thicken.

2 Attach the stems with plastic twist ties (not ones with wire centers) that are easy to remove and adjust. Or use cloth strips, string, or nylon fishing line. Weave flexible stems directly through the mesh.

3 Trim extra stems at the base of the plant to direct energy to the longest stems. Trim fast-growing annual vines weekly once they get established.

4 Woody plants, such as this barberry, are slower growing and take years to climb a support. Early training pays off in future years with a lovely display.

controlling vines

Vines need to be kept in their place. Clip and retie stems periodically on vines trained to trellises. Trim those clinging directly to brick or stone walls to prevent them from straying too far. Ivy tends to overwhelm windowsills and gutters and force its way under roof shingles. In midsummer, check its growth and prune back wandering stems.

seasonal vine care checklist

Cool Climates

Spring

- ☐ Sow seeds of annual vines indoors in early spring.
- ☐ As temperatures rise, remove winter mulch from beds.
- ☐ Prune perennial vines that bloom on new wood to stimulate flower and leaf buds.
- ☐ Fertilize vines with a granular, slow-acting product.
- ☐ Plant new vines.

Summer

- ☐ Transplant annual vine seedlings into the yard in early summer.
- ☐ If rainfall is scarce, regularly water vines.
- ☐ Train new vines as they produce longer runners. Trim established ones.
- ☐ Optional: Clip pieces of stem from vines to root in water or damp vermiculite.

Warm Climates

Spring

- ☐ Sow seeds of annual vines indoors in early spring. Sow hardy ones directly outdoors.
- ☐ Prune perennial vines that bloom on new wood to stimulate flower and leaf buds.
- ☐ Rake, weed, and trim vine plantings as growth proceeds.

Summer

- ☐ Transplant young homegrown or purchased annual vines outdoors.
- ☐ If rainfall is scarce, regularly water vines.
- ☐ Train vines as their growth spurts by tying main stems and pruning stray branches.
- ☐ Optional: Clip pieces of stem from vines to root in water or damp vermiculite.

Fall

- ❑ Continue to water vines in dry periods.
- ❑ Continue to clip climbing vines.
- ❑ As weather chills, move vines growing in containers to a sheltered area.
- ❑ After hard frost, mulch in-ground vines.

Winter

- ❑ Record information on the selections, care, and performance of vines—especially new ones—over the past season.
- ❑ Clean and sharpen garden tools to guard against rust.
- ❑ Order seeds and seedlings from mail-order nurseries and suppliers.

- ❑ Plant vines when weather cools.
- ❑ Shape up planted areas by clearing debris and spreading fresh mulch.
- ❑ Continue to train vines by tying them to supports. Trim only if necessary, as pruning stimulates new growth that might not survive winter chill.

- ❑ Record information on the selections, care, and performance of vines—especially new ones—over the past season.
- ❑ Clean and sharpen garden tools to guard against rust.
- ❑ Order seeds and seedlings from mail-order nurseries and suppliers.
- ❑ Prune grapes toward the end of winter before their sap begins to rise.

trees and shrubs

the value of trees

Trees are the unsung heroes of our landscapes. Individually and collectively, in yards across the nation, they contribute enormously to our quality of life—even though they are largely taken for granted. However, when a tree is cut down or falls in a storm, the hole it leaves in the sky reminds us of its extreme importance. The wonderful hardwood forest that greeted the European settlers on the east coast of North America helped sustain them, just as it had the native population eons before. It sheltered abundant wildlife to hunt, yielded fruits and nuts to eat, and preserved the soil for agriculture. Its wood warmed and housed the settlers. It moderated the heat, blocked the wind, and caught the rain. So as the settlers migrated westward in their restless search for more and better land and opportunities, they carried in their being the sense that trees are part of a good life. Even the farmers among them—although they cleared trees to make fields for crops—knew how essential it was to preserve some of the trees. For settlers, trees were an integral part of the home

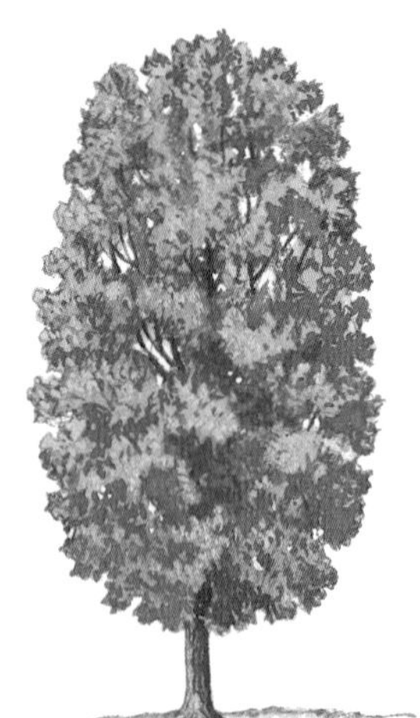

columnar

Columnar trees are shaped like columns or cylinders, with branches of uniform length—top to bottom. They aren't necessarily narrow, but they appear to be because of the branching pattern. Many commonly known trees are available in columnar versions.

examples:
Cherry, crabapple, European hornbeam, Lombardy poplar, red maple, quaking aspen, sugar maple, tuliptree

open-head irregular

The branching pattern of these trees is irregular and random, creating an open, asymmetrical canopy shape. They offer wonderful shade, and after their leaves fall, their branch architecture creates dramatic silhouettes against a winter sky.

examples:
Ash, buckeye, catalpa, hickory, pawpaw, sycamore (London plane), silver maple, smoketree

weeping

The branches of weeping trees droop downward and are covered with graceful cascading foliage. These typically smaller, ornamental trees soften the hardscape. Many commonly known trees are available in a weeping form.

examples:
Birch, cherry, crabapple, hemlock, katsura, larch, sourwood, willow

pyramidal

These broad, cone-shaped trees have triangular canopies—wider at the base and narrower toward the top. Many deciduous trees and conifers have this classic shape. The large ones are stunning on properties where they have room to grow.

examples:
American beech, American holly, baldcypress, blue spruce, cucumber magnolia, fir, linden, oak (pin, scarlet), sweetgum

landscape, wherever their home would be. Understandably, one of the great trials of life on the prairie was the absence of trees—living entities that seemed to sustain the human spirit as well as guard the environment and beautify the landscape. Today, trees still nurture us. They provide continuity with our history and influence our climate and quality of life. We plant trees to make our properties more beautiful, valuable, and comfortable. Trees define our yards by establishing their scale, marking their borders, and roofing them with leafy canopies. By filtering light and creating shade, trees make our homes more livable. They contribute shelter and food to wildlife, health to the overall landscape, and beauty to all of us in the form of lovely flowers, fruit, and bark. And they enhance our properties' values, as well. Each healthy, mature shade tree can contribute up to $1,500 toward the value of a lot.

globe

The canopies of these trees—with their regular, rounded shape—are ideal for formal landscapes. Stately rows provide a strong linear feature, softened by the billow of their canopies. When alone on a spacious lawn, they make handsome specimens.

examples:
American hornbeam, American yellowwood, bur oak, black maple, flowering dogwood, hackberry, redbud

fastigiate

These trees have an elongated, narrow, tapering profile and a strong vertical habit that draws the eye upward. When planted in rows, they serve beautifully as hedges to define boundaries, as windbreaks, and as effective screens against noise or undesirable views.

examples:
Arborvitae, baldcypress, European beech, ginkgo

vase

Trees that have vase-shaped canopies work well near streets and walks because they don't block the view of traffic or pedestrians. Branches grow at a sharp upward angle from the trunk, flaring outward at the tips. Canopies resemble upside-down triangles.

examples:
Boxelder, elm, fringetree, hawthorn, striped maple, zelkova

horizontal spreading

With strongly horizontal branches, even at the top of the canopy, these trees seem very wide. Usually massive, they overwhelm small properties and can dwarf single-story homes. But their spreading habit contrasts well with a narrow house.

examples:
Beech, Eastern redcedar, fir, honeylocust, hornbeam, Korean dogwood, larch, oak (red, white), witchhazel

choosing trees

Because trees can live for decades —even centuries in some cases—it's important to choose varieties that are appropriate for their site. Take time to consider what you want the tree to do—just look pretty, shade the driveway, block the wind or neighbor's view, or provide flowers or fruit. Will it be part of a formal planting area or grove, or will it stand alone? Consider its size at maturity. Will there be enough room for it? A tree's growth rate also may have a bearing on your choice. The slower-growers are hardwoods and tend to live longer. If it's important to establish shade or have flowers relatively quickly, choose a fast-growing tree. They're usually smaller, have soft

judging tree size

A small tree is not always a young tree. If it's small from lack of vigor, the condition of its bark will give it away. A weak one will have thicker bark that's textured with ridges, furrows, or flakes, rather than the smooth, tender bark of youth.

Japanese maples grow 3 to 20 feet tall and offer fine-textured foliage, rich color, interesting shapes, and a tolerance for some shade. Use them to adorn beds, pools, and lawns. Hardy in zones 3 to 6.

Callery pear is fast-growing and has small, white flowers in the spring and colorful foliage in the fall. Its pyramidal canopy reaches 30 to 45 feet at maturity. Early versions called 'Bradford' tend to split in storms, so choose 'Aristocrat' or 'Chanticleer'. Hardy to Zone 4.

Korean dogwood has white spring flowers with pointed petals. Dangling, fleshy red fruits hang from its distinctly horizontal branches in fall. Zones 6–9.

Citrus trees bear lovely, fragrant, white flowers and edible fruits. These small trees easily deteriorate if you don't spray them properly. Zones 9 and 10.

wood, and don't live as long. Scale trees to their surroundings. Use small or medium-sized varieties for smaller houses and yards. On any site, put smaller trees near the house and taller ones farther out in the yard or at its edge. Trees and shrubs are either deciduous or evergreen. *Deciduous* trees lose their leaves in the fall and are bare all winter, though the leaves often give a final show of beautiful colors before they drop. *Evergreen* trees and shrubs retain their foliage year-round. Some, such as southern magnolia, feature broad leaves. Others, such as pines, have needled foliage.

Crabapple grows 15 to 25 feet tall and is covered in spring with deep pink flower buds that become white blossoms; they, in turn, give way to small red or yellow apples that the birds love. The tree spreads to an irregular shape. Zones 3–5.

Honeylocust is tough and adaptable, grows 30 to 50 feet tall, and drops pods. Its foliage turns yellow in fall. Choose the thornless variety. Zones 3–9.

Redbud bears tiny pinkish purple flowers along its stems and bare branches in early spring. They give way to rows of wide heart-shaped leaves. Pods become visible as leaves turn yellow in fall. Mature trees grow 25 to 30 feet tall. Zones 5–9.

Saucer magnolia is deciduous and grows to about 30 feet tall. It bears 6-inch-long, pale pink flowers early in spring. Hardy to Zone 6.

choosing trees

Of course, there are always exceptions. The soft, fine-textured needles of larch and baldcypress turn color in the fall and then drop off—just to confuse things. Every kind of cultivated tree has assets that suit it for some landscape use. Each also has certain requirements that are critical to its survival in the yard. Some are more cold-hardy than others, so check their hardiness-zone rating. Many do best in rich, moist, woodsy soil that's definitely on the acid side. Others prefer more alkaline soil that tends to be dry because it's not as rich in moisture-holding organic matter. Some trees, like swamp red maples and baldcypress, can handle

urban trees

Certain trees are more tolerant of typical urban conditions than others. They're able to handle atmospheric pollutants from industry and cars, compacted soil, poor drainage, night lighting, and salt spray from snow plows. City trees generally have much shorter lifespans than their suburban or country counterparts. Those that do best include Norway maple, oaks, Washington hawthorn, ginkgo, honeylocust, sweetgum, crabapple, linden, and zelkova.

Serviceberry is a tough and adaptable large shrub or small tree at 6 to 20 feet tall. Its early spring clouds of white flowers become edible dark fruits by June. Yellowish pink fall foliage entertains in a woodland setting or near a patio. Hardy to Zone 4.

Sorrel, or sourwood, grows to 75 feet tall and is a multiseason beauty. Its July flowers are drooping strands of tiny white urns among slightly leathery and glossy, medium green leaves that turn to a brilliant red early in the fall. Hardy to Zone 5.

White cedar is a type of falsecypress that grows to a narrow, conical 40 to 50 feet tall. It begins with a slender shape, then turns spirelike when it matures. At home in the eastern United States, it has light green or grayish foliage and likes wet soil. Zones 4–8.

Willow oak has narrow and pointed foliage and forms a fine-textured, dense conical canopy rising to about 50 feet at maturity. It makes a good street and shade tree and is easy to transplant. Foliage turns yellow before it drops in the fall. Hardy to Zone 6.

even truly wet soil. Trees also have their liabilities. Some have thorns that make them unsuitable for homes with children. Others are weedy; some are messy—sycamores and the relatives of the London plane tree drip fuzzy balls, bark, and twigs all over the place. The spiked balls from sweetgum trees and the runaway roots of willows present challenges as well. However, if you choose the right place for some of these less-desirable varieties, you can overlook their faults and enjoy their virtues.

Tuliptree grows quickly to its 25-foot height. Beautiful tulip flowers with orange centers snuggle among interesting leaves. Hardy to Zone 5.

Weeping cherry varieties typically grow 15 to 25 feet tall and spread as wide. They bear a blizzard of pink or white, single or double flowers. Zones 6–9.

Pine foliage is evergreen for year-round beauty and is comprised of bundles of soft, long needles. Though some pines are a bit brittle in harsh weather, they're often used for wind and privacy screening. Hardy in various zones, depending on variety of tree.

Spruce trees are fragrant needled evergreens—perhaps the ultimate Christmas tree. They range in height from dwarves no more than 5 feet tall to giants that tower over 100 feet high. Depending on variety, the hardiness range extends as cold as Zone 3.

choosing shrubs

A yard without shrubs is, well, not really a yard. With all their wonderful diversity of size, shape, foliage, and flower, shrubs can turn a mundane piece of property into a beautiful showplace. Shrubs make the yard inviting and livable. You've probably noticed that builders always plant a few shrubs around newly constructed homes. There may be no trees or grass, but there are shrubs.

Shrubs, with their deciduous or evergreen foliage, are enormously decorative and highly useful. Like trees, evergreen shrubs may have broadleaf or needled foliage and can offer colorful berries or cones, interesting bark, and lovely flowers. Even in the winter, their leafless, contorted trunks and

weather

In many areas of the country, rainfall is never generous. And it's becoming less dependable in many other areas, too. If you live where water is likely to be restricted, choose shrubs that don't require much water. Some examples are olive, butterfly bush, potentilla, and barberry.

American holly can grow 30 to 40 feet tall and is pyramidally shaped. This hardy evergreen has leathery, glossy, spined leaves. Female trees bear red or yellow berries that attract birds. Hardy to Zone 5.

Andromeda, or pieris, is a 4- to 12-foot tall, broadleaf evergreen. It bears pendulous clusters of fragrant, white, urn-shaped florets in the spring. This slow-growing shrub likes some shade. Zones 6–9.

Forsythia bears rows of bright yellow, trumpet-shaped flowers on its bare stems in early spring. It becomes 8 to 10 feet tall. Hardy to Zone 5.

Harry Lauder's walking stick is actually a filbert used as an ornamental shrub. It has coarse, veined leaves and grows 8 to 10 feet tall. Zones 4–9.

interesting architecture enhance the landscape. Their size provides a pleasant transition between tall trees and groundcover plantings, softening the edges of boundaries, foundations, buildings, and walls. At the same time, they protect the soil and support and shelter all kinds of wildlife. Shrubs are versatile. Use them as groundcovers on slopes, as living walls, as backdrops for flower borders, and as screens to block street noise and dust. Put them where they'll obscure landscape eyesores, such as heating and cooling units, swimming pool mechanicals, utility meters, and trash can areas.

avoiding deer damage

Visiting deer damage shrubs by nibbling their twigs, fruit, and foliage. Homeowners across the country are searching for ornamental shrubs that deer will ignore. Lists vary by region—even by neighborhood—but certain types of plants appear on many of them. Consider shrubs with thorns or prickers, resinous wood, aromatic foliage, and silver or gray fuzzy leaves.

Boxwood is an evergreen covered with tiny, oval, glossy leaves. It tolerates shearing into hedges very well. Common boxwood grows to 20 feet tall and accepts sun or light shade. Hardy to Zone 6.

Sumac grows up to 20 feet tall and bears clusters of greenish yellow flowers in late summer. Its foliage puts on a show of flaming red, yellow, or orange in the fall. It can form colonies in poor soil. Zones 4–9.

Japanese barberry grows 2 to 5 feet tall and is tough and versatile, even in poor, dry soil. Its small red berries persist all fall. Hardy to Zone 5.

Korean stewartia has delicate white blossoms in early summer. Its leaves turn orange-red in the fall, then drop to expose patchy bark. Zones 5–7.

choosing shrubs

Use shrubs to accent pools, patios, and dooryards. Or plant thorny varieties to redirect children and animals using your yard for shortcuts. Conifers are generating renewed interest. These cone-bearing, needled evergreens are available in dwarf forms—a much more suitable scale for today's smaller properties. They offer an amazing array of foliage color—soft blue, variegations in yellow or cream with green, as well as the traditional green. Whatever the colors, they really stand out in a winter landscape. Conifers also come in many forms—weeping, prostrate, and topiary, in addition to the usual upright configuration. Native shrubs

using native shrubs

Native shrubs that combine the virtues of beauty and low maintenance include:

- *American arborvitae*
- *American beautyberry*
- *American holly*
- *Bayberry*
- *Bottlebrush buckeye*
- *California lilac*
- *Carolina allspice*
- *Chokeberry*
- *Dwarf fothergilla*
- *Mountain laurel*
- *Oakleaf hydrangea*
- *Oregon grapeholly*
- *Rhododendron (some)*
- *Serviceberry*
- *Sweet pepperbush*
- *Viburnum (some)*
- *Virginia sweetspire*

Lace-cap hydrangea features flat clusters of tiny, tight, fertile flowers ringed by petaled, sterile ones. The blue or pink flowers nestle among green foliage in early summer. Hardy to Zone 6.

Lilac boasts fragrant sprays of tiny, tubular florets in pink, white, and shades of lavender during the spring. Heart-shaped, smooth, bluish green leaves continue through the season and drop in the fall. Lilac grows slowly but lives a long time. Zones 4–9.

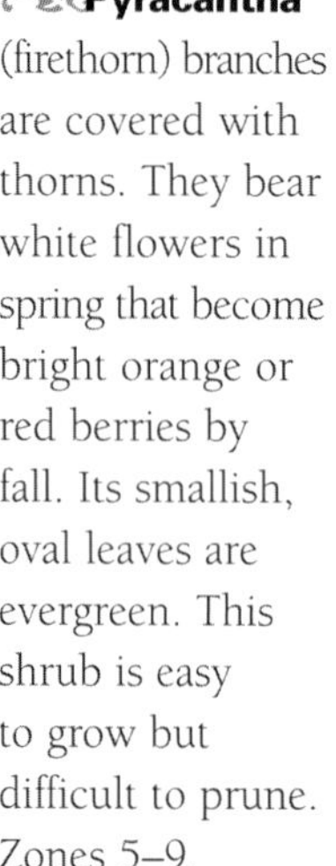

Pyracantha (firethorn) branches are covered with thorns. They bear white flowers in spring that become bright orange or red berries by fall. Its smallish, oval leaves are evergreen. This shrub is easy to grow but difficult to prune. Zones 5–9.

Plum-leaf azalea, native to the Southeast, bears its fragrant, orange-red flowers in midsummer, later than most azaleas. Shrubs have evergreen foliage and grow to 10 feet or more. Zones 5–8.

also are enjoying long-overdue attention. Because they have existed in the same region long before European settlers arrived, they're adapted to local climate and soil conditions. Unfortunately, Americans temporarily lost interest in them, while other countries happily adopted them. But now we're recognizing their many low-maintenance virtues. They don't require extra watering and tend to resist pest insects and disease. And they're big favorites of local wildlife.

Mountain laurel is a broadleaf evergreen that grows to 15 feet tall. It's vigorous and bears globes of intricate, starlike florets in late spring. Use it as a specimen or in woodland settings. Zones 4–9.

Oleander tolerates heat, drought, and salt and takes any soil. Narrow evergreen foliage lines thin branches tipped with colorful flowers all season. Caution: All parts of the plant are poisonous. Zone 9.

PJM rhododendron is a compact evergreen that grows 3 to 6 feet tall. Resembling an azalea, its leaves are small and leathery, turning purplish in the fall. Spring flowers are pinkish-lavender. Zones 4–9.

Seven-sons flower's soft green foliage shows off its 6-inch-long clusters of fragrant ivory flowers in late summer. It likes moist, woodsy soil (but tolerates less) and grows to 15 feet. Zones 5–8.

attracting wildlife

Some shrubs with berries that attract birds and other wildlife include:

- *Barberry*
- *Bearberry*
- *Beautyberry*
- *Blueberry*
- *Brambles*
- *Cotoneaster*
- *Dogwood*
- *Euonymus*
- *Firethorn*
- *Holly*
- *Juniper*
- *Viburnum*
- *Wax myrtle*

four-season interest

Don't underestimate the ornamental value of a shrub. Even if you want to plant shrubs for a practical purpose—such as to prevent soil erosion or screen the view of the neighbors—choose ones that can bring beauty to your yard during one or more seasons. Every shrub will have its particular showy feature at some point, so choose an assortment of shrubs that have a variety of peak times. That way, you'll have something attractive to enjoy all year long. A peak time isn't necessarily limited to showy blossoms—it also might include magnificent fall foliage color and dramatic pods, nuts, bark texture, or overall form. Another way to achieve year-round beauty is to

spring

Scotch broom grows quickly to 6 feet. Lined with fragrant, yellow, pealike flowers in midspring, its bare, bright green stems add color to the yard in winter. Zones 6–9.

Flowering dogwood offers white or pink spring flowers and scarlet fall foliage and berries that are favorites of birds. It can grow to 40 feet in an irregular pattern. Zones 5–8.

Crapemyrtle bears clusters of crinkly petaled flowers in shades of pink and white in summer at tips of branches. Its flaking, patchy bark and sinuous shape give winter interest. Zones 6–9.

California lilac grows 4 to 6 feet tall with white or pink spring flowers and bears showy, bright red seed capsules in summer. Its leaves turn yellowy tan in fall. It likes dry soil. Zones 4–6.

Korean azalea (*foreground above*) is a deciduous rhododendron with magenta flowers that appear on leafless stems in early spring. It is lovely paired with magnolia or forsythia. Zones 4–8.

Doublefile viburnum has a double row of white flowers along its branches in spring that give way in summer to bright red berries that attract birds. It grows 6 to 12 feet tall. Zones 3–8.

choose those special shrubs that are constantly interesting, such as evergreen hollies. Their shiny leaves are attractive year-round and the berries in fall through winter—only on female shrubs—are an added bonus. Choose plants that will give a succession of bloom. You'll find many that bloom over the summer into fall—even winter in the coldest states. Add witchhazel (late-winter bloomer), serviceberry (early-spring bloomer), and crapemyrtle (summer bloomer) to your mix. Follow up with fall-blooming Japanese bush clover or sweet autumn clematis if they're suitable for your region.

summer

Bluebeard, or blue spirea, blooms in late summer. The scented blue flowers blend nicely with its gray-green foliage. The leaves and stems are scented, too. It takes dry, sunny sites. Zones 6–9.

Japanese rose, or kerria, grows 4 to 6 feet tall and creates yellow flowers in midspring on slightly arching branches. Its leaves yellow and drop in fall, revealing green stems for winter. Zones 4–9.

Colonnade™ apple is ornamental as well as productive. Spring blossoms yield colorful fruit by midsummer. Grows about 6 feet tall and 2 feet wide, perfect for a container. Zones 4–7.

Peegee hydrangea grows upright 6 to 12 feet tall and bears fat clusters of ivory blooms in midsummer. Flowers turn pinkish in fall, remain attractive all winter, and dry well. Zones 3–8.

Beach rose combines a sturdy constitution with lovely flowers. Textured, leathery leaves resist disease and look good all summer. Enjoy the orange hips through fall. Zones 2–7.

Rose daphne is a low-growing, fine-textured, mounded, semi-evergreen shrub—likely to keep its leaves in mild winters. It bears fragrant, bright pink flowers in spring. Zones 4–7.

four-season interest

The word "ornamental" isn't just about flowering. It's also about berries and cones, bark texture and branching pattern, habit and silhouette. And mostly, it's about leaves. The glory of many shrubs is their foliage. Sometimes it's the shape of the leaves, sometimes the color or variegation pattern, sometimes both. The appeal of needled evergreens, for example, is the fine texture and color of the needles all through the year—especially winter. Many deciduous shrubs, on the other hand, offer a bonus show of fall foliage color before the leaves drop. Don't underestimate the value of colorful berries either. Hollies, firethorn, beautyberry, and others peak in the fall as their fruit ripens, then extend their ornamental display well into winter. After frost, when the leaves have fallen,

fall

Beautyberry has inconspicuous flowers and plain green leaves. Suddenly, in late summer, clusters of vibrant magenta berries appear along the stems and remain through fall. Zones 5–8.

Pyracantha, or firethorn, follows up its white spring flower show with a fiery display of bright orange to red berries in fall. It's best in sun and dryish soil. Beware of thorns. Zones 6–9.

Burning bush, or winged euonymus, has distinctive flared stems covered by plain green leaves. In fall, its foliage turns a stunning crimson that lights up the yard before dropping. Zones 4–8.

Wintergreen is a low evergreen groundcover. Tiny white flowers become red berries that last from summer until spring and are fragrant when crushed. Leaves are reddish in winter. Zones 3–6.

Aucuba has dense, shiny evergreen leaves speckled with yellow, which upstage the purple spring flowers and red fall berries. Take cuttings in fall in cold areas and grow indoors. Zones 7–10.

Japanese maples are prized for their fall color—bright yellow, reddish orange, or deep scarlet. Some change leaf color from spring to summer as well. Many handsome varieties. Zones 5–9.

deciduous shrubs with textured and colorful bark can show it off, no longer hidden from view by leaves. Of course, the easiest way to assemble an assortment of shrubs that will provide beauty through the four seasons is to choose a few individual ones that have everything—or almost everything—going for them. Oakleaf hydrangea, for example, has gorgeous spring flowers that persist all summer, coloring gradually into ivory and pink as fall approaches. Its handsome green foliage takes on beautiful colors, eventually dropping to expose the shrub's rustic, peeling bark. Virginia sweetspire is another delight, offering spring flowers, decorative capsules, and colorful fall foliage.

winter

River birch, a handsome tree in any season, shows off in winter. In fall, its leaves turn yellow. Its bark—a patchy, reddish tan—peels back in strips to create gorgeous winter interest. Zones 3–9.

Paperbark maple has lovely bark that is overshadowed by leaves most of the year. Growing 20 to 30 feet tall, it boasts cinnamon brown, peeling bark that gets better as it ages. Zones 5–7.

Holly has handsome, spiny, glossy evergreen leaves, which dramatically set off the red or yellow berries that mature in midfall and last most of the winter. It attracts birds to the garden. Zones 5–9.

Japanese maples have sinuous branches and great architectural form that can be best appreciated after the leaves have dropped. A dusting of snow highlights the form. Hardy to Zone 5.

Witchhazel blooms from early to late winter, but there are fall- and spring-blooming varieties, too. Fragrant, yellow, ribbonlike flowers unfurl on sunny days. It boasts handsome fall color. Zones 5–8.

Cornelian cherry has dark green foliage that turns purplish in fall then drops to reveal flaky, gray-brown bark. In late winter, it bears flat, yellow flowers just before its leaves return. Zones 4–7.

attracting wildlife

Wildlife is an integral part of almost any backyard. Birds, butterflies, and other creatures add color, sound, and movement to the scene. At the same time, an assortment of wildlife is essential to a healthy landscape. Plants wouldn't survive without the help of pollinating and predator insects—or squirrels to bury nuts and seeds to grow new plants. Birds patrol for pest insects and eat those they find lurking in the bark of trees and shrubs and under the soil. In return, plants sustain the creatures by providing shelter in their dense branches and foliage and by supplying seeds, nectar, pollen, berries, bark, and cones for food. This reciprocal arrangement benefits all species in your yard.

weather

Seasonal storms are hard on backyard wildlife. Heavy winter snows, torrential spring rains, and thunderstorms in summer and fall are stressful for birds, rabbits, squirrels, and others. Shrubs and trees, especially twiggy and heavy-foliaged ones, provide important shelter.

Gourd birdhouse trees appeal to purple martins. Site the gourds in an open area near fresh water to attract many insect-eating families.

Fresh water is essential to birds, insects, and butterflies, as well as to the occasional visiting duck or goose. Make sure it's available during the winter, when natural sources freeze.

Pets help control undesirable wildlife. While cats occasionally may catch a bird, they also hunt voles, shrews, and mice. Dogs will chase deer.

trees and shrubs to attract wildlife

plant	part of the plant	wildlife it attracts
American beech	Nuts	squirrels, chipmunks, bears, porcupines
	Leaves	butterfly larvae
Buckeye	Flowers	hummingbirds
Butterfly bush	Flowers	butterflies, beneficial insects
Buttonbush	Flowers	bees, butterflies
	Seeds	ducks, deer
Cotoneaster	Berries	squirrels
Desert willow	Flowers	hummingbirds
Dogwood	Berries	squirrels, birds, rabbits
Glossy abelia	Flowers	hummingbirds
Hawthorn	Berries	birds
	Shelter	birds
Hickory	Nuts	squirrels
	Bark	insects for woodpeckers
Holly	Berries	birds
	Shelter	birds
Juniper	Cones	birds
Lilac	Flowers	bees, butterflies
	Leaves	deer
	Shelter	birds
Maple	Seeds	squirrels
Oak	Nuts	birds, squirrels, deer, wild turkey, raccoons, mice
Oregon grapeholly	Flowers	bees
	Berries	birds
	Shelter	birds, mammals
Paperbark birch	Seeds	birds
	Leaves	butterfly larvae
Pine	Cones	squirrels, chipmunks, birds
	Twigs	browsing game
	Shelter	squirrels, chipmunks, birds
Salal	Berries	chipmunks, birds, bears, deer
Serviceberry	Berries	songbirds, wild turkey, bear
Viburnum	Flowers	beneficial insects
	Berries	birds, chipmunks, fox, deer
	Shelter	birds, butterflies, larvae

attracting wildlife

A yard that attracts and supports wildlife has lots of different kinds of plants. The more diverse the offerings of food and shelter, the more diverse the visitors. Include some native plants among them. Plant all kinds: trees and shrubs as the backbone and then vines, wildflowers, aquatic plants, and grasses. Choose annual and perennial flowers that are colorful, flat, and open faced. Herbs and many food crops also support wildlife. If you truly want to attract wildlife, don't use broad-spectrum pesticides; they don't discriminate between good and bad pests and they kill off the beneficial ones, too. The pest problems are likely to get worse,

hedgerow habitat

Hedgerows are ideal for attracting wildlife. To start your own, choose from several types and sizes of shrubs—and perhaps vines—that offer a wide variety of berries, cones, and seeds over the entire year. The informal, somewhat unruly arrangement of these woody plants provides excellent cover for birds and small mammals, such as rabbits. They also require much less maintenance than a more formal hedge.

Viburnum varieties, such as highbush cranberry, black haw, and possum haw, produce spring flowers that have nectar for butterflies. In fall, their showy berries attract birds and deer. Zones 4–8.

Flowering dogwood bears fruits in late summer. Birds and squirrels wait and watch them redden before they descend and devour them. This doesn't affect the flowers the next spring. Zones 5–8.

Crabapple flowers attract honeybees and other insects in spring. By summer, they have developed into miniature apples that dangle enticingly from their branches. From late summer into fall—until the birds finish feasting—the red and gold hues of the fruit enliven the garden. Deer, rabbits, and foxes eat the apples that drop to the ground. Zones 4–8.

rather than better. Instead, use biological (natural) products on pest insects, or use barriers or repellents where certain animals, such as deer and rabbits intrude. A yard that attracts wildlife offers housing. The best shelters for rabbits, chipmunks, hibernating butterflies, and birds that nest on or near the ground are brush piles and weedy grasses. Waterfowl prefer streams or ponds. Leaf litter and debris provide nesting materials. Hedges, shrubs, and trees supply cover and places to hang birdhouses.

Oregon grape holly is widely distributed across the country. A generous host to wildlife, its fragrant, yellow spring flowers are usually covered with honeybees. Its fall berries attract birds. Zones 6–9.

Butterfly bush is a magnet for adult butterflies. Its florets, packed in tapered clusters, are full of nectar. It begins to bloom in early summer when the butterflies appear. Zones 6–9.

Hibiscus flowers are classics for hummingbirds. They're trumpet shaped, the nectar deeply recessed for a perfect hummingbird fit. Red is the best color, then orange, yellow, pink, and purple. Zones 6–9.

Rose hips in shades of red and orange remain after garden roses have bloomed. People covet the vitamin-C-rich hips for jams and tea. Birds eat these brightly colored treats just as they find them. Zones 2–7.

attracting wildlife: birdbath

Songbirds are attracted to shallow water. Add a birdbath to your garden and you'll be amazed at all the birds that will stop by. Nestle this lovely handmade birdbath in a flower bed; admirers will never know that it was so easy to make. You don't need a fancy mold to fashion the basin. You can even use a cardboard box instead of the ground, as long as the box is at least 4 inches wider than the basin's width. Fill it 10 inches deep with soil, then scoop a basin shape in the soil. Work quickly with the concrete mix to shape the basin; concrete starts to set within minutes. You can inset some crushed glass, attractive stones, or shells into the basin.

YOU WILL NEED

- hoe or shovel
- spray bottle and water
- rubber gloves
- face mask
- 2—3 cups peat moss
- 3 gallons pre-mixed concrete
- crushed, colored recycled glass
- sheet of plastic

1 Dig and shape an 18- to 20-inch hole in the ground. Spritz it with water; pack the soil down firmly. Tamp a flat area in the center so the finished basin will sit securely on a flat surface.

2 Wear gloves and mask. In a wheelbarrow, mix the peat moss and concrete. Stir in about 2 gallons of water to make a stiff "batter." If it is too thin, add more concrete; if too thick to hold together, add water.

3 Shovel the wet mix into the mold; pat in place, working from the center to the outside rim. Pat smooth. Spritz with water to keep concrete moist.

4 Sprinkle on glass and gently press into place. Cover basin with a plastic sheet for 3 to 7 days. Uncover; let it age a month before filling with water.

planting trees & shrubs

Trees and shrubs bought by mail order are often shipped with bare roots and arrive in late winter while they're still dormant. Deciduous ones have bare branches; their leaves dropped the previous autumn. Evergreens do have their foliage, but they're also in their rest period. All the soil is washed off their roots, which are usually wrapped in moist, shredded paper, moss, or sawdust for shipment. This way, they're easy and relatively inexpensive to ship. Bare-root plants tend to be very young, so are smaller than those sold in containers or balled and burlapped. They're less expensive, and many more varieties are available through specialty mail-order sources. Keep plant roots moist if you'll

planting depth

Planting depth is critically important when you plant trees and shrubs. Whether they're bare root, containerized, or balled and burlapped, don't plant them too deeply. Check often while positioning them in the hole to ensure that the root flare—where the roots begin at the base of the stems or trunk—is visible at or above the level of the ground.

planting bare-root trees and shrubs

YOU WILL NEED

- garden gloves
- shovel or spade
- bare-root plant
- bucket
- water
- mulch

1 Dig a hole that accommodates the roots when you spread them out. Make it deep enough so the soil mark—it's probably still visible on the stem—is level with the soil surface.

2 Unwrap the roots carefully and gently rinse off any sawdust, moss, or debris so they're bare. Cleanly clip off any dead rootlets, and cut broken ones back to healthy tissue.

5 Cut away any broken or dead stems. Unless the shipping and planting instructions specifically tell you to cut away a portion of healthy top growth, don't prune anything more.

6 Set the crown of the plant—where the roots join the stem—over the soil cone and drape the roots evenly over its sides. Make sure the soil mark on the stem or trunk is at ground level.

be delaying planting. Keep them wrapped and stored in a cool, dark place. Several hours before planting, unwrap the roots and set the plant in a container of tepid water so that its roots are immersed. Be careful not to damage the roots. The tiny root hairs are important because they will spearhead the growth in the soil. Once planted and watered, bare-root plants need less water than others until they leaf out. Delay fertilizing until they produce stems and foliage growth.

heeling-in

Sometimes it's not possible to plant bare-root nursery stock right away. Heeling it in—a sort of temporary planting—ensures that the roots stay moist and protected during the delay. Dig a trench or slot in the soil or in a pile of leaves, mulch, or compost. Then set the tree or shrub so its roots lay in it. Cover the roots with soil or compost in a loose heap and wet it down thoroughly. You can keep plants heeled-in for up to three months.

3 Soak the roots in a bucket of tepid water for several hours so they can take up water. The more hydrated the plant's tissues are, the better it can handle the planting process.

4 Press loose soil at the bottom of the hole into a cone to support the root system. Make it high enough so the roots drape freely and the plant crown is level with the soil surface.

7 Fill the hole with the soil removed from digging. Pour water into the half-filled hole to help reduce air bubbles, settle the roots in position, and show if you need to adjust the depth.

8 Fill with soil up to ground level. Firm it gently over the root zone to support the plant. It's not necessary to create a water reservoir around the plant; the latest studies show it does more harm than good.

9 Water again to settle the soil. Mulch with a 2- to 3-inch layer of chopped leaves or aged wood chips over the root zone. This will discourage weeds and keep the soil moist. Don't fertilize yet.

planting trees & shrubs

More and more trees and shrubs sold these days arrive in containers. In fact, some nurseries grow trees in them from the outset, so the first time they're ever in the ground and develop roots freely is when you plant them in your yard. Before you purchase a containerized tree or shrub, check to see if it's rootbound. Be suspicious if roots are swelling above the soil level, wrapped around the trunk, or trailing out the bottom of the container. Ask the salesperson to lift the plant out of its container so you can see if the roots are wrapped in circles around the soil ball. Choose a plant that's still comfortable in its pot. It will be less stressed and more willing to wait quite a while in case planting is delayed. The idea is to encourage the tree's or shrub's roots to leave

time to plant

Fall is the best time to plant many trees and shrubs. Spring is the next best time to plant and transplant and it's better for certain trees, such as oaks, beeches, birches, and willows. You can plant ones that come in containers almost any time the soil isn't frozen.

planting container-grown trees and shrubs

YOU WILL NEED

- garden gloves
- shovel or spade
- containerized plant
- burlap or tarp
- pruners
- water
- mulch material

1 Dig the planting hole just as deep as the tree's or shrub's container. Slope the sides a bit so the hole is wider near the top to encourage the roots to grow laterally outward into the soil.

2 Slide the root ball out of the container carefully. If the soil is moist, the ball should come out easily. If it's stubborn, check to see if roots protruding from the bottom of the pot are snagging it.

6 Fill the hole with the plain dirt that you dug from it. Don't add materials to improve it unless the ground is solid clay. The plant has to learn to handle its new soil environment.

7 Firm the soil around the buried root ball to remove any air pockets. Create a watering basin by mounding the soil several inches high just beyond the edge of the planting hole.

their pampered environment of loose, rich container soil and venture out to find food and water on their own in a strange, more daunting soil. Don't put any special soil amendments in the hole or add them to the fill soil. They might encourage roots to stay put and wrap around themselves. Withhold fertilizer—which mainly fuels foliage growth—while the tree or shrub concentrates on root growth. Once the planting is established and new stems and foliage appear, sprinkle some granular, slow-acting fertilizer over the root zone and let the rain soak it in. Use lots of organic mulch to keep the soil moist, and give the new tree or shrub plenty of moisture the first year or two. Water it in winter when the ground isn't frozen.

3 Loosen and untangle any circling or snarled roots. Cut any that are broken, dead, or hopelessly tangled. Those protruding from the soil ball will have a head start growing outward.

4 Loosen any bottom roots that have matted. If they don't come loose easily, cut or slice through them to get them to hang freely. Cut off impenetrable masses; it won't harm the plant.

5 Set the plant in the empty hole. Step back to see if it looks right. Then check its depth. The top of its soil ball should be even with—or slightly above—the surrounding ground.

8 Water the tree or shrub thoroughly, filling the reservoir, then letting it drain. Do this several times, waiting a while between waterings for the water to soak in deeply.

9 Stake trees only if they are threatened by wind. Insert two or three stakes into the soil, equidistant around the root zone. Loop soft tie material around the trunk and tie one loosely to each stake.

10 Mulch the root zone with a 2- to 3-inch layer of organic material, such as aged wood chips, pine needles, or chopped leaves. Don't pile mulch against plant stems, and don't fertilize at this time.

planting trees & shrubs

Trees sold with their roots in soil wrapped in burlap tend to be larger and more mature. These "B & B" (balled and burlapped) trees grow in the ground and are dug out in late winter or spring, wrapped, and shipped to garden centers. The burlap-wrapped root ball is sometimes covered with a wire cage to stabilize it and make carrying it easier. Although they're more difficult to handle, B & B plants generally transplant successfully. When properly cared for, they can sit safely for months at the nursery, where the root balls may be buried in mulch to keep them moist. When the tree is sold, its branches are bound loosely with twine to prevent damage during transport and planting. In the past, suppliers traditionally used standard burlap because it's tough, its natural

getting off to a good start

Because the first priority for a newly planted tree or shrub is to establish and grow roots, use a kelp or mycorrhiza growth product at planting time to help it get started. Delay spreading granular, slow-acting fertilizer until the plant shows its roots are established and functioning with new stem and leaf growth visible.

planting balled and burlapped trees and shrubs

YOU WILL NEED

- shovel or spade
- burlap-wrapped plant
- tarp
- water
- mulch
- stakes (optional)
- tree wrap (optional)

1 Examine the tree before you buy it. Reject those with gouges, scrapes, or wounds on the trunk. Look, too, for girdling roots encircling the base of the trunk under the burlap wrapping.

2 Spread a tarp for the soil. Dig a hole with sloping sides exactly as deep as the root ball is high and at least half again as it is wide. Don't add anything to the hole or soil.

5 Use the plain loose soil on the tarp to fill in the hole around the root ball. Water it when the hole is half full to prevent air pockets. Check the root ball level again and raise it if it has sunk.

6 Finish filling the hole and firm the soil. Arborists say you shouldn't create a water reservoir around the base of the tree because that can cause root rot. Water slowly and deeply.

fibers rot in the hole, the soil around the roots isn't disturbed, and it makes planting easier. Today's "new" burlap is made from synthetic fibers. It's difficult to detect and doesn't decay in the soil. Cut away as much of it as possible from the sides of the root ball after you've positioned it properly in the hole. Because most roots grow laterally, this will ensure unobstructed progress. If the ball is encased in a wire cage, cut it away, too. Then you can get at the burlap and remove it.

3 Remove any protective outer wrapping, but leave the burlap on to hold the roots while you position the plant in the hole. Untie the branches to determine the most pleasing aspect.

4 Cut away as much burlap as you can. Roots grow laterally, so fabric under the ball can remain. Be sure the top of the root ball—where the roots flare out from the trunk—is at or above ground level.

7 Spread a 2- to 3-inch layer of organic mulch over the root zone to discourage weeds and retain soil moisture. Unwrap the branches if they are still tied; they will soon regain their normal posture.

8 Use tree wrap to protect the tender bark on young trees threatened by rodent or sun damage. Follow the instructions on the package to ensure proper application.

staking a tree

1 Use straps around the tree's trunk if you have to stake it. The wide, soft material doesn't cause abrasions on its tender bark. Attach supporting wire or rope to the grommets in the straps.

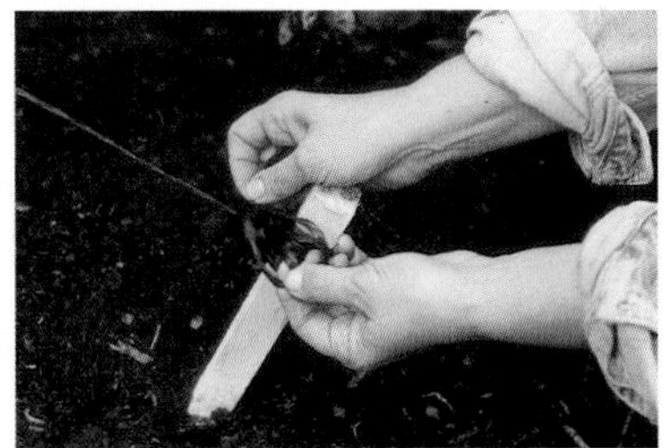

2 Insert two or three stakes in the soil just outside the planting hole and equidistant around it. Attach a supporting wire or rope to each stake. Be sure to leave some slack in the wire or rope to allow the trunk to flex properly.

3 Never leave staking on a newly planted tree for more than six or eight months. Throughout this period, check the straps around the trunk to make sure they're loose enough to avoid damaging the tender bark.

planting bare-root roses

Hundreds of varieties of roses are featured at local nurseries or in mail-order catalogs. These days, many roses—especially landscape (shrub), rambling, and old garden roses—come planted in containers, already in bloom. Plant them, following the step-by-step procedure suggested on pages 230 and 231, allowing 4 to 6 feet between plants. Hybrid tea roses and their cousins—floribunda and grandiflora—typically are shipped bare-root and dormant. Their canes have no leaves—but buds are visible where leaves will soon appear—and their roots are wrapped in moist paper or sawdust. The roots easily dry out, so be sure to keep them wrapped and moist until you're ready to plant.

YOU WILL NEED

- bare-root rose
- pail
- water
- compost or other organic material
- gypsum (optional)
- shovel
- heavy gloves
- pruners
- mulch

1 Soak bare roots in a pail of water overnight. Prepare the soil in the planting area by adding compost or other organic material. Ensure good drainage in heavy clay by adding gypsum.

2 Dig the planting hole about 2 feet deep, and wide enough to fit the roots and several inches of stem. Fill the hole with water to test for drainage; it should drain within an hour.

5 Set the roots on the soil cone so the swollen graft union is 2 inches below ground level (but at ground level in areas that have frost-free winters).

6 Partially fill the hole with soil. Water, then fill the hole to ground level. Mound soil around the crown temporarily to keep the canes moist.

Site roses carefully. Once established, they resent being moved. Grow hybrid teas and their cousins in a bed of their own. Their stiff canes and upright growth habit don't blend well with other plants. They need frequent attention and rich soil; they are easier to provide at one location. All roses need protection from wind and at least six hours of bright sun daily. Sunlight dries their leaves, reducing the chance of fungal disease. In hot climates, some shade from afternoon heat is welcome. Space hybrid teas at least 24 inches apart so you can prune and cut the flowers without getting pricked by the thorny canes.

3 Prune any roots broken during shipping or packaging. (Be sure to wear heavy gloves.) Even after you've done this, each plant still should have three or four healthy canes 8 to 10 inches long.

4 Use loose soil to form a tall cone at the bottom of the hole. This will support the bare roots in the correct position—and in proper alignment in the hole—until the hole is backfilled.

7 Create a water reservoir over the roots by firming a ridge of soil around the perimeter of the planting area. Fill it with water to soak the soil.

8 Spread mulch over the planting area. Prune canes by one-third to stimulate new growth. Make cuts just above a swollen leaf bud that faces outward.

quality roses

Since 1938, All-America Rose Selections (AARS) has encouraged rose growers to improve the vitality, strength, and beauty of roses for America's gardens. At trial plots around the country, promising new varieties are observed for superior vigor, bloom, and disease resistance under controlled conditions. Those selected as AARS winners have the AARS emblem on their package labels and stem tags. Look for this sign of quality.

planting an evergreen

Because they're living walls, your hedges are prominent features of your landscape. So your choice of shrubs and the way you prune them can set a style for your entire yard. All kinds of shrubs have the qualities to make a good hedge. Tall or short, deciduous or evergreen—a shrub needs only a reasonably uniform growth habit, heavy branching, and attractive, dense foliage. However, those intended for a formal hedge must be able to handle the close shearing they get on a regular basis. The purpose of the hedge influences your choice of shrub. Faster-growing deciduous shrubs provide a better seasonal show—spring flowers, colorful fall foliage, and berries. They also make

instant hedge

One way to hurry a hedge is to space the shrubs so they're actually too close together. This provides an instant hedge look. As the shrubs grow and start to crowd each other, dig up every other one and transplant them somewhere else. Another way is to plant shrubs in a staggered pattern to look like a filled-in hedge, even though they're the correct distance apart.

YOU WILL NEED

- shrubs
- stakes
- strings
- shovel or spade
- measuring tape
- water
- mulch

1 Choose nursery stock that's uniform in color, size, and shape. Check to see whether the roots are healthy and well-developed. Buy all the plants you will need at the same time and place.

2 Tie string to stakes to mark the area where the shrubs will be planted. The line will guide your digging so the bed will be straight and uniformly wide. Keep plants moist until planting.

5 Set the plants—still in their pots—alongside the trench to establish the correct spacing. Allow for their width at maturity although they might look very far apart at this stage.

6 Remove each plant from its container and check the roots. Loosen or untangle any that are matted because they were confined in the pot. Clip off any broken ones.

hedge

good accents and boundaries. Evergreen shrubs—especially needled ones, such as juniper, arborvitae, or falsecypress—grow more slowly. Their year-round foliage provides privacy and shelter from wind. Shrubs with thorns—especially barberry, holly, and landscape roses—are particularly useful in a hedge that's a barrier to foot traffic and unwelcome visitors. When you shop for needled evergreens, choose ones that have uniform size and color. Be sure all shrubs are healthy. If a sickly one dies after a couple of years, it can ruin forever the uniformity of the hedge. Choose a hedge site that has the appropriate amount and exposure of sun over its entire length, because any portion that's in the shade won't grow uniformly.

3 Dig within the string guides. Although it's possible to plant shrubs for a hedge in a row of individual holes, a trench is more efficient. Remove turf sod and put it aside, then dig the soil.

4 Dig the trench as deep as the plants' containers. Slope the sides to encourage roots to grow outward. Don't put any loose material in the bottom of the trench.

7 Position the shrubs in the trench. Make sure that they are at the correct depth. Adjust them, if necessary, so that the tops of their root balls are at—or just above—ground level.

8 Fill in the trench with plain soil. Firm it gently over and around each root ball, then water well. Spread a 2- to 3-inch layer of organic mulch over the planted bed, then water again.

windbreaks

Burlap serves as a temporary windbreak for young evergreen shrubs in a site exposed to drying winter winds and sun. Remove it when spring arrives.

Straw stacked as bales forms a temporary wall to protect evergreens from wind and sun damage in the winter. Loose straw makes an excellent soil insulator.

planting a shrub border

Shrub borders are truly freewheeling affairs. Unlike hedges, where a considerable degree of uniformity of plant type, size, and design is necessary to achieve the correct look, shrub borders are all about diversity. The most attractive and interesting ones owe their beauty to their variety—in size and shape of plants, foliage color, and texture. Some also boast delightful seasonal displays of flowers, fruit, cones, or bark. The interplay of these features gives the borders structure and interest over all the seasons. Although hedges are planted in more or less formal rows for a linear effect, shrub borders may vary in width—and may even curve pleasingly. They will also vary in depth,

YOU WILL NEED

- spade or shovel
- organic material
- garden rake
- shrubs (a mix of deciduous and evergreen)
- water
- pruners
- mulch

1 Site preparation is important if your planting area is new, or if your soil needs help. Remove sod and set it aside. Turn over the soil to loosen and aerate it.

2 Add organic material—compost, chopped leaves, or Canadian sphagnum peat moss—to improve soil's ability to hold water, drain, and add nutrients.

5 Start your layout by temporarily arranging the potted shrubs on the prepared soil. Then move them around until you find a pleasing arrangement.

6 Dig a hole for each plant exactly as deep as its container. For easy access, start at the back of the border and move to the front.

depending on the site and purpose—15 to 20 feet deep to cover the area between a driveway and a wall—or only 6 to 8 feet deep. And they're typically longer than they are wide. Shrub borders work well on uneven ground, too. On a slope, they help control erosion in ornamental style. When planted on a berm—a constructed mound of soil that raises the elevation along boundaries—a shrub border screens the noise and view of traffic. One that's composed of understory plants, such as azaleas, rhododendrons, and mountain laurel, makes a good transition between a woodland and the lawn area.

3 Sprinkle granular, slow-acting fertilizer on the soil. Mix it in as you rake the soil smooth and level the bed. Remove any stones and debris.

4 Keep the plants moist while they await transplanting. Containers dry out rapidly, so shelter them in the shade if the weather is warm.

7 Prune discolored, broken branches while the shrubs are in their pots. You can spot problems easier when the plants are at eye level.

8 Set each shrub in its hole with the top of its root ball exactly at, or even slightly above, the adjoining surface. Fill in with extra soil, firm it gently, and water.

weather

Evergreen shrubs in a border often are exposed to harsh sun and wind during the winter, so they're in danger of drying out. That's because their leaves continue to release moisture that their roots can't replenish if the ground is frozen. Shelter them with a windbreak, spray their foliage with an antidessicant before cold weather sets in, or do both.

planting a shrub border

A simple shrub border may be a bed of various ornamental shrubs planted more or less in a row. It may front a wall or fence, or even the foundation of the house or garage. A more elaborate one may accommodate several rows of shrubs of various heights. Plant them irregularly, staggered so that every one is seen from the front of the border. Position the taller ones toward the back, medium ones in the center, and low-growing and groundcover types at the front of the border. Leave plenty of space for them to grow to natural size at maturity—plus a bit more to allow you room to move between them to water, feed, and prune. You can plant a shrub border using only one type of shrub—for instance, just evergreens, or even just conifers. They're available in so many

optimizing space

Take advantage of the extra space at the front of your shrub border by planting some flowers. Incorporate a few hardy spring-blooming bulbs, such as daffodils, when you plant the bed. Add petunias or impatiens for the summer months, then replace them with chrysanthemums in the fall. Be careful not to disturb the shrubs' shallow root systems when you do your planting.

9 Some shrubs have unruly habits. Prune off excessively long or damaged branches. They are easier to handle while still in pots.

10 One by one, remove each plant from its pot. Loosen any roots that are tangled or wrapped around in circles, or score the root ball with a knife.

13 Fill the hole with soil, firming it around the roots to eliminate air pockets. After watering, the soil may sink; add more soil if necessary to level the area.

14 Water the border after it's planted. To avoid compacting the soil, don't walk on it. The more aerated it remains, the more water it will hold.

colors, sizes, shapes, and textures that such a border can provide plenty of year-round interest. Another option is to use a mixture of deciduous and evergreen shrubs. This gives you a perfect opportunity to incorporate shrubs that are popular with birds and other wildlife so you can develop a backyard wildlife habitat. Choose shrubs that are relatively self-reliant and need little maintenance. Allow them to develop their natural shape and size so you can minimize pruning. Choose shrubs that are well-suited to the soil as well as the available light and water. Mulch them well to reduce weeds and keep soil moist.

11 Plant broadleaf evergreen shrubs the same way as needled evergreens. Dig a planting hole in prepared soil as deep as the container and a bit wider.

12 Adjust the depth so the shrub is at or above the level of the surrounding ground. Make sure each shrub has room to spread to its mature size.

15 Spread a 2- to 3-inch layer of organic material over the bare soil to discourage weeds, preserve moisture, and protect the soil.

16 For finishing touches, include colorful annuals near the front and edge of the border. In autumn, plant some hardy bulbs among the shrubs.

pruning woody plants

Pruning is essential to plant health and beauty. It disciplines growth and coaxes the best performance from woody plants, such as trees, shrubs, and perennial vines. Some homeowners who don't understand the process delay it too long or avoid it altogether, making their plants suffer. But pruning isn't all that difficult, if you know the specific need. Prune *to repair* injury and prevent disease and insect problems whenever they arise, whatever the season. Jagged stubs from a broken branch provide an entry for disease and insects into the interior of the plant, so make a smooth cut near the base of the limb to promote healing. Prune out branches with tents that harbor caterpillars. Eliminate

more pruning hints

- *For your safety and for the health of your plants, keep your pruning equipment sharp. Don't leave pruners outdoors; they could rust and become dull.*
- *To prevent browning, clip the tips of needled evergreens when they're damp.*
- *Don't paint or seal wounds where tree limbs are removed. Exposure to air prevents decay while the healing callus tissue gradually grows over the area.*
- *Hire a professional if the job requires using a chainsaw on a ladder.*

removing a large limb

1 Undercut the designated branch away from the trunk. This prevents a tear that may strip the bark down onto the trunk when you cut through the cumbersome, large limb from above later.

2 Top-cut the limb just beyond the undercut. Make this cut all the way through the limb to remove it entirely. Because it's a preliminary cut, it doesn't have to be aesthetically pleasing.

3 Remove the heavy limb before making a final, smooth cut. Identify the branch collar at the base of the branch. Cut the branch just beyond it.

4 This incorrect cut leaves a big stub that the tissues in the branch collar cannot close. Make another cut, 2 inches from the trunk and parallel to it.

rubbing branches and weak crotches. Prune *to train* the structure and stimulate growth of young plants while they're dormant in late winter. Thin crowded branches and saw off one of the competing branches to establish a single leader where necessary. Remove branches that rub on the roof. Shear hedges and renovate old, overgrown shrubs early in the season by cutting back all stems to the ground or removing just the thickest. Prune *to reduce growth* or remove errant branches during the growing season. But don't expect to *control growth*, because many plants react to pruning by generating new leaves and flowers.

when to prune trees and shrubs

plant	when to prune	why
Andromeda	after spring bloom	shape growth; remove winterkill
Arborvitae	late winter when dormant	shape; prune out winterkill
Azalea	after spring bloom	shape growth
Barberry	spring/summer	shear for hedge; renovate/shape
Boxwood	late winter when dormant	shear as hedge; prune out winterkill
Butterfly bush	early spring	cut back stems to start new wood
Daphne	after flowering	shape growth
Falsecypress	late winter	shape
Forsythia	after spring bloom	shear for hedge; shape or renovate
Holly	winter, early spring	boughs for decoration; shape
Hybrid tea roses	late winter–early spring	remove winterkill, shape; stimulate new growth
Juniper	late winter	shear for hedge
Lilac	after spring bloom	groom: deadhead, remove suckers
Mock orange	after spring bloom	thin stems; trim unruly branches
Mountain laurel	after spring bloom	renovate overgrowth
Nandina	early spring	cut off dead berries; shape
Pine	late spring	clip "candle" growth for size
Rhododendron	after spring bloom	shape growth; deadhead flowers

pruning fruit trees

Fruit trees are both ornamental and productive, so annual pruning is doubly beneficial. The best time to do major pruning is late winter or early spring, because you're stimulating rapid growth of new stems. Leaves haven't emerged yet, so the branch layout is clearly visible. Yearly pruning establishes—then maintains—the shape you want. The *central leader system* is common primarily for ornamental fruit trees. Prune to establish a single leader—or trunk—then encourage lateral branches at regular intervals around it. The *modified leader system* features a central leader and three or four equally important major branches. Cut away all other large branches. Use the *open center system* for orchard

pole pruners

Long-handled pole pruners are ideal for clipping thin upper branches from the canopy of a small tree. They allow overhead work without the nuisance and danger of a ladder. Look for models tipped with small saws or cord-operated, crook-shaped cutting blades. Pole pruner handles extend up to 8 feet.

Remove root suckers that sprout from the base of the tree—they actually come from its roots—as soon as they appear. Use loppers to cut them off as close to the base as possible.

Water sprouts are suckers that grow vertically from tree limbs. Because they divert valuable energy from the fruit-bearing branches, immediately clip them off cleanly with your loppers.

1 Use a pruning saw to remove large branches that are injured or rubbing a neighbor. Make the first cut upward, several inches out from the trunk.

2 Make the second cut at the trunk but leave the branch collar—the ring of transition bark at the crotch—to grow callus tissue, which heals the wound.

trees. Prune to encourage three or four major limbs instead of a central trunk. The limbs should angle out widely and support six secondary, fruit-bearing branches each. This flattened shape opens the canopy to air, and the lower profile makes the fruit more accessible.

Always prune bottom to top, inside to outside, and remove any dead or damaged wood. If two branches are rubbing together, cut off the poorer-positioned one all the way back to the trunk or main limb. Encourage branches that grow upward and outward from the tree's center or that fill an opening in the overall profile of the tree.

rejuvenating an apple tree

Apple trees live a long time. It's possible to restore a venerable tree that has been neglected for years by carefully pruning it over several seasons. First determine that it doesn't have any trunk rot or root rot that has compromised its basic health. Then clear away brush and prune back neighboring trees that shade it. Cut off suckers and twiggy growth throughout the branch canopy to let in sunlight. Each year afterward, prune away only one-fourth to one-third of the new growth so you can control suckering. Water and fertilize the tree.

forcing branches to bloom

Force flowering trees and shrubs to bloom prematurely by bringing a few cut branches inside and giving them an early spring. Because most plants need a dormant period of rest and cold, wait until early February to do your cutting. The length of the cold spell they need varies by plant variety, but this timing works for most. Choose plants with many new flower buds formed just after last year's bloom. Flower buds are typically plumper than leaf buds, which are usually slim and pointy and lie nearer the stem. The closer to their normal bloom time, the faster the branches will bloom indoors. So cut early bloomers—such as spirea, forsythia, witchhazel, fragrant honeysuckle, quince,

YOU WILL NEED

- hand pruners
- pail
- tepid water
- floral preservative or chlorine bleach
- display container

1 Your goal is not only to cut a branch to force inside but also to preserve the natural shape of the shrub or tree and ensure a good outdoor bloom display later. Cut branches with lots of plump buds.

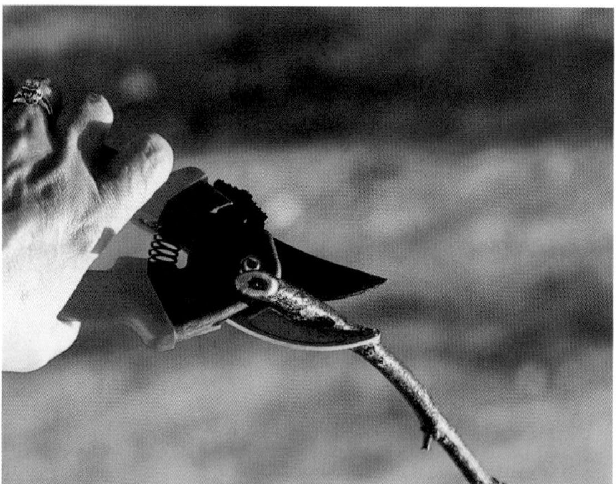

2 Ensure maximum water uptake by recutting the stem ends at a sharp angle to expose as much surface to the water as possible. Clean off buds from the part of the stem that will be underwater.

branches for form and berries

Many shrubs and trees have interesting shapes or colorful berries that can be cut and added to flower arrangements or displayed on their own. Some possibilities include firethorn, Harry Lauder's walking stick, beautyberry, viburnum, corkscrew willow, and winterberry holly.

3 Promptly put the cut stems in a pail of tepid water with commercial floral preservative—or a drop of chlorine bleach—to fight bacteria.

4 Set the pail in a cool place for a week or two. Change the water periodically if necessary. When buds begin to swell, bring it into warmth and light.

and wintersweet—in early February. Cut later bloomers —crab apple, cherry, azalea, rhododendron, flowering dogwood, and redbud—in early to mid-March. Cut branches during the warmest part of a mild day, when buds have the most sap. Allow them to adjust indoors for a week or two. Pamper them with moisture.

5 Rearrange the stems in fresh water and floral preservative in the container of your choice for display. Set it in bright light but not sunlight. The warmer the room, the faster the buds will open. However, for longer display life, keep them in a cool area. Once they've bloomed, as in the above photo, you have a miniature version of your outdoor plant that can bring spring's beauty indoors well ahead of its normal arrival.

other plants you can force

Callery pear bears small, musky-scented white flowers in rounded clusters with emerging leaves. Cut in mid-March for bloom in two to three weeks.

Cherry trees bear clusters of pink flowers. If cut in mid-February, earliest varieties bloom indoors in two weeks, the later ones in three to four weeks.

Redbud bears pealike purplish pink (sometimes pink or white) flowers along bare branches. Cut branches in March for indoor bloom in three weeks.

Apple blossoms start as clusters of deep pink buds. They open to 1-inch, dainty, scented white flowers with emerging leaves. Cut stems in March.

Flowering quince is forced indoors easily in January to early February. It bears 1½-inch-wide red, pink, orange, or white flowers on spiny stems.

Forsythia bears 2-inch-long, trumpet-shaped yellow florets along its arching branches. If cut in early February, it will bloom indoors in two weeks.

pruning evergreens

Most evergreens have neat, symmetrical habits and don't require much pruning. Some, such as eastern white pine, are brittle and suffer damage in rain- or snowstorms. Cleanly prune away injured branches to avoid more damage from disease or pests. Otherwise prune evergreens just to maintain symmetry and encourage denser foliage. Stimulate the development of more twigs by cutting individual branch tips with shears or clippers.

Some conifers—cone-bearing, needled evergreens—branch out randomly and sprout new growth wherever latent buds appear. Arborvitae, hemlock, and yew—good hedge material—respond well to aggressive shearing by producing dense, new

pruning for size

YOU WILL NEED

- gloves
- hand pruners or hedge shears
- debris container
- household bleach
- hot water

1 Cut back branches of broad-leaved evergreens, such as holly, with hedge shears to encourage denser growth. Create a more natural look by cutting individual stems with hand pruners.

2 Use pruners or loppers to clip off dead and injured branches as soon as you discover them. Cut back to where fresh foliage occurs or where the branch joins the trunk.

avoiding browned tips

To prevent temporary browning on cut ends of needled evergreens, prune them when they're wet. Choose a time just after a spring rain or early in the morning when the dew is heavy.

3 Prune to guide the natural growth of each shrub. If you need to do heavy pruning each year to control its growth, it's the wrong plant for the space.

4 Clean up all debris afterward. If there are signs of disease, bag trimmings in plastic for the trash. Disinfect tools with household bleach and hot water.

foliage. Other conifers, such as pine, juniper, fir, and spruce, branch out differently. All their main branches grow directly from their trunks, radiating outward like spokes of a wheel. Simply trim branch tips. They won't grow new foliage if pruned back too far. Don't constantly prune a shrub to keep it squeezed into a space that's too small for it, because you'll stress and disfigure it. If it's too large for the space, move it to a place that can handle its mature size. Choose cultivars that will mature to the size of your space. You'll find many dwarf conifers these days that are just right for small yards and gardens.

pruning for shape

1 Make cuts to maintain a shrub's natural shape. Clip the individual stems of needled evergreens when their soft "candles" of new growth appear in late winter. Cut back each candle by about one-half.

2 Replace a shrub's central leader if it breaks or fails to develop. Select a nearby stem and bend it upward, fastening it if necessary so it's dominant.

common pruning errors

Incorrect pruning mars appearance, undermines vigor, and compromises health—good reasons to avoid these errors:

- **Topping –** Cutting off the top of a tree forces it to develop new, weaker, multiple replacement stems. It will struggle to achieve its genetically programmed height.
- **Heading back –** To shorten a branch, cut where another branch or side twig emerges rather than at just any point along the way.
- **Cutting back stems to bare wood –** Many shrubs don't generate new twigs and foliage from branches that have no existing leaves or twigs (usually those near the trunk).
- **Shearing into tight shapes –** Except for certain shrubs that easily withstand shearing for hedges, repeated shearing promotes dead twigs and foliage loss inside the shrub.
- **Leaving a stub –** Cleanly cut off branches at the trunk and leave only the branch collar to heal into a small knob.

pruning to reveal bark

You can improve a tree's appearance by removing its lower limbs, especially when it's young and just forming its branching structure. In its ungainly adolescence, it may develop branches that are too close together or that cross and rub bark against bark. Sometimes branches form at such a severe angle with the trunk that the crotches are weak and break easily in storms. In all of these cases, you'll want to prune excess or ill-formed limbs to improve the tree's health, as well as enhance its ornamental appeal. And if you selectively remove tree limbs, you can open up a tree's canopy to more light and air. Limbing-up a tree—removing one or more lower limbs—is a common practice where trees

sprucing up

As Colorado blue spruces age, their lower limbs often become scraggly and flop on the ground. You can improve their appearance immensely by cutting off these unkempt branches to expose 6 to 8 feet of the trunk.

limbing-up a tree

1 Use loppers—long-handled pruners that require two hands—on branches up to 1 inch thick. Cut just beyond the branch collar to promote healing.

2 Remove low branches—those less than 6 feet above the ground—that block the way of passersby and anyone using a lawn mower.

3 Proper cuts stimulate the branch collar, healing it to a rounded knob that's barely detectable on trunks covered with colorful, textured, peeling bark.

4 Use hand pruners to remove spindly suckers that emerge from the base of the tree. Prune away thin, vertical watersprouts on branches, too.

share space with people. It may be necessary to allow more light to reach a planting area below the tree or enable people to pass easily under it. Many trees have striped, patchy, or peeling bark that is obscured by dense branching. By removing the lower branches of these trees, you can expose the bark to year-round enjoyment. Branches that grow low on a tree will always be at that same low height, because trees grow from their tips, gradually elongating at the top, not from their base. If you need to remove the lower branches of a tree, do so when it's young so the wound heals quickly and properly.

5 Groves of trees, such as these 'Heritage' river birches, are limbed-up to show their bark. A bench encourages you to pause and enjoy their beauty.

trees with attractive trunks

- *Crapemyrtle*
- *Franklinia*
- *Japanese tree clethra*
- *Kousa dogwood*
- *Lacebark elm*
- *Lacebark pine*
- *London planetree*
- *Mexican paloverde*
- *Paperbark maple*
- *Parrotia*
- *River birch*
- *Shagbark hickory*
- *Stewartia*
- *Striped maple*
- *Sycamore*
- *White birch*

pruning roses

You can enjoy incomparable blossoms from your hybrid tea roses all summer long if you prune them back—a step that's probably harder on you than on the plant. Although the idea of cutting back each bush to a few small, short canes (stems) may be difficult for you to conceive, it's essential to the rose's health and well-being. Hybrid teas and their close relatives, grandiflora and floribunda roses, respond to annual early-season pruning with vigorous new growth. When you remove winter-killed wood, excess canes, and rubbing branches, you groom the plants and shape their growth so they stay relatively compact in size and produce lots of flowers. Without this care, the bushes usually become tall and

YOU WILL NEED

- heavy gloves
- hand pruners
- loppers (optional)
- pruning saw (optional)

foiling fungus

The foliage of many hybrid tea roses is vulnerable to fungal disease. Prune them down to outward-facing leaves to maintain good air circulation in the center of the shrub. This is the first line of defense. Mulch plants well to prevent rain from splashing spores up onto foliage.

1 In late winter—just as leaf buds begin to swell—prune hybrid tea, grandiflora, and floribunda roses. Remove all deadwood, then stimulate growth by cutting back healthy canes (stems) to 6 inches.

2 Make clean, slanting cuts about ¼ inch above a leaf bud that faces outward. This encourages outward growth and keeps the center of the plant open for good air circulation.

3 Remove any canes that cross others. When you're finished pruning, you want three or four healthy canes. Remove all others, stubs and all.

4 A properly pruned rose looks small and vulnerable. However, it will grow properly in just a few weeks and produce beautiful blossoms.

rangy and produce fewer, smaller flowers. Prune roses with the correct equipment. Sharp bypass pruners will handle most of the cutting. Use long-handled loppers—also with bypass blades which won't crush the stems—or a pruning saw for extra-thick canes, old and neglected bushes, or where thorns on nearby stems make access difficult. Remove any part of the shrub that's brown and brittle; after a severe winter, this might amount to a lot. Entire canes might be brown to their base and part of the crown at the soil level could be dead. Remember: Pruning does the plant a favor.

pruning roses in bloom

Cutting rose blossoms for indoor display is a form of pruning. Take care to prune each stem back to where its leaves are composed of at least five or more leaflets. Cut on a slant just above an outward-facing leaf. Use the same technique to remove any faded blossoms on the shrub. This promotes a neat, compact shape and grooms the plant.

better late than never

Prune roses about the time that forsythia begins to show its yellow buds, but it might be impossible to prune on schedule. Fortunately, it's never too late to thin stems from the center and cut away deadwood. In fact as the shrub leafs out, you can tell right away which canes need removal. Just prune away all of the dead brown parts.

roses that need minimal pruning

Roses that are designated shrub or landscape don't require much pruning. Although they respond to shaping and look better when the dead stems are cut away, their growth habits are less formal:

- Rugosa hybrids
- 'The Fairy'
- 'Carefree' roses (Carefree Beauty™, 'Carefree Wonder', Carefree Delight™)
- Dream™ roses (yellow, pink, orange, and red)
- Flower Carpet™ roses (pink, white, red, and appleblossom)
- Meidiland hybrids (Bonica™ and others)

shaping shrubs

Many shrubs grow rapidly, and in their enthusiasm, they become overgrown, excessively twiggy, and weighted down with excess foliage. This bushiness eventually obscures their structure, reduces flowering, and invites fungal disease. Periodic pruning makes them more attractive and healthier. Pruning to control size is a waste of time—they will just grow back. Instead, guide them so they grow to their mature size with strong stems and healthy foliage. Experienced gardeners usually do their major structural pruning when shrubs are dormant, then perform follow-up shaping during the growing season, after the spring growth spurt. Prune your flowering shrubs to shape them after

dormancy

Whether deciduous or evergreen, trees and shrubs have a dormant period. Except for certain tropical trees, this rest time is usually during the cold winter months. During the period when days are short and the ground is cold, they suspend active growth and live off of stored energy. Warm weather triggers new vitality.

shaping forsythia

1 Overgrown shrubs look unkempt and unattractive and don't bloom well. Thinning the dense foliage-covered branches of this forsythia allows light and air to penetrate and improve its health.

2 The first step is to cut back excessively long branches. Clip them off where a leaf emerges back on the stem near the main mass of foliage. Avoid making them all identical lengths.

3 Reach deep within the dense tangle of branches and clip off particularly large or twiggy ones at the point where they join a main branch.

4 Once its general shape is established, give the shrub a final once-over. Be sure no branches rub against walls or tangle in nearby plants.

they've bloomed and before they set buds for the following year, so you don't inadvertently remove the buds and ruin next year's bloom. Plan to shape spring bloomers, such as rhododendron, azalea, and forsythia, in early to midsummer. Wait to shape summer bloomers, such as crapemyrtle and glossy abelia, until autumn. They form their buds for the new season early in the summer. Clip branches individually, and reserve shearing for hedges. The idea is to groom the shrub to curb unruliness, not to change its appearance. Properly shaped, the shrub should look essentially the same, only neater.

shaping shrubs

When shaping shrubs, you'll get the best results when you honor their natural habits. Use restraint. Appreciate that each shrub is genetically programmed for a certain size, profile, and branching pattern. Make cuts that support these features and preserve the essential character of the plant. Lollipop shapes are not attractive on the front lawn. Leave the highly stylized pruning—topiary, pollarding, and bonsai—to the experts.

shaping evergreen hedges

1 If the foliage on the sides of the hedge doesn't get sufficient sunlight, it will die back. Taper the sides of the hedge so that the lower branches are wider than those at the top.

2 To stimulate growth, trim a hedge with hedge shears or electric clippers below the desired height in spring. When you prune later in the season, don't remove all new growth.

shaping boxwood

1 Boxwood shrubs are commonly used as hedges because they tolerate repeated shearing well. However, when planted individually, they contribute attractive, fine-textured evergreen foliage to the scene. Periodically clip them to maintain their appearance.

2 Use hand pruners, rather than the hedge shears shown here, to clip off individual branches that protrude from the main foliage body of the shrub. Cut the branches at slightly different lengths to avoid creating a round profile.

renovating shrubs

It's easy to take shrubs for granted. Annual and perennial flowers get most of the attention, while the shrubs gradually grow older and bushier. Those that expand by sending up new shoots at ground level develop into wide clumps of increasingly crowded stems. This preponderance of thick, woody stems causes the shrubs to lose vitality and become vulnerable to disease and insect attack. You can save the cost and effort of replacing a valued, otherwise healthy, overgrown shrub by using good pruning techniques to revitalize it. Renovation involves cutting the oldest and thickest of the stems down to ground level and removing them. Because most are likely to be

spring growth

Spring is the period of greatest plant growth. When shrubs emerge from dormancy, all systems are go. If stems are cut back to the ground, the new surge of energy will produce replacement shoots that vibrantly arise from the crown of the shrub and give older shrubs a new lease on life.

1 After several years, shrub stems become crowded. Their leaves and flowers are sparser, and they look disheveled. Thin the shrub when it's dormant by removing the oldest and thickest stems.

2 Use long-handled loppers to cut stems up to an inch in diameter. Cut each stem 1 to 2 feet above the ground and remove it so there is room to cut the stub properly at ground level.

5 With about a third of the thick, old stems removed, there's plenty of space for this shrub to send up vigorous new replacement shoots.

6 Cut back extra-long stems to normal length. If the leaves have emerged, don't cut them all off, or the shrub may not grow new shoots.

pruning candidates, the basic rule of thumb is to cut out no more than a third of them at one time so the shrub continues to have a presence in the yard. Meanwhile, the pruning stimulates its root system to send up supple, vigorous replacement stems. If done gradually over a period of six years, this process completely renews an old shrub. Some shrubs that respond well to renovation are lilac, mock orange, quince, deutzia, weigela, privet, barberry, forsythia, and bottlebrush buckeye. Others include shrub dogwoods, beautyberry, spirea, bluebeard, rose of Sharon, Japanese kerria, and staghorn sumac.

yearly pruning

You can increase the beauty of certain shrubs, such as red-twigged dogwood, by cutting back all of the stems every year. This stimulates them to send up new shoots. The new young growth may have brilliantly colored bark. Shrubs that bear flowers on new growth, such as butterfly bush, produce more and better flowers.

3 A pruning saw is handy for stems that are larger than 1 inch in diameter. This narrow, pointed folding saw fits into tight spaces between crowded stems. It also makes a smooth cut.

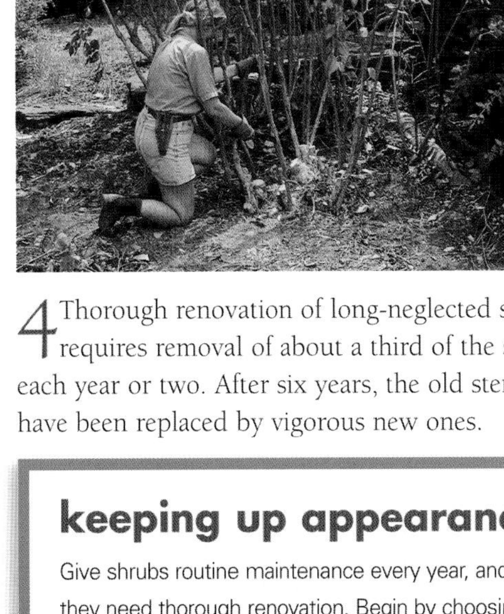

4 Thorough renovation of long-neglected shrubs requires removal of about a third of the stems each year or two. After six years, the old stems will have been replaced by vigorous new ones.

keeping up appearances

Give shrubs routine maintenance every year, and they will never reach the point that they need thorough renovation. Begin by choosing the correct plant for each site, so that each has sufficient space to grow to its mature size. Don't overfertilize shrubs. If their soil is decent and they are mulched, they won't need granular, slow-acting fertilizer after the first three or four years. Overfertilization encourages excessive growth and bushiness, which restricts their access to light and air. This stresses plants and makes them vulnerable to pest and disease attack. Water shrubs well whenever rainfall is sparse. Most importantly, prune them lightly and regularly as they grow to establish their structure and shape. Thin their foliage branches if necessary. To prevent overcrowding, annually remove obviously aging stems before they become thick and woody. This helps a shrub constantly and gradually regenerate without undergoing a radical renovation pruning. It's particularly important in preserving the uniform look of a hedge year after year.

regional tree & shrub

Cool Climates

Spring

- ❑ Prune woody stems of butterfly bush to about 6 inches from the ground.
- ❑ Prune any broken or injured limbs on trees and shrubs. Also, prune away water sprouts, suckers, and rubbing branches.
- ❑ Begin renovation of overgrown shrubs by pruning one third of the oldest stems.
- ❑ Sprinkle granular, slow-acting fertilizer on the soil around any trees or shrubs that weren't fertilized in the fall.
- ❑ Mulch bare soil over tree and shrub root zones with a 2- to 3-inch layer of organic material.
- ❑ Plant or transplant trees and shrubs.
- ❑ Inspect trees that are staked to be sure the supporting lines aren't too tight.

Summer

- ❑ Prune spring-blooming shrubs and trees—such as azalea, rhododendron, magnolia, and forsythia—as soon as blooming is over to control their size and shape and to stimulate new buds for next spring.
- ❑ If rainfall is sparse, mulch newly planted trees and shrubs. Water them deeply when the soil beneath the mulch feels dry. Unmulched plants will need watering every few days.
- ❑ Prune diseased or damaged branches from trees promptly. Make smooth cuts, leaving the branch collar to encourage healing. In case of disease, disinfect tools by dipping them in hot water mixed with household bleach.
- ❑ Watch for and pull off dangling bagworm cases on needled evergreens.

Warm Climates

Spring

- ❑ Prune stems and branches that were damaged during the winter.
- ❑ Fertilize ornamental trees and shrubs with granular, slow-acting fertilizer.
- ❑ Plant camellias and azaleas while they are in bloom. Delay fertilizing until late in summer.
- ❑ Inspect needled and broad-leaved evergreens for signs of insect damage.
- ❑ Renew organic mulch under trees and shrubs.

Summer

- ❑ Except in extremely hot inland areas, plant tropical and subtropical trees and shrubs such as hibiscus, gardenia, orchid tree, and palms.
- ❑ Water established trees and shrubs deeply but infrequently to encourage their roots to reach far into the ground.
- ❑ Mulch all plants heavily (but don't pile mulch against their stems) to prevent evaporation of moisture from the soil.
- ❑ Watch for—and pull off—dangling bagworm cases on needled evergreens.
- ❑ Promptly prune diseased or damaged branches from trees. In cases of fireblight on pear, cotoneaster, cherry, and others, cut branches at least 8 inches below the visible infection. After each cut, disinfect tools by dipping them in hot water mixed with household bleach to avoid spreading disease.

care checklist

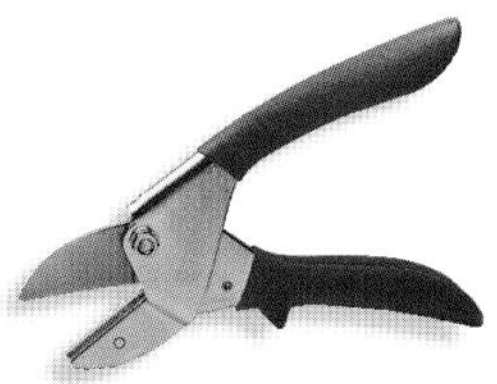

Fall

- ❑ Transplant shrubs or young trees to new locations on the property in early fall.
- ❑ If rainfall is sparse, deeply water trees and shrubs—especially evergreens—before the ground freezes.
- ❑ After the ground freezes, spread a winter mulch—up to 6 inches thick—of organic material such as chopped leaves.
- ❑ Fertilize young trees and shrubs that have been in the ground for at least a year. There's no need to fertilize old, established trees and shrubs, especially if they're mulched.
- ❑ Winterize roses by mounding mulch over the lower parts of their canes. In cold regions, shelter them with a burlap screen.
- ❑ Take down and clean out birdhouses. Make repairs over the winter.

- ❑ Water citrus and avocado trees well to prevent the fruit from splitting.
- ❑ Disbud camellias for larger blooms. Water camellias regularly to prevent buds from browning and dropping off. Mulch with pine needles.
- ❑ Stop feeding tropical trees and shrubs in September to give them time to harden off for winter dormancy.
- ❑ Plant or transplant nontropical trees and shrubs around the property. Delay fertilizing until spring.
- ❑ Prune injured branches from trees and shrubs.
- ❑ Take down and clean out birdhouses. Make repairs during the winter.
- ❑ Rake leaves or collect pine needles to use as mulch under trees and shrubs.

Winter

- ❑ Erect a screen of burlap, shade cloth, or similar material (never plastic) to protect broad-leaved evergreens exposed to drying winter winds.
- ❑ Brush heavy snow off evergreen boughs to keep them from breaking. Start with the lower branches, then work upward.
- ❑ Spray foliage of broad-leaved evergreens with antidessicant to help them retain moisture.
- ❑ Allow the ice on branches to melt on its own.
- ❑ Prune off ragged stubs of broken or injured branches with a smooth cut just in front of the branch collar.
- ❑ Prune large shade trees while they're dormant and the branch architecture is visible.
- ❑ Cut branches of early-flowering trees and shrubs (forsythia, flowering quince, crabapple, dogwood, star magnolia) and bring indoors to force bloom ahead of schedule.

- ❑ Prune and spray fruit trees, other deciduous trees prone to problems, and hybrid tea roses with dormant oil prior to leaf bud break. If leaves are out, use light (superior) oil.
- ❑ If frost threatens, shelter tender shrubs with polyspun garden fabric or a bedsheet.
- ❑ Plant bare-root trees and shrubs and transplant any others to new sites.
- ❑ Promptly prune any injured or broken branches from trees and shrubs.
- ❑ Buy and plant sasanqua camellias while they're in bloom.
- ❑ Cut branches from early-flowering shrubs and trees and bring them indoors for early bloom.

ornaments in the garden

ornaments in the garden

Ornaments are the finishing touches to a garden. They personalize the space, making it truly yours. In their main role as decorative objects, they can add elements of color, shape, texture, mood, and whimsy—all reflecting the interests and personality of you, the owner. Your garden is a wonderful venue to display art of all kinds. If you choose ornaments with design features that reflect bygone eras, they'll evoke nostalgia. You can use ornaments to carry out period themes such as a Victorian garden or a French estate garden. Urns, gates, fences, sculpture, fountains, old tools, and artifacts punctuate the overall effect of your garden—sometimes with a period, sometimes with

weather

In regions with cold winters, outdoor ornaments have to stand up to alternating freezing and thawing over several months. Unless they're made of wood, concrete, metal, or other frost-proof materials, they'll crack. When in doubt, move them indoors before the first frost. Bring in ceramic or terra-cotta plaques, figurines, and containers.

Ornaments with animal motifs are popular in gardens. If you're a fan of frogs, owls, snakes, rabbits, or other animals, you can have fun displaying your collection throughout the landscape.

Informal art pieces, such as this Southwestern-style metal sculpture, work well in open meadow gardens and lawn areas. They're especially effective when grouped and viewed from a distance.

Sculptures of wildlife enhance a natural-looking garden. These ducks blend with the rocks and add a suggestion of movement at the edge of the pond.

Objects that reflect light are welcome additions to gardens. Gazing balls and birdbaths brighten shaded spots and add perspective.

an exclamation point. Garden ornaments can be practical, too. They're useful in establishing focal points to guide the eye toward an intersection of paths or to a vista. As accents, they draw notice to a nook, a special plant, or steps. Decorative bridges, stepping-stones, and lights direct foot traffic. Distinctive furniture invites visitors to rest and reflect in the garden. Other ornaments, such as sundials and weather vanes, provide practical information for those inclined to notice. In some cases, the ornaments precede the garden or are added to define the design. Structural ornaments,

Birdhouses are decorative and functional, whether they are mounted or hung. Those with proper-sized holes and ventilation attract feathered friends to patrol your garden for insect pests.

Humor is important, too. Here, the colorful menagerie adds an element of surprise and delight because these animals are foreign to this environment.

Add fun and whimsy to a garden by tucking a bashful figure under foliage where mythical gnomes are said to hide.

ornaments in the garden

such as arbors, tuteurs, gazebos, and pergolas, support plants and help define spaces and boundaries. Matched objects, used repetitively, reinforce a sense of balance and symmetry in a formal design. Ornaments also contribute to the life and health of your garden. Can you imagine a garden without any sounds—especially bird song? Birdhouses, bird feeders, birdbaths, and fountains invite singing winged friends to visit the garden. Birds are among the unsung heroes of the garden, keeping many insect pests at bay—completely or at least within tolerable limits. The sight and sound of birds in the garden are relaxing and help to drain the

round and round

Orbs and spheres are enjoying renewed popularity as garden accessories. Gazing balls, concrete or marble balls, crafted willow-branch spheres, round paper lanterns, and colorful plastic bubbles have many uses in the landscape. Hang them from trees, float them on water, or wrap them in lights to evoke the music of the planets.

For the best effect, integrate ornaments and plants. Daisies floating in this birdbath seem to emphasize the interdependence of the flowers, the moisture, and the creatures who visit both.

A pedestal provides vertical interest. Topped with a round object—armillary sphere, gazing ball, or sundial—it suggests a flower on a stem. Its inanimate features contrast with the living plants nearby.

Achieve a special effect by using familiar ornaments in new ways. This gazing ball nestled among the plants at ground level surprises passersby when they notice its reflections in the sun.

Collectors enjoy displaying their treasures in the garden. Some collectibles, such as these watering cans, are already at home. Anything that can endure weather is a potential garden ornament.

The presence of cherubs, fairies, and mythical figures endows a garden with a spiritual dimension.

Placement of ornaments enhances their effect. Here a swan glides on a lake of grape hyacinths.

Natural materials such as wood, stone, and clay harmonize well with any natural setting.

Ornaments borrowed from England, such as this staddle stone, pay homage to their source.

ornaments in the garden

stress of the day away. Siting plays an important role in attracting birds. Place a birdhouse near the outside of a tree so the bird can fly straight to it without having to duck other branches. Hang a birdfeeder where there are trees or shrubs nearby so birds can sit and wait their turn at the feeder. Avoid hanging it where cats have easy access. Birdhouses and bird feeders add beauty to the garden while attracting wildlife that helps control insect pests.

Every garden has a special character and feeling; the ornaments heighten the character of the garden. Use ornaments that have pleasing color, good proportion, and unique design. Or, put something outrageous in the garden—bowling balls in the midst of a groundcover such as bishop's weed for

weather

In regions with cold winters, outdoor ornaments have to stand up to alternating freezing and thawing over several months. Unless they're made of wood, concrete, metal, or other frost-proof materials, they'll crack. When in doubt, move them indoors before the first frost. For sure, bring in ceramic or terra-cotta plaques, figurines, and containers.

Recycle an old chair as a display area for a plant or two. Either set a potted plant with trailing foliage on the chair or remove the seat and replace it with a sphagnum moss basket and fill with flowers.

Incorporate animal sculptures as foils for plantings in the garden. Here, a lamb sits in front of a stand of lavender. The lavender softens any harsh lines of the lamb and gives a sense of scale to the sculpture.

Add globes—whether Victorian gazing balls, blown glass balls, bowling balls, or even a painted basketball—to contrast or coordinate with the plants.

Attract butterflies with a slice of papaya or banana. They'll also come to very shallow water—or a birdbath with a rock on which they can perch.

contrast. And there are always the ubiquitous pink flamingos. If you want to use them, put a new twist on these plastic birds and place them in the shallows of a pond. There are no rules for garden art, except possibly to avoid overdoing it. Even that's all right if the spirit moves you. Some garden designers say that it's not what you put in your garden; it's the intent with which you use yard art that counts. For example, one or two pink flamingos may be considered tacky, but a whole flock of them—or even flamingos that light at night—is gaudy and makes a strong statement.

Make sure planters have drainage holes. If they don't, put a layer of gravel at the bottom of the planter and place a potted plant in it. After a rain, check the planter and empty out any excess water.

Grace a meadow planting with a rustic table and chair. The scale is right for the space—perfect for a child to hold a tea party with garden fairies.

Spruce up the entry to a vegetable garden by painting the the top of the post a vivid color. A garden hat, basket, or bunch of garlic—seemingly thrown on the fence—gives the impression that the gardener is nearby.

maintenance

using fertilizers

Fertilizer, rather than plant food, is the true source of soil nourishment. It's designed to supplement the nutrients that occur naturally in soil, enabling it to produce healthy and productive plants. The key to choosing the right fertilizer is understanding the nature of the soil on your property. The less fertile it is, the more fertilizer is necessary. Even if your soil is well aerated and contains some organic matter, it's safe to assume you'll need to add fertilizer. That's because residential landscapes are not only typically planted more intensively than are natural areas, they also contain plants and lawns, which are big feeders.

Over the years, many garden plants tend to use

weather

Temperature affects the rate at which organic fertilizers release nutrients into the soil. Because this release is a function of microbial activity in the soil, these nutrients are more available to plants in hot weather, when soil microbes are most numerous and active. Coincidently this also is the time when plants are growing most actively and need a nutritional boost.

foliar feeding

1 Mix liquid or powdered water-soluble fertilizer with tepid water at half the strength listed on the product label. Stir thoroughly. Spray plant foliage when the temperature is below 80 degrees Fahrenheit.

2 Use a watering can—or hand or pump sprayer—to moisten leaves thoroughly. Cover all leaf surfaces as much as possible. The fertilizer won't harm blossoms or fruits.

Hose-end sprayers are the most efficient way to foliar-feed large gardens and lawns. Measure the fertilizer into the jar, then attach it to the hose.

N-P-K: what it means

- Plants require three major nutrients: nitrogen (N), phosphorus (P), and potassium (K).
- **Nitrogen** fuels leaf and stem growth. It's the most quickly depleted nutrient.
- **Phosphorus** stimulates root growth and seed formation. It's in greater proportion in fertilizers sold for use in fall, a time of major root growth.
- **Potassium** promotes flowering, fruiting, and disease resistance.
- The proportions of NPK are indicated on fertilizer packages by three numbers, such as 5-10-5. Manufacturers alter the ratios for specific categories of plants, such as roses, vegetables, evergreens, and lawns.

up soil nutrients faster than natural processes can replace them. Fertilizer compensates for the loss. If your soil is more deficient in some nutrients than others, special fertilizer products redress the balance. In cases where soil is compacted and low in nutrients, a complete slow-acting fertilizer will sustain it until you can aerate it and add organic material. Fertilizer is food for the soil, not the plant. It adds fresh supplies of nitrogen, phosphorus, and potassium to soil where these naturally occurring nutrients have been depleted. In areas where plants have been growing for a long time or are planted

using granular, slow-acting fertilizer

1 Use granular, slow-acting fertilizer in spring to provide uniform, consistent nutrition over most of the season. Scratch the soil around existing plants, being careful not to harm shallow plant roots.

2 Sprinkle the granular fertilizer on the roughened soil in the amounts suggested on the package label. Water it in or allow the rain to soak the area thoroughly. Then cover with mulch.

3 Dig the granular fertilizer into the top 10 inches of the soil of a new bed. Add it to the potting mix for container plants before planting.

organic fertilizer

- Nutrients in granular, slow-acting fertilizers may be derived from natural sources or synthesized in a laboratory. Both provide exactly the same nutrition, but it's released to plants from the soil by different mechanisms. The nutrients in synthetics are coated to slow down the rate at which they're released when in contact with soil moisture. Those in natural or organic products are released by the activity of microorganisms that live in the soil and convert nutrients into a form that plant roots can absorb.
- Organic fertilizers are formulated from a wide variety of natural materials—animal manures, fish meal, rock phosphate, seaweed, wood ashes, seed hulls—that supply nitrogen, phosphorus, and potassium.

using fertilizers

repeatedly, such as lawns, flower beds, and vegetable plots, the plants use up the primary nutrients over time. Plants that are expected to produce flowers or fruits continuously over an entire season use up soil nutrients faster than even the most fertile soil can provide. Fertilizer fills the deficiencies, but it's not a substitute for healthy soil. Thin, compacted soil that has virtually no organic matter needs a lot of help from fertilizer if it's to do anything more than hold plants up.

Fortunately, you can reduce the amount of fertilizer you'll need in future years by amending the soil by adding organic matter every year. The resulting rich, fertile soil needs less help from fertilizer. Look for fertilizers that are slow-acting and granular. For general use, choose those labeled

pH and plant nutrition

Depending on the pH of the soil, plants may not be able to take up dissolved nutrients through their roots. If you find that your plants are not thriving, despite applications of fertilizer, check the soil pH and adjust as necessary.

1 When preparing a new garden bed, cultivate the soil first. Sprinkle granular, slow-acting fertilizer on the soil, following label instructions, then rake it in.

"balanced" or "all-purpose." You can buy specialty products for certain groups of plants, such as lawns, roses, acid-loving trees and shrubs, bulbs, and vegetables. Their formulations are adjusted to the needs of these plant groups. Although plants take up nutrients mostly from the soil, they can also absorb them in liquid form directly through their leaves. Water-soluble fertilizers deliver nutrients rapidly for the short term, but they must be used repeatedly throughout the season. Take care not to foliar feed if the temperature is over 80 degrees Fahrenheit, or you risk burning the leaves.

2 The action of a rototiller incorporates granular fertilizer into the soil down 4 to 6 inches. Follow label instructions for the amount of fertilizer to use.

3 Spread fertilizer on beds in early spring to supply plants with uniform and consistent nutrition for up to 16 weeks—a good main meal.

4 Follow the application of granular, slow-acting fertilizer with periodic snacks of water-soluble fertilizer. Spray it directly on foliage (foliar feeding) with a hose-end sprayer or spray bottle, to deliver a quick boost to plants about to flower or fruit. Follow label directions for dilution ratios to avoid harmful overfeeding.

fertilize with caution

Keep this advice in mind whenever you are using fertilizers.

- *Avoid overuse of fertilizers.*
- *Water plants and lawns well before using water-soluble products.*
- *Delay fertilizing newly planted trees and shrubs for a year.*
- *Do not fertilize plants stressed by drought, disease, or pests.*
- *Do not fertilize and lime the lawn simultaneously.*

using fertilizers

Container-grown plants require special fertilizers, because planting mixes intended for container use are typically soil-less—lighter, disease-free, and devoid of nutrients. Unless the manufacturer chose to add slow-acting fertilizer—an action that, fortunately, is becoming more common—you must provide all the nutrition to your container plants, whether they are indoor or outdoor, ornamental or food plants. Fertilizers are sometimes categorized as organic or synthetic. Both provide the same nutrition, but they vary in their sources of nutrients and the way the nutrients are released into the soil. The nutrients in synthetic

Type of fertilizer
Each fertilizer label prominently indicates the type of fertilizer. It may use the terms, "lawn," "houseplant," "nursery" (for trees and shrubs), or similar language.

Water-soluble fertilizer
Water-soluble fertilizer is delivered with moisture. Its nitrogen acts very quickly but only for a short time. You need to apply it repeatedly to provide uniform, continuous nutrition.

How much to use
Different plants need different amounts of nutrients. Carefully follow label instructions for diluting fast-acting, water-soluble products to avoid harming the plant and the soil.

ALL-PURPOSE WATER-SOLUBLE FERTILIZER

15-30-15

GUARANTEED ANALYSIS

Total Nitrogen (N) 15%
  6.8% Ammoniacal Nitrogen
  8.2% Urea Nitrogen
Available Phosphoric Acid (P_2O_5) 30%
Soluble Potash (K_20) 15%
Boron (B) 0.02%
Copper (Cu) 0.07%
Iron (Fe) 0.15%
  0.15% Chelated Iron
Manganese (Mn) 0.05%
  0.05% Chelated Manganese
Molybdenum (Mo) 0.0005%
Zinc 0.06%

Nitrogen from Ammonium Phosphates and Urea; Phosphoric Acid from Ammonium Phosphates; Potash from Muriate of Potash; Boron from Boric Acid; Copper from Copper Sulfate; Chelated Iron from Iron EDTA; Manganese from Manganese EDTA; Molybdenum from Sodium Molybdate; Zinc from Zinc Sulfate.
Chlorine (Max Avail.): 12.5%

SUGGESTED FEEDING INSTRUCTIONS

TYPE OF PLANT	AMOUNT OF PLANT FOOD SOLUTION	HOW OFTEN
LAWNS	1 gallon/25 square feet	Every 4 weeks
DECIDUOUS TREES (Ornamental and fruit that drop leaves in fall)	1 gallon/10 square feet soak soil	3 times a year
EVERGREENS Broadleaf and needle-leaved types	1 gallon/10 square feet	Every 2 weeks
ROSES Large bushes – (greater than 2 ft. diameter)	1 gallon/bush	Every 2 weeks
Medium to small bushes (less than 2 ft. diameter)	½ to 1 gallon/bush	Every 2 weeks
DECIDUOUS SHRUBS (Ornamental and fruit that drop leaves in winter)	1 gallon/10 square feet	Every 2 weeks
ALL FLOWERING PLANTS	1 gallon/10 square feet (annuals, perennials)	Every 7-14 days
ALL VEGETABLES	1 gallon/10 square feet	Every 7-14 days
TOMATOES	1 gallon/plant	Every 7-14 days
BERRIES and other small fruits	1 gallon/10 square feet	Every 2-4 weeks

DON'T WASTE PLANT FOOD.
Small, newly planted plants need just enough plant food to wet their root areas.

NPK Ratio
These numbers indicate the relative proportion of nitrogen, phosphorus, and potassium—the major nutrients in the product. Lawn fertilizer is always heavy in nitrogen.

Guaranteed analysis
The "guaranteed analysis" box indicates the kinds and percentages of nutrients in the formulation. A large proportion of WIN, or water-insoluble nitrogen, means it's slow-acting.

Frequency of feeding
Plant roots and leaves quickly take up the nitrogen in water-soluble fertilizers. It rapidly greens up their foliage. However, because it's also used up quickly, it requires repeat doses.

fertilizers are manufactured from chemicals. In slow-acting products, they are coated to prevent them from immediately dissolving in water. They break down gradually in moist soil so they are available over time to the plants. The nutrients in organic products are derived from natural plant and animal sources, such as manures, wood, paper, fish and bone meal, and seaweed. The activity of microbes in the soil releases the nutrients and makes them available to the plants.

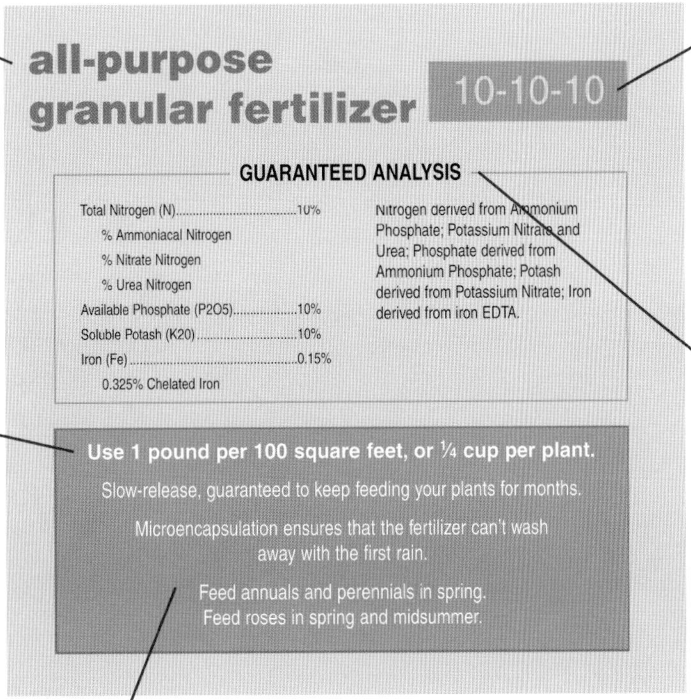

All-purpose fertilizer
All-purpose fertilizers are appropriate for many kinds of plants. They have a wide variety of nutrients, including the major ones, plus micronutrients and trace minerals.

Coverage
Although granular fertilizer is packaged by weight, that is not an indication of how much you need. Look for a phrase on the label indicating how many square feet the bag's contents cover.

all-purpose granular fertilizer 10-10-10

GUARANTEED ANALYSIS

Total Nitrogen (N).....10%
% Ammoniacal Nitrogen
% Nitrate Nitrogen
% Urea Nitrogen
Available Phosphate (P2O5).....10%
Soluble Potash (K20).....10%
Iron (Fe).....0.15%
0.325% Chelated Iron

Nitrogen derived from Ammonium Phosphate; Potassium Nitrate and Urea; Phosphate derived from Ammonium Phosphate; Potash derived from Potassium Nitrate; Iron derived from iron EDTA.

Use 1 pound per 100 square feet, or ¼ cup per plant.

Slow-release, guaranteed to keep feeding your plants for months.

Microencapsulation ensures that the fertilizer can't wash away with the first rain.

Feed annuals and perennials in spring.
Feed roses in spring and midsummer.

Don't overfeed
Over-fertilizing a plant stresses it. Too much nitrogen encourages overproduction of tender foliage that tempts pest insects. The result: stalled fruit or flower production.

Reading the numbers
In balanced, all-purpose fertilizers, the numbers that indicate the ratio of the basic nutrients—nitrogen, phosphorus, and potassium (NPK)—are typically much closer together numerically.

Guaranteed analysis
The "guaranteed analysis" box indicates the kinds and percentages of nutrients in the formulation. A large proportion of WIN, or water-insoluble nitrogen, means it's slow-acting.

controlling weeds

Weed seeds lurk in almost all soil. Most weeds don't cause a problem because they never get the light they need to germinate. However, when you cultivate ground for planting, weed seeds inevitably surface and sprout beside the new plants. From the outset, weeds compromise the health and welfare of ornamental and food crops by crowding plants and competing for nutrients and moisture. They often harbor disease pathogens as well as insects and their eggs. The best way to prevent weeds is to cover the soil with mulch to deny the seeds of annual weeds and the emerging perennial weeds the light they need to grow.

To be effective in thwarting weeds, a material used

weeding tips

- *Remove weeds as soon as they appear, while their roots are undeveloped.*
- *Use a regular hoe or scuffle hoe to scrape the surface of the soil to dislodge the tender sprouts—roots and all.*
- *Take care not to disturb the roots of nearby shrubs and plants.*
- *Rake up the weed seedlings or leave them lying on top of the soil to dry out in the sun.*
- *Never put any aggressive weeds on the compost pile.*

mulches

Straw is an ideal mulch for vegetable gardens, where appearance is not critically important. It easily allows moisture through, cushions ripened vegetables that drop, and doesn't decompose for many months.

Small stones allow moisture and air through to the soil. They also hold heat from the sun to moderate nighttime soil temperatures. However, they don't improve the soil.

Cocoa hulls make a handsome, fine-textured cover. They allow air and moisture through to the plant's roots. And they smell like chocolate!

Pot shards block sun from weeds and retain moisture. Their color attractively sets off certain ornamentals. But shards don't feed the soil.

as mulch must block light, yet allow air and moisture into the soil to benefit the roots of nearby garden plants. There are all sorts of mulches, such as landscape fabric, decorative gravel, and colored plastic. But the best mulches are organic—plant material that eventually decomposes. Organic mulches are superior because they improve the soil as they discourage weeds. Over time, they break down into a spongy humus teeming with living organisms, which enrich and condition the soil. Plants mulched with straw, chopped leaves, grass clippings, or other organic matter benefit from this bonus.

Shredded bark gives a neat, finished look to soil around landscape plantings. It holds up well for months before gradually decomposing to enrich the soil. Replace it each spring.

Compost offers the ultimate in soil enrichment and blocks light from weed seeds in the soil. However, seeds that blow in from elsewhere readily take root in this mulch.

Shredded leaves make an excellent mulch and are a good way to recycle leaves from your yard. They effectively block weeds and enrich the soil.

Pine needles have a finished look and lovely color. They control weeds effectively, break down slowly, and are ideal for plants that like acidic soil.

handpicking weeds

Handpick larger weeds (including those you missed on other weed patrols) that are growing in or around ornamental or food plants. Wait until the soil is moist. Grasp the weed stem at the soil level between your thumb and forefinger. Pull with a steady, gentle pressure to coax the entire root out of the ground. Mulch the area immediately to prevent the emergence of more weeds.

identifying garden pests

A typical landscape teems with insects, fungi, bacteria, and other organisms, most of which are benign or beneficial if the environment is healthy. Only a small number of insects and organisms are harmful. The trick is to know good from bad. Most of the time, populations of harmful insects and pathogens are kept in balance with the good ones. However, sometimes this balance is tipped because of weather, pollution, or the death of beneficials from overuse of pesticides. The usual result: a population explosion of undesirables. Infestations might show up as blemished or chewed leaves, clusters of bugs on buds or tender stem tips, or rotted roots. Some diseases, such as

pesticide alert

Broad-spectrum chemical pesticides often cause more

problems than they solve, as seen on this damaged plant. Because the pesticides kill indiscriminately, they destroy beneficial insects, too. Then when pest insect populations rebound, there are no predators in the garden for several weeks to control them.

fungal diseases

Blackspot is a fungal disease commonly found on the foliage of hybrid tea roses. Spores splashing up from the soil during a heavy rain create moist, infected dark spots that are easily visible.

Powdery mildew, a gray coating of fungus on leaf surfaces, appears when plants are crowded and lack good air circulation. Humid summer weather encourages mildew.

Holes can indicate a number of different problems. Before using chemicals indiscriminately, identify the pest that has caused the holes.

Botrytis is a fungus that creates water-soaked spots on food crops and ornamental plants. The spots, once enlarged, become covered with grayish mold.

bacterial and viral infections, kill plants quickly; the problem and outcome are never in doubt. But fungal diseases, such as mildew and blackspot, rarely kill a mature plant. Sometimes ants signal trouble by congregating around the sweet liquid produced by pest insects feeding on infested plants. Yet you shouldn't assume that because you see ants congregating around a plant that there are problems. For example, ants are always found on peonies just before the flowers open. In that case the ants are actually eating a substance off the bud that helps the flower open. Good bug or bad?

beware of bugs

Rose caterpillars, the larvae of a number of moths and butterflies, chew holes in or skeletonize rose leaves and flowers. Leaf-roller types curl the leaf edges around them.

Japanese beetles (green and copper wings) chew holes in plant foliage. Their soil-dwelling larvae—plump, curled, cream-colored worms with brown heads—eat grass roots.

Colorado potato beetle larvae are humped blackish worms that chew foliage. Adults (yellow with black stripes and orange heads) lay bright yellow eggs on leaf undersides.

Aphids are soft-bodied, pear-shaped, and tiny with long antennae. Colors may be green, black, brown, or pinkish. They cluster on new plant growth and suck juices from the cells.

Snails and slugs may be brown, black, yellow, or gray. They lurk in dark, moist places during the day and sustain themselves by chewing on plant fruit and foliage at night.

Leaf miner adults are minute black flies. Their yellowish larvae tunnel between leaf surfaces, marring them with pale tracings. These insects sometimes carry disease.

controlling garden pests

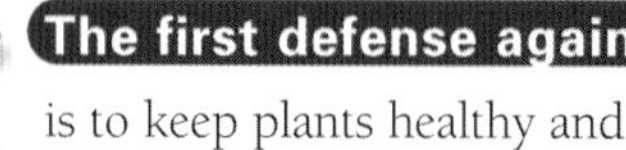

The first defense against insect-related problems is to keep plants healthy and happy. A stress-free plant has its own effective defenses against attack by insects, caterpillars, and beetles. Sometimes, though, plants are unable to fight back. The best way to limit damage and preserve plant health is to catch the infestation early. Several times a week, walk through the garden and routinely inspect your plants. Check young ones and tender new growth on others—both likely victims for insects that suck plant juices and chew on leaves. Try to catch and treat plant pest problems early to prevent the diseases that often strike plants weakened by insects. Some insects even carry disease that they

insecticide alert

Use all insecticides—even those labeled "organic" or "natural"—with respect. Follow the instructions on their labels for use, storage, and disposal. Always protect skin and eyes; when using powdered products, wear a pollen mask.

fungicide recipe

An effective spray for blackspot and mildew is a mixture of 1 teaspoon of baking soda, 2 drops of vegetable oil, and 2 drops of dishwashing liquid in 1 gallon of water. Spray the top and bottom of the leaves at the first sign of a problem. Don't spray if the temperature is going to be over 80°F.

Japanese beetle traps, with their pheromone and floral lures, attract beetles from a wide area. Hang bags at distant corners of the property.

Insecticidal soap kills soft-bodied insects on contact by penetrating and dissolving their tissues. Spray it on aphids, whiteflies, and mealybugs.

Floating row covers temporarily protect plants from insects. The polyspun garden fabric allows light, air, and moisture to penetrate but bars insects. Remove it to allow pollination of food and flower crops.

Water spray is effective against aphids, mites, and mealybugs. It can disrupt their life cycle when directed at the spots where pests congregate—stems and both sides of the foliage.

introduce into the plant as they feed. Make sure that the insects are actually pests and not beneficials, such as parasitic wasps, ladybug larvae, and soldier beetles. When in doubt, leave them alone. Beneficial insects (which you can buy at garden centers or mail order) can often handle the problem. However, if infestation should threaten to overwhelm a plant or garden bed, you'll need to intervene. Start with the least toxic measures such as traps, handpicking, or a forceful spray of water. Then turn to light horticultural oil, neem, or insecticidal soap sprays. Remember that they kill the good bugs as well as the bad.

reducing plant stress

Plants that are happy seldom suffer from pest or disease attacks. Stress from environmental conditions, such as too much sun, too much or not enough water, and wind or storm damage, tends to weaken a plant's natural resistance. Competition from weeds, excess fertilization, and compacted soil also stress plants. Protect them from stress as much as possible. Mulch and water them during times of drought, and prune damaged stems or faded flowers.

Slug traps can be as simple as a slate or board laid on the ground. During the day, slugs seek shelter from the sun. Scrape them off daily.

Wire cages are effective against pest animals such as squirrels, birds, rabbits, woodchucks, and deer. More utilitarian than decorative, they're most often used in the vegetable garden.

good bugs

Spiders help control pest insect populations by preying on their eggs in the soil. A thick lawn cut at 2½ to 3 inches tall shelters and protects them.

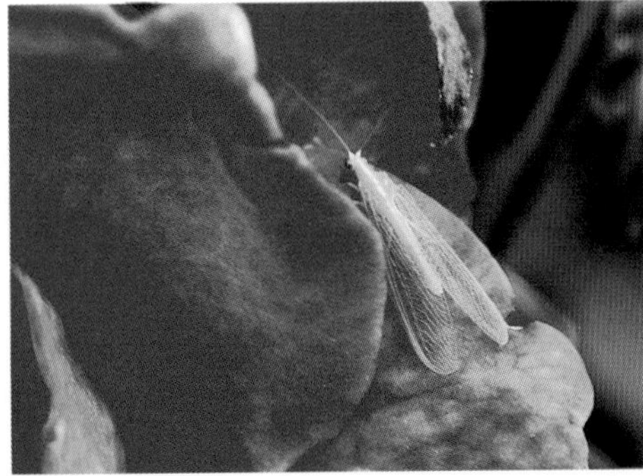

Lacewings feed on pollen and nectar produced by plants. Their larvae are predators of aphids, mites, scale, mealybugs, whiteflies, and other offenders.

extending the season

Extending the season means lengthening the growing time beyond the regular summer season. If you live in a region with real winters, you'll probably want to stretch the vegetable growing season by starting earlier in spring and ending later in fall. The result: fresh produce from the garden almost year-round. In spring the key is to have the soil warmed and dried out quickly. Most plants and seeds like the soil to be at least 55 degrees Fahrenheit; many need it to be even warmer. You can achieve that by covering the soil with black plastic, which absorbs heat from the sun, several weeks before planting. Protect the transplants by fashioning tunnels of clear plastic over them to admit the sun's rays. Be

weather

Light frost and hard frost are two different stories. Many plants can survive a brief, light frost overnight and thrive for weeks in the sun of Indian summer. Hard frost is a killer. It freezes the soil and blackens plants. In many regions, it signals the arrival of real winter.

For an inexpensive cold frame, set old windows on railroad ties surrounded with bales of straw to keep in the warmth. Prop the windows open for ventilation on sunny days and close them at night.

The curved double-glazed fiberglass top on this cold frame accommodates tall plants. The water-filled black drum at the end absorbs and stores the sun's heat to moderate overnight temperatures.

Commercially made cold frames have hinged tops so they can be opened to allow ventilation when the temperature gets above 40 degrees Fahrenheit.

The cover on the top of this cold frame is made of inexpensive plastic sheeting that's easily rolled up to open the area to fresh air during warm spells.

sure to cut ventilation slits in the plastic. Cold frames are useful in extending the traditional season at each end. Set them over planting beds to warm the soil and protect the growing plants inside. Automatic vent openers, available from mail-order suppliers, open the cold frame when it's too warm inside and close it during chilly or cloudy weather. Cold frames also make good transition nurseries for young seedlings awaiting transplanting. A stay of a few days or weeks in the cold frame gradually acclimates them to the outdoors. so they suffer less stress when they're finally planted. There are other

hardening off

Most vegetables are annuals and aren't constitutionally cold-hardy. However, some can adjust to cold if they're gradually acclimated to it, or hardened off. This process happens in two stages. First, the cold slows, then stops, the plant growth. Then the plants produce natural sugars in their foliage that depress the freezing point of the water in their cells. This protects them from bursting. Cool-season vegetables have this ability.

This 3- by 4-foot cold frame is a portable version that's easy to make out of clear plastic sheeting and redwood lumber. It's sized to fit comfortably over a raised bed.

extending the season

techniques for protecting plants when chilly weather threatens. Cover individual plants with some type of cloche (originally used in France) to trap and warm the air on sunny days. Homemade versions fashioned from plastic milk jugs, old-fashioned bell jars, or terra-cotta pots effectively insulate plants from brief nighttime frosts. Water-filled plastic tepees maintain even temperatures in the soil and around extended-season plants. Throw a light blanket over plants when frost threatens, or use polyspun garden fabric—a lightweight cover that's available in various thicknesses. It allows air, light, and moisture through, but not frost. Mulch effectively

weather

Frost is most likely when the sky is clear and the air is still and dry, with no breeze and low humidity. If the temperature is low already, expect it to drop quickly at sunset. Unsheltered plants may be frosted. Some cool-weather vegetables taste even better after a touch of frost. Kale, collards, arugula, and Brussels sprouts become milder. Root crops such as carrots, parsnips, turnips, leeks, and beets become sweeter after frost.

Plastic milk jugs with their tops cut off fit easily over young plants to protect them from overnight frosts. Weigh them down with stones or bricks in windy weather. Remove the jugs during the day.

Wall O Water™ tepees protect individual plants with water. The water-filled chambers in the plastic support it around the plant. The water collects warmth from the sun and holds it through the night.

Tepee-style cloches accommodate plants as they grow taller. The tops of the tepees are vented to prevent overheating. As the plants increase in height, they can poke out the top.

Recycled panes of glass work as shelters for plants. When fastened together with aluminum clips, they form a tent to trap heat from the sun. The space at the top of the glass provides ventilation.

insulates the soil and protects plant roots. Spread a 2- to 3-inch layer of organic material such as chopped leaves, straw, aged wood chips, or pine needles on the bare soil. Try to maintain soil warmth as long as possible to extend the gardening season into fall. Plastic covers (for beds and rows) or a cold frame allows you to grow a second crop of cool-weather vegetables such as chard, broccoli, and spinach. There's nothing like fresh vegetables from the garden for Thanksgiving dinner.

Loosely thrown polyspun garden fabric shelters beds of early-spring or late-fall crops if a light frost threatens. Temporarily weight the edges with bricks or stones. Remove the cover the next morning.

Row tunnels made of plastic protect entire rows of warm-season vegetables from late-spring frost. The black plastic floor warms the soil, and the clear plastic top collects and holds warm air.

building a plastic tunnel

To use a plastic tunnel, the plants you want to protect must be in raised growing beds that are boxed in. Collect your building materials: 1-inch flexible PVC pipe, string, and a roll of plastic. Bend the PVC pipe into hoops or ribs and insert them into the soil every 3 to 4 feet. Link them with a length of string tied at their tops and along both sides to stabilize them. When weather conditions require action, cover the unit with plastic or polyspun garden fabric (also known as garden fleece or floating row cover) and anchor it firmly to the ground. Tunnels covered with clear polyethylene plastic help extend the growing season at each end. In spring they protect newly planted tomatoes and other warm-season crops while they become acclimated to the outdoors. If frost is still possible, stretch a sheet of the plastic or polyspun garden fabric over the hoops. Use stakes, soil, or a row of bricks or rocks to anchor it at the sides and ends. Be sure to cut ventilation holes in the tunnel. When frost arrives for sure in fall, keep the cover on crops that are still producing.

putting the garden to bed

Putting the garden to bed for the winter is mostly a matter of cleaning up and covering up. As fall progresses and temperatures drop, those plants that aren't killed outright by frost prepare for dormancy. Clear out the blackened stems and foliage of annual flowers and vegetables to prevent the possibility of their harboring disease pathogens and insect eggs over the winter. The cool weather is a good time to make a cold frame, dig and box in raised beds, and make general repairs. While it appears as if all activity in the garden has stopped, there's a lot going on under the soil until it freezes. Newly transplanted trees and shrubs, divisions of perennials, and hardy bulbs are all growing roots,

weather

Snow both protects and endangers plants. A good snow cover insulates the soil like a mulch. However, snow piled on evergreen branches weights them down, risking breakage. Knock snow from the bottom branches first, then work upward. This way snow from above will not add weight to the already burdened lower branches. If branches are bowed by ice, don't try to free them. Instead let the ice melt and release them gradually.

protecting plants

Cut back dry stems of perennials to soil level after frost to neaten the garden and remove pest eggs and disease spores that may linger. Leave stems with attractive seed heads for winter interest.

Compost dead plant debris to create an organic soil conditioner. Hot, active piles kill weed seeds and disease pathogens; passive, inactive piles do not. Throw questionable plant material in the trash.

Cut off diseased foliage from evergreen plants and shrubs and discard it in the trash. Rake up and discard the old, disease-bearing mulch, too.

To prevent rodents from nesting in the soil, wait until the ground freezes before adding a 6-inch layer of organic material as winter mulch.

drawing on soil nutrients and moisture around them. Earthworms and various microbes in the soil are still processing the organic material they're finding. Most likely, the organic mulch you spread to protect the soil during the summer months has substantially decomposed. It's important to spread new mulch now —a thicker winter layer—to protect plants and soil over the winter months. The idea is not so much to keep the soil warm as it is to keep the temperature even. Once the soil is frozen, mulch keeps it frozen. So if you have shade trees, convert the fallen leaves to mulch and use it throughout your property.

Mulch perennial and shrub beds with pine needles or chopped leaves. This protects both plant roots and the soil and moderates the effects of extreme temperature changes during winter freezes and thaws.

Mulch bulb beds with evergreen boughs to protect the soil from shifting and cracking during the winter. Otherwise plants, especially small, shallowly planted bulbs, can be heaved to the surface.

Protect the tender bark of young trees from gnawing critters by wrapping stems or trunks with wire or commercial tree-guard products.

Screen evergreens, particularly exposed broad-leaved types, from drying winter wind and sun by setting up burlap screens or shade cloth shelters.

winterizing roses

Roses are so beautiful that it's difficult to begrudge them the extra attention they require over the growing season. As cool fall weather brings on their dormant period, one final job remains for you: preparing them for winter. As a group, hybrid tea roses are the most vulnerable to winter cold and need the most preparation. The complexity of this job depends on how severe the winters typically are in your part of the country. It's important to stop fertilizing in late summer in most areas. Make the last feeding of the season two months before you expect the first frost. Also refrain from major pruning, and stop cutting blossoms. This avoids stimulating any more new, tender growth, which will be killed by the first frost. Remove all old mulch from under and around the roses; it might harbor insect eggs or disease spores from infected fallen leaves. Just before the first hard or killing frost of the season, spread fresh mulch of wood chips, shredded bark, or chopped leaves around the base of the plant, extending as far out as the branch tips. Wait until

YOU WILL NEED

- stakes
- burlap
- string
- organic mulch

getting tree roses ready for winter

1 Tree roses, or standards, are vulnerable to the cold, so you'll want to help them cope with winter. Begin by setting four stakes in the ground around and just beyond the mulched root zone.

2 Wrap a protective barrier of burlap around the stakes and tie it in place with string. Then fill in the middle with an insulating layer of shredded dry leaves.The rose is now shielded from harsh winds.

weather

Spring weather is fickle. Delay removing mulch until leaf buds swell. Keep polyspun garden fabric handy to cover exposed roses if frost threatens after you've removed the winter mulch.

cold-hardy hybrid tea roses

- **'Chicago Peace' –** pinkish double flowers turning apricot at their base
- **'Chrysler Imperial' –** deep red double flowers; spicy fragrance
- **'Double Delight' –** cream-tinged with red, becoming redder with maturity; extremely fragrant
- **'Garden Party' –** double-flowered with pink-tinged white petals
- **'Mister Lincoln' –** velvety, dark red double flowers; highly fragrant
- **'Pascali' –** white flowers; lightly fragrant
- **'Perfect Moment™' –** double flowers, red with yellow bases
- **'Tiffany' –** pink double flowers; sweetly scented
- **'Tropicana' –** brilliant orange flowers and fruity fragrance; also a climbing form
- **'White Delight' –** double flowers, ivory with pink centers

after the ground freezes to spread the mulch if rodents are a problem in the yard. Mice, especially, like to build their nests in mulch. Water the rose well, especially if it's been through a dry summer.

Once the ground freezes, it's time to add more mulch. If you live in an area with relatively mild winters, simply mound the mulch over the plant crown 6 to 12 inches up the canes. This insulates the soil to maintain an even temperature in spite of the normal alternating winter freezes and thaws. This thick mulch is especially important when there is no reliable snow cover to protect plants. If winter temperatures often drop well below zero, build the mound of mulch, then add more material after every freeze to make the mound higher. Eventually, the mulch should virtually cover the bush. Sometimes it's easier to enclose the shrub in a cylinder and fill it with mulch.

cold-hardy roses

To minimize winter rose care, choose varieties that are reputed to withstand cold temperatures. Landscape (shrub) roses, old garden types, and miniatures are quite hardy. Hybrid teas and grandifloras generally require the most care, although certain varieties are hardier than others. Look for roses grown on their own roots rather than grafted ones if hardiness is a concern.

protecting roses with mulch

Enclose shrubs in cylinders of cardboard, metal, or plastic or in commercially made foam rose cones for maximum protection. Fill them with shredded bark, paper, or leaves for added insulation.

Protect the graft (or bud union) and crown of roses by mulching with loose soil, wood chips, shredded bark, or shredded leaves. Mound the mulch to a foot high over the base of the plant.

The canes of climbing roses are vulnerable to winter wind and sun. They need special attention in regions where winter temperatures typically drop below zero. Either wrap the canes with burlap or detach them from their supporting trellis and lay them horizontally on the ground. Cover them with a mulch of leaves, wood chips, or soil.

winterizing garden tools

Quality tools deserve quality care. And tools that are in top condition make your work easier and time spent shorter. A sharp spade slices through a tough clump of tangled roots in practically one motion. Sharp pruner blades cut through branches cleanly, minimizing the possibility of disease and further damage. Sharp lawn mower blades cut grass cleanly, preventing excess moisture loss through frayed foliage tips. Every month or so, take a few minutes to smooth off nicks or gouges on tool edges before they become worse. Carefully file the bevel to maintain an edge. Clean the dirt from tools after each use. Use a wooden stick to wipe or scrape off shovels and rakes; the wood won't scratch

keeping tools clean

An effective way to clean dirt from the metal parts of shovels, spades, and digging forks is to shove them into a 5-gallon pail of sharp builder's sand saturated with used oil from your car, lawn mower, or other gasoline-powered equipment. Move the metal part of the tools in and out of the sand several times to scour and rustproof them for winter storage.

If you use a moistened whetstone to sharpen a shovel, be sure to maintain the same angle of bevel. To smooth out nicks, make repeated strokes the length of the whetstone along the entire shovel edge.

When you use a file to sharpen a shovel, hold the file at a 20- to 30-degree angle to the blade edge. With a smooth motion and medium pressure, stroke the length of the file across the cutting surface.

To sharpen loppers with a moistened whetstone, stroke across the upper of the two bypass blades, following the established angle.

If you use a file to sharpen loppers, make several gentle passes along the upper, sharpened, blade of the two bypass blades.

the metal, so rust is avoided. Remove dried clippings that cake under the mower. Put tools away after each use. At season's end, rub wooden handles with linseed oil and replace those that are split. Oil metal blades to prevent rust. Replace worn blades on pruners and mowers. Store everything in a dry place.

Sharpen a hoe with a file just as you do a shovel. Stroke the length of the file at medium pressure across the hoe edge. Try for a clean bevel rather than a knife-sharp edge.

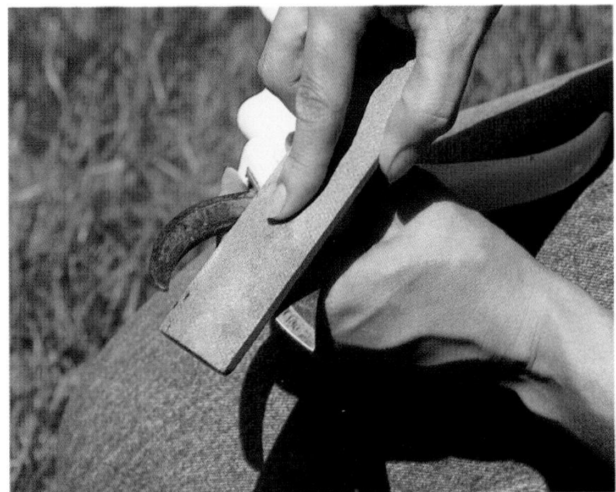

Sharpen shears with a moistened whetstone by stroking the cutting edges of the blades. Be sure to move across the bevel at the same angle.

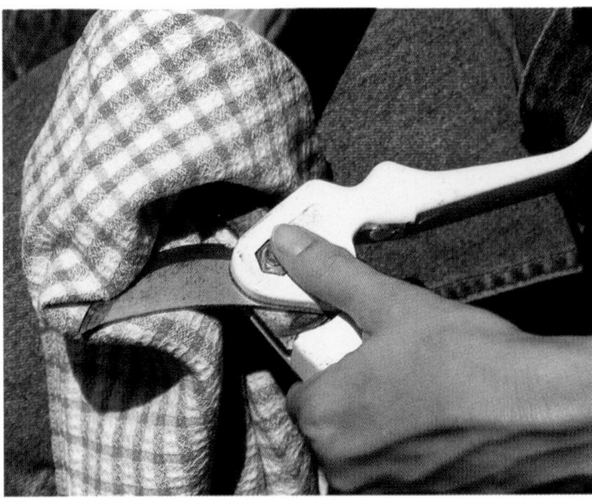

Regularly wipe cutting blades of pruners, loppers, and hedge shears with a cloth to maintain their edge as long as possible between sharpenings.

tools and resources

the basic tool kit

There is no denying that gardening is hard physical work. But it's *pleasurable* hard work, made all the easier by good quality tools. Just a few basic tools, well-designed for comfort and carefully crafted from the best materials, will serve in most situations. If you care for them properly, they should last a lifetime. When purchasing tools, always choose quality over quantity. Today's tools are ergonomically designed to spare backs, shoulders, and wrists. Space-age materials make them lighter, more balanced, and easier to grip and use without developing calluses. Look for tools with features such as replaceable parts, easy cleaning, rust-proof

garden spade

A spade is not the same tool as a shovel. A spade is short-handled and has a flat, squared-off blade. It is ideal for edging beds, digging planting holes, slicing under sod, and working soil amendments into the garden. In a pinch you can even use a spade to chop ice on walks. Its versatility makes it a staple in the tool shed.

garden fork

Dig into the soil with the four straight, sturdy steel tines of a garden fork. Also known as a spading fork, it's a good tool for turning and aerating the soil. Use it to break up chunks of soil and to work organic matter, fertilizer, and other amendments into the soil. A garden fork copes easily with occasional buried roots or rocks and comes in handy for dividing clumps of perennials.

shovel

A garden shovel typically has a dished (concave) blade that is rounded or mildly tapered at the tip. Most shovels are long-handled, although you can buy them with short handles, too. Because the blade is canted at an angle to the handle for greater leverage, a shovel is ideal for attacking piles of soil, sand, and other materials you need to load or move.

hoe

Cultivate the soil and remove young weeds in a garden bed with a hoe. The simplest hoe is basically a straight-edged, square blade attached at a right angle to a long wooden handle. It's useful for chopping clumps of soil and scraping the soil surface to cut off sprouting weeds. When tilted at an angle, the corner of the blade traces neat planting furrows in prepared soil. There are many different types of hoes. A swan hoe has a curved neck. A diamond hoe has a head that is diamond-shaped, perfect for pulling weeds from between plants.

metal parts, and a hole in handles so you can hang the tool on a peg. Try out tools in the store before you buy them. Check out their grips to make sure they will be comfortable after repeated use. Good pruners, for example, come in different sizes to fit your grip. You want ones with handles that don't open wider than your hand. For hoes, handle length is important; it should come up to nose height. Hold the hoe upright and use only your hands and forearms to move it forward and backward. This means no bending—and no backache!

steel rake
Also called a garden rake, this tool features 12 or 14 short steel tines mounted on a sturdy steel bridge at the end of a long handle. Use a steel rake to dress and smooth out prepared soil in a planting bed. Its tines simultaneously break up small clods of soil and corral stones and debris. Use a flathead style to level the soil for planting. Flip the rake over so its bridge scrapes along the surface of the soil.

trowel
The basic hand tool for digging, a trowel is indispensable for planting bulbs, seedlings, and other small plants in a garden bed. Trowels are available with sturdy handles and narrow or wide, cupped metal blades with tapered tips. Different sizes—widths and lengths—suit different planting jobs.

flexible rake
The business end of this type of rake, sometimes called a lawn or leaf rake, is a fan of flat, flexible tines. Typically bent at their tips, the tines are made of lengths of metal, bamboo, plastic, or even rubber in a variety of styles. The tines are attached to a long handle for easy control. Use a flexible rake to gather light debris that is spread out on beds, lawns, and walks, and to rake up leaves.

hand weeder
This tool is basically a miniature hoe, which most gardeners use for down-and-dirty weeding. The short handle at the end of a flat, straight-edged blade allows you to maneuver between plants in a bed. The blade may be square or triangular and mounted at various angles for flexibility. Position the blade on the soil and draw it toward you to cut weeds off at—or just below—the soil level. Or turn the blade upward, so its corner digs deeper to dislodge stones or pry out larger weeds.

the basic tool kit

Some essential gardening and yard care equipment aren't always thought of as tools. However, they are as useful and labor-saving as familiar tools such as shovels and pruners. Watering devices, gardening garb, and equipment to carry things are included in this group. So are storage facilities and maintenance tools from your household tool kit. They increase your efficiency and safety as you care for the plants in your yard and the power tools that help you with these tasks. Even what you wear while doing yard work is important. Protective clothing with long sleeves and long pants, as well as safety glasses and ear protectors, are essential. Remember to wear a hat and sunscreen to protect your skin from harmful rays of the sun. Pay particular

preventing hearing loss

Repeated and long-term exposure to noise causes progressive hearing loss. Even sound that is not terribly loud can gradually impair your hearing over many years. Wear ear protection when you use any power equipment for more than 10 minutes. Ear protectors designed for shooting ranges offer the best protection.

watering can

Because water is crucial to the well-being of plants, the watering can is an old standby. Originally made from galvanized metal—and now in a variety of materials from brass to plastic—it retains its classic form. A bucket-like reservoir that holds the water is flanked with a bowed handle on one side. On the opposite side, a long spout capped with a sprinkler head, or rose, protrudes. Choose a can that feels balanced when full and holds a generous amount of water without straining your arms as you carry it.

hose

A hose is a must for maintaining plants in any yard or garden larger than a few square feet. It will save you from carrying a watering can during hot weather. At every life stage, plants need water for good health, and a hose can bridge periods of scant rainfall. Buy the best hose your budget will allow. Choose a rubber or vinyl hose made of several layers of mesh and with sturdy connectors to ensure long life.

watering tools — hose attachments

A **nozzle**—which used to be made of brass and now comes in a variety of materials, sizes, and shapes—is essential to control the stream of water coming out of the hose. A **watering wand**—long tube extension with a sprinkler head at the tip—converts the hose to a long-distance watering can. Use it to water containers, hanging pots, and beds. The wand should have a shutoff at its connection to the hose to prevent wasting water. Another key tool is a **sprinkler**, which is attached to the hose and place on the ground. It oscillates or rotates to deliver water to beds and lawns. The best sprinklers have timers and adjustments to control the width and direction of the stream.

sprayers

Fertilizers, tonics, fungicides, insecticidal soaps, and many other products are water-soluble and most effective if sprayed on plant foliage. Although many are packaged ready-to-use in spray bottles, they are more economical if you buy them in concentrated form that you mix in water. Convenient sprayers attach to the hose and dilute automatically. You might want to have a one- or two-gallon pump sprayer for small jobs. Larger backpack units are useful for spraying fertilizer over broad areas such as lawns.

attention to sensitive skin areas such as the back of your neck and your ears. Be sure to protect your feet with sturdy shoes. They will prevent injury from equipment and will properly support your legs and back. Non-skid soles—used on athletic shoes and rubber gardening shoes or boots—reduce the danger of slipping on wet grass or ice. Wear heavy work boots when working with a chainsaw, log splitter, or similar equipment. Whenever you use a ladder, wear non-skid shoes or boots that are flexible enough to allow you to safely negotiate the steps.

safety glasses

Special glasses made from sturdy plastic are a must. Choose from various styles that feature wraparound lenses to protect your eyes from flying objects while mowing, sawing, chopping, or tilling. Some models are designed to fit over prescription eyeglasses. Others are tinted for work in the sun or can be attached to a hard hat for construction or arbor work. Be sure they fit snugly over your ears to prevent slipping.

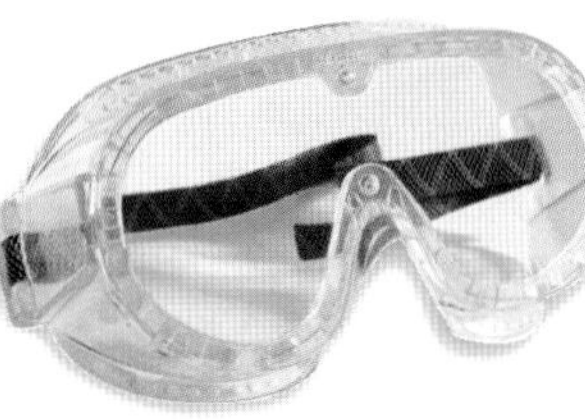

wheelbarrows, carts, wagons

Yards and gardens generate a lot of debris that you need to transport to the compost pile. They also benefit from the loads of organic matter and mulch you haul in and distribute. Garden carts and wheelbarrows do these jobs and many others. Use a stable, two-wheeled cart with high sides for large, bulky loads. It can handle up to 500 pounds on its pneumatic tires. The smaller, nimbler wheelbarrow —available in one- or two-wheel models—is easier to maneuver around small spaces.

gloves

Different types of gloves protect hands from different injuries. Have several pairs available for yard-care tasks. Choose leather or cloth gloves to avoid blisters from repetitive tasks such as sawing, pruning, and shoveling. Wide-cuffed or long gloves coated with nitrile or plastic protect wrists and forearms when you're working with thorny plants. Latex or rubber gloves protect against soil-borne fungi that cause dermatitis. Check the fit by making a fist, then feel for finger fit at the tips of the glove fingers.

kneelers and seats

While one of the many attractions of gardening is the opportunity to kneel down close to the soil, getting up effortlessly afterward can become a problem as age takes its toll on your knees and back. Kneelers of various kinds cushion the contact with the hard ground. Those with a metal frame and tall side bars also help you stand up. Low gardening seats—either on metal frames or on wheeled tool carts—also ease back and knee strain. Some knee pads strap on over pants to protect your knees and keep your pants clean.

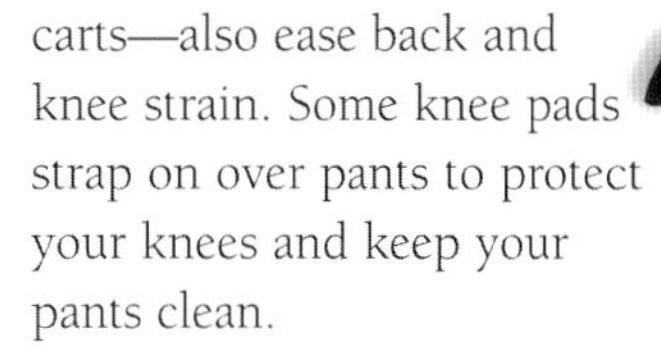

lawn-care tools

Lawns are high-maintenance landscape features. However, for those of us who grew up with front and back yards covered with grass, it's difficult to imagine not having at least some lawn. Nothing equals grass as a soft place for children to tumble and play and as a rich green backdrop to showcase landscape plantings. That beautiful surface of emerald green is greedy for water, fertilizer, and your time and energy. That means regular mowing, edging, repairing, aerating, and topdressing. Homeowners with small lawns—under 4,000 square feet—can do most of these maintenance jobs with a small assortment of hand tools. If you prefer the quiet and enjoy the exercise,

weather

For the healthiest grass and most uniform cut, mow the lawn when it is dry. When it is damp with early-morning dew or wet from rainfall, blades don't cut cleanly and clippings clump. Any existing fungal disease will be tracked onto healthy lawn areas.

power lawn mower

A gasoline- or electric-powered rotary lawn mower is appropriate for lawns over 4,000 square feet. If the lawn has a large expanse, self-propelled models are particularly helpful. Today, almost all power lawn mowers are designed as mulching mowers with a special blade and higher bell that suspends clippings long enough to be cut several times before they fall back into the grass as mulch. There's no need to collect them.

drop spreader

Use a drop spreader to precisely sow grass seed, lime, or granular fertilizer. The granules or seeds flow from a rectangular hopper in measured amounts in a row along its wheelbase. An adjustment on the handle alters the amount you dispense. With each pass across the lawn, this spreader evenly distributes the material in spreader-width rows. It's perfect for lawns with straight edges, but think about your pattern of passes so you don't leave any missed strips.

rotary spreader

Rotary spreaders broadcast seed or granular fertilizer in a wide, circular pattern. When you push the spreader, a spinner—under the hopper that holds the material—rotates, throwing out the seed or granules at a rate regulated by a lever on the handle. Because the spreader casts the material widely on both sides of it, there's no danger of missing areas that later show as streaks in the lawn. To ensure uniform coverage, make vertical and horizontal passes over the area.

manual (reel) mower

The old-fashioned lawn mower has been updated for modern times. It's now made of lightweight, space-age materials, and most models have pneumatic tires, easy blade-height settings, and handle-length adjustment. The horizontal blades on this type of mower have always given a superior cut. They are mounted on a reel that's geared within the wheel assembly, and they slice the grass against a lower, rigid bar. Spectacularly quiet and, of course, pollution-free, these manual mowers are especially useful for smaller lawns.

hand tools also will save money. A manual mower, broadcast seeder, edger, and aerating tool work just fine. Use a lawn rake to spread organic material for topdressing in the fall or spring, and use hand grass clippers to clean up weedy patches along walls and fences. Medium lawns—4,000 to 10,000 square feet—are usually too big for hand tools. A powered rotary mulching mower is faster, and a self-propelled version is easier. Fall mowings with this type of mower also provide your lawn with an organic topdressing—chopped leaves—if you have deciduous trees on your property.

hand edger

A hand edger consists of a sharp, straight-edged steel blade mounted at the end of a long wooden or Fiberglass handle. This English-style version has a rounded semicircular blade with a broad top edge that forms a tread for your foot. Place the tool along the edge of the turf where it meets pavement, then push the blade downward to cut a neat border.

dethatching rake

The steel tines on this special rake penetrate the thatch layer on a lawn. They are mounted on a sturdy bridge that's attached to a long wooden handle. When you pull the tines through the grass with a raking motion, they snag the matted strands of dead grass plants that make up the thatch layer. They bypass the healthy grass and loosen and pull up only dead material. On some models, you can adjust the angle of the row of tines.

electric-powered edger

For edging long stretches of lawn along walks and driveways, a powered edger is the most efficient. If you have a large property or a lot of lawn that you want to keep perfectly edged, this tool is for you. Electric-powered edgers are available in corded and battery-powered models. Before choosing one, consider the length the electric cord would have to be to reach the nearest electrical outlet from the farthest area you will be edging. When using a powered edger, be aware of where any shallowly buried electric or water lines might lie—a consideration if you have an in-ground irrigation system for the lawn. You don't want to accidentally cut any lines.

hand core-aerator

Hand core-aerators consist of two or more hollow tines connected by a narrow, steel bridge that serves as a foot plate. A waist-high, steel handle, topped by hand grips, attaches to the bridge. When you press your foot against the steel bridge, the 6-inch-long tines penetrate moist turf and fill up with a core of soil. Then when you withdraw them, each one leaves a narrow hole in the turf that admits air and moisture to the root area. Each time you press the tines into the turf, a soil plug pops out the top and lands on the lawn where it will decompose in the rain.

lawn-care tools

On medium-size lawns, rent a power core-aerating machine to aerate properly. Lawns of this scale are likely to have many more feet of edges to manicure, so a powered edger is a good idea, too. Use power string-trimmers to clean up weeds around fence posts and walls. Large lawns—over 10,000 square feet—require even more sophisticated equipment. A large powered rotary mulching mower can do the job, but a riding mower might be more appropriate. The powered core-aerator, edger, and weed trimmer are essential. Whatever the lawn size and whichever the tools, choose them carefully, based on

lawn mower troubleshooting checklist

If the lawn mower doesn't start, ask yourself:

- ❑ *Is there gas in the tank?*
- ❑ *Is the starter switch on or is the baffle engaged?*
- ❑ *Is the engine primed?*
- ❑ *Is the spark plug old or disconnected?*
- ❑ *Is anything obstructing the blade?*
- ❑ *Is last season's gas still in it?*
- ❑ *If it has an electric motor, is the cord plugged in?*

1 To sharpen the mower blade, disconnect the spark plug or unplug the mower. Then turn the mower over and remove the nut that attaches the blade to the motor.

2 Stabilize the blade in a vise and use a medium file to smooth out imperfections along the blade edge (at the ends of mulching blades). Don't try to hone a sharp edge.

3 After you smooth the cutting edge on both halves of the blade, check to see if the blade is balanced. If not, remove more metal from one of the halves until the blade does balance.

bagging attachments

In most cases, it's best to allow your grass clippings to fall onto the lawn rather than collect in a mower bag attachment. Mulching blades on modern power rotary mowers chop clippings into tiny pieces that fall among the grass blades and give the lawn a little extra moisture and nitrogen. The clippings don't cause thatch.

There are some instances, however, when it's really handy to have a bag attachment for your mower. For example, before you overseed a lawn, mow closely and catch the clippings so you don't have to rake them up to expose the bare soil. Moreover, if annual weeds, such as crabgrass, have formed seeds, a bag attachment will catch the seedheads along with the clippings and prevent self-seeding; throw the contents into the trash.

craftsmanship, design, and materials. Wherever possible, try them out to be sure they are comfortable to use and appropriate for your situation. Durability is an important factor, too, as are ease of maintenance, convenience, and safety features. Look for mowers that instantly shut off the mower blade when you release the handle baffle, and spreaders that will hang on a wall. The ultimate test of a tool's performance is its owner. Use all tools correctly —for your safety and for the health of your yard.

choosing the right mower

mower type	advantages	disadvantages
Push (reel) mower	▪ Quiet, lightweight, maneuverable. ▪ Easy to store. ▪ Has superior cutting blades.	▪ Hard to sharpen. ▪ Operator must be in good physical condition. ▪ Requires overlapping rows to ensure uniform cut.
Gasoline-powered, mulching rotary mower	▪ Cuts clippings small, requiring no raking or bagging. ▪ Easy to adjust cutting height. Mulches fallen leaves into lawn as topdressing. ▪ Most offer self-propel, bag-attachment, and side- or back-discharge options. ▪ Variety of horsepower ratings available.	▪ Noisy and pollutes atmosphere. Needs frequent maintenance. Sometimes hard to start. ▪ Needs periodic refueling, oil change, new spark plug.
Corded, electric-powered rotary mower	▪ Non-polluting. ▪ Cuts clippings small, requiring no raking or bagging. ▪ Easy to adjust cutting height. ▪ Mulches fallen leaves into lawn as topdressing. ▪ Requires little maintenance. ▪ Side/back discharge.	▪ Noisy. ▪ Cord can become a danger, as well as a nuisance, especially when mowing location is significant distance from electrical outlet.
Battery-rechargeable electric rotary mower	▪ No cord to worry about. ▪ Fairly quiet. ▪ No engine maintenance. ▪ Cuts clippings small, requiring no raking or bagging. ▪ Easy to adjust cutting height. ▪ Mulches leaves into lawn as topdressing.	▪ Must be plugged in between uses to recharge battery. ▪ Bulky to maneuver. ▪ Not available everywhere.
Riding mower	▪ Covers large areas quickly. ▪ Useful for operators with physical limitations. Automatic transmission, mulching blade, and cart options available.	▪ Most expensive of all alternatives. ▪ Requires larger storage area than others. ▪ Repair and maintenance more extensive.

pruning tools

You need to prune trees and shrubs to keep them healthy. In fact, you might already routinely clip rubbing branches, shear hedges, remove an occasional injured or inconvenient tree limb, renovate old shrubs, and perform general grooming throughout your landscape. And if you live on a spacious, heavily wooded property, you might occasionally need to cut down a small tree, or cut up wood from one that has fallen. For each of these tasks there is a tool. Sometimes a simple hand tool does the job. In other instances, a powered version is your best choice. The trick is to know which one will help you do the job most efficiently. For example, don't use a hand pruner to cut thick

chainsaw safety

Because chainsaws are extremely dangerous, manufacturers go to great lengths to develop and equip them with many safety features. Never remove or disable chainbreaks, anti-kickback chain links, tip guards, or throttle interlocks, even if they seem to reduce efficiency.

hand pruner (bypass type)

Also known as secateurs, this pruner works one-handed. Its two steel blades bypass each other—the top, sharpened blade slices through twigs and stems up to ¾ inch thick. Some models have soft-grip or swivel handles.

hand pruner (anvil type)

Its sharpened top blade cuts by pressing twigs and stems against the thicker lower blade in a crushing, rather than slicing, action. Although this type isn't as versatile and maneuverable as a bypass pruner, it's more stable. And it requires less wrist and hand strength to operate.

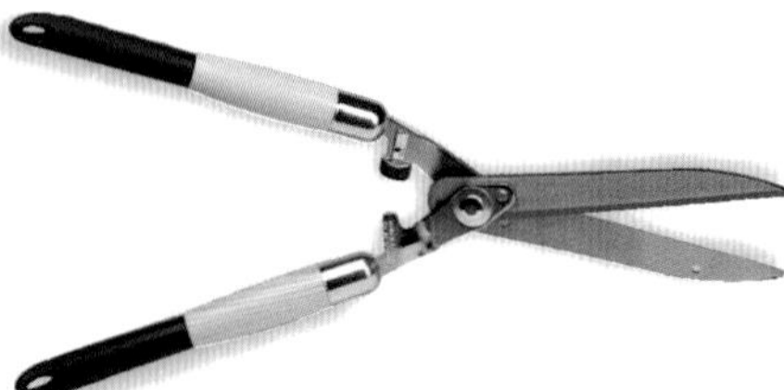

hedge shears

This long-handled tool with 8- to 10-inch-long carbon steel blades cuts twigs and branches up to ½ inch thick. Use it to clip hedges and cut back ornamental grasses.

long-handled pruning saw

This 14- to 16-foot-long tool is ideal for pruning low-hanging tree branches up to 1½ inches thick. It typically has telescoping or extension handles made of wood or fiberglass. The very sharp steel saw at the tip easily slips between foliage-covered branches.

ratchet pruner

This type of pruner, although touted to cut almost anything, is best used on twigs and stems less than ½ inch thick. It was designed for people who lack the hand strength to operate other types of pruners. The racheting action allows you to keep squeezing the handles until the blades cut through the stem.

loppers

Essentially long-handled pruners, loppers require two hands to use. Available with bypass or anvil blades, they cut small branches and stems as thick as your thumb. They also extend your reach and give you improved cutting leverage.

branches or a saw to cut twigs. Pruning tools are sophisticated engineering designs. The best ones—made of carbon steel, aluminum, and contemporary plastics—make pruning easy, as long as you care for them properly. Wipe off pruners, loppers, and saw blades after each use and sharpen them regularly. Keep power tools clean and oiled. Store all tools indoors, away from dampness. Look for extra features that improve the tools' performance. The best pruners and loppers have bumpers where their handles meet. Others have swivel handles, cushioned grips, and ratchet action to enhance your comfort.

compact pruning saw
The extremely sharp teeth on this compact, wooden-handled saw make quick work of medium-sized stems and branches. Those models that allow the blade to fold into the handle are equipped with a latch to prevent it from folding while you're using it.

bow pruning saw
The light weight of this saw makes it useful for cutting fallen branches. Its thin, toothed blade is attached at each end to a curved metal handle with a grip at one end. It quickly cuts any log that's no thicker than the length of the replaceable blade.

straight pruning saw
Once the workhorse for cutting major limbs, this straight-edged saw has been eclipsed by the chainsaw. But it still comes in handy when you don't want to get out the chainsaw to prune one or two large limbs. Some models offer a choice of coarse teeth on one edge, fine teeth on the other.

powered hedge clippers
Various models have 18- to 24-inch-long blades—the longer ones typically on heavy-duty models—with moveable cutting teeth. Some feature double blades that move in opposite directions to cut twiggy hedges more efficiently. The motor gets its power from an electrical cord or a portable battery pack.

chainsaw
Chainsaws cut with teeth linked together on a chain that's propelled around a grooved guide bar. They are powered by either a gasoline engine or electric motor at speeds up to 45 mph.

watering tools

Shopping for a watering device can be quite a challenge. In fact, you can choose from literally dozens of models of sprinklers for just about any situation. Most are relatively inexpensive, so it makes sense to have several. Look for evidence of durable construction, because sprinklers have to endure a lot of abuse. They not only spend most of the summer in the hot sun, but they also suffer from hazards, such as run-ins with the family car, lawn mower, and children's play vehicles.

Whatever the style of sprinkler, modern design offers several watering options. Many models feature mechanisms for adjusting the pattern, volume, angle, and direction of the water flow. Some are equipped

drip irrigation

Drip irrigation is the most efficient method of watering plants in the garden. By delivering water slowly and directly into the soil, it eliminates waste from evaporation or runoff. Plant leaves remain dry, discouraging fungal disease. ***Emitter systems*** *feature intermittent nozzles along the pipe that deliver the water. They are good for rows of shrubs.* ***Soaker (porous) hose systems*** *leak water droplets along their entire length. They work well for closely planted flower, groundcover, or vegetable beds.*

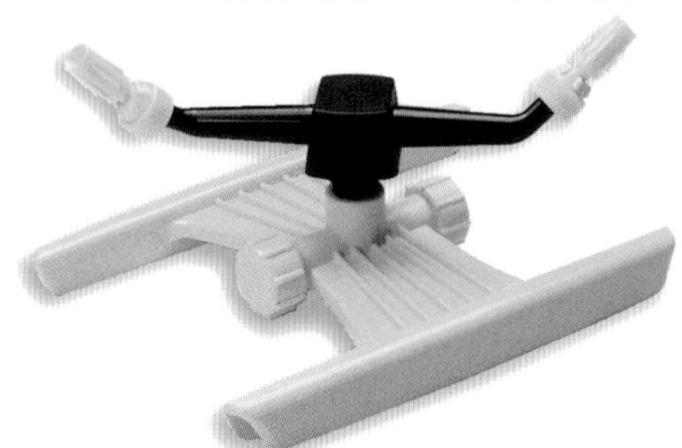

whirlybird sprinkler

As its nickname suggests, this rotating sprinkler throws water in a distinctive circular pattern as its arm rotates from the force of the water coming out of the hose. Because the stream of water is interrupted by the action of the arm, it covers the areas both in the vicinity of the sprinkler and at some distance away from it. The spray is in larger droplets and falls fairly low to the ground.

fixed-spray sprinkler

Water from a fixed-spray sprinkler extends high into the air so it creates an umbrella pattern on small areas of groundcover or lawn. The fine, rain-like spray falls on foliage as well as soil, and some of the water is inevitably lost to evaporation in its travels. Choose a model with a stable base so it won't tip over.

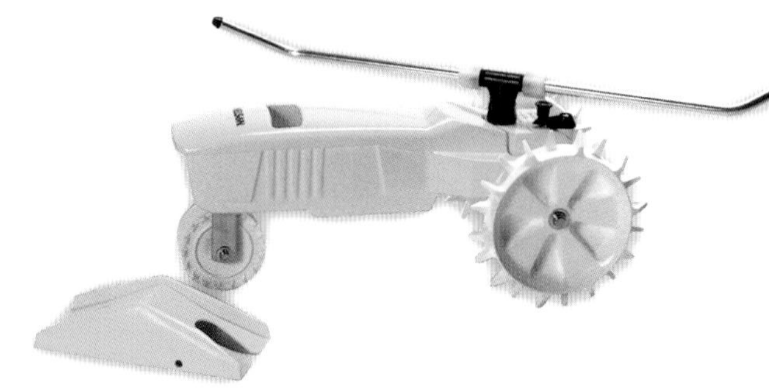

tractor sprinkler

As if by remote control, this sprinkler travels as it delivers water. The force of the water propels the rotating sprinkler head on wheels guided by the hose. You can adjust the speed to vary the amount of water that reaches the area it traverses. Its watering pattern is not as wide as that of impulse sprinklers, but it's quite effective on broad, open lawns.

impulse sprinkler

Mounted on either a flat base, a tall tripod, or a spike you insert into the soil, these sprinklers throw rhythmic pulses of water over a wide area, relatively low to the ground. They can cover an area around their entire circumference or in just one sector. Water may reach as far as 100 feet away. They are ideal for lawns and under trees and shrubs. Their low arc minimizes evaporation.

with practical manual timers that shut them off automatically. Because most areas of the country have concerns about their fresh-water supplies, these timers help conserve water. An essential part of any watering system is the hose that supplies the water. Choose the best quality that you can afford. Look for a rubber or vinyl product that is constructed of several layers of mesh. The more substantial hoses are kink-free and can withstand UV rays. Make sure yours has sturdy metal fittings to prevent leaks that waste water and reduce the effectiveness of the sprinkler.

pop-up sprinkler
This device is typically part of a professionally installed automated sprinkler system and is most common in warm areas of the country, where lawns require frequent moisture, or on very large properties. The sprinkler head is permanently installed, flush with the ground. When the water is on, it pops up and sprays water in a fixed pattern. It can be programmed to deliver different amounts of water in different patterns.

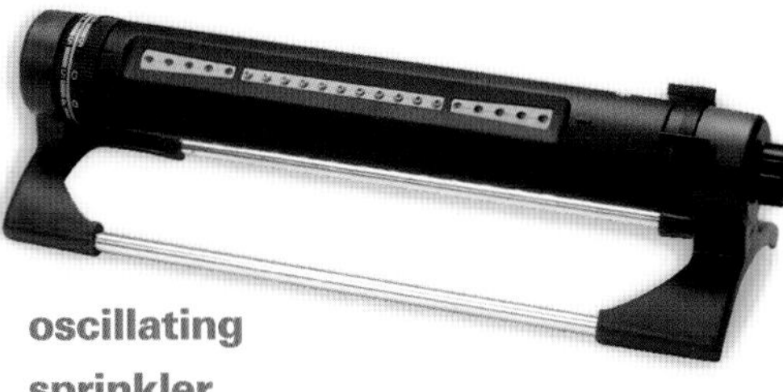

oscillating sprinkler
Use this type to cover wide lawn areas or beds of tall plants best watered from above. It emits regular arching sprays of water from holes in its oscillating bar. You can adjust it to water on just one side in varying degrees or to swing in a full arc, from one side to another. On some models, you also can adjust the width of the spray patterns.

best times to water

Lawns – Water turfgrass deeply but infrequently. Wait until the grass shows it needs it—turning dull and grayish. A footprint will remain hours after a person steps on it. The signal for watering may come just a few days after a watering where the soil is compacted or lacking moisture-holding organic matter. Water early in the day so that the grass blades have time to dry off before nightfall to discourage fungal disease.

Trees and shrubs – Water newly planted trees and shrubs every couple of days when rainfall is scarce and the weather is hot. Even long-established plants need water during droughts. Allow a hose to drip slowly at various spots under the foliage canopy to achieve deep watering over the broadly spreading root system. Be sure the mulch layer is not too thick; 2 or 3 inches will admit the water and then retard its evaporation from the soil. Water must penetrate at least 10 to 12 inches into the soil—the depth of most tree and shrub roots.

Flowers and vegetables – Annual plants, such as petunia, impatiens, nasturtium, basil, beans, and peas, are relatively shallow-rooted. Even if they're properly mulched, water them every couple of days in dry, hot weather. Those in containers might need daily watering. Perennial plants, such as chrysanthemum, aster, pachysandra, astilbe, asparagus, and rhubarb, have deeper roots. In good loam soil with proper mulch, they need water every five to eight days, depending on the heat. Water early in the day so they have time to dry off by nightfall.

weeding tools

It seems that weeds are always with us. Their seeds lurk in the soil for decades, remaining viable, and lying in wait for a chance to see some sun so they can germinate. Because some weeds typically produce up to 250,000 seeds from a single plant, it's no wonder that they are everywhere. Every time the soil is disturbed—even when weeding—more seeds surface. That's why weeds are so common along roadsides and other edges where the soil is disturbed. Fortunately, you can discourage weeds by keeping the soil covered with dense groundcover plantings or mulch. Because the best defense is a good offense, attack weeds as soon as they appear. Young ones are easier to eliminate than

weather

Rainy weather is ideal for weeding. It's much easier to pull weeds from softened, moist soil than from dry, hard soil. After the rain, wait until the moisture has a chance to soak deeply into the soil, then start pulling with a tool or by hand. In dry periods, water, then weed.

dandelion weeder

Also called a fishtail weeder, this traditional tool is designed to penetrate deeply into the soil to capture and pry out taproots of plants, such as dandelion and thistle. It is also useful for prying weeds from narrow spaces. You can buy it in either a short- or long-handled designs. On the best models, the wooden handle is ergonomically shaped at a slight angle to give you an especially good grip. The notched blade at the tip is typically made of steel and has a sharp edge.

pronged-foot weeder

This heavy-duty tool is easy on the back. Sturdily made from steel, it features a set of five round, pointed prongs mounted on a spring-loaded steel plate. This assembly is, in turn, attached to a larger steel foot plate with a tread on the back. Insert the prongs vertically into the soil by pushing on the waist-high wooden handle. Then step on the foot plate to lever the prongs upward, popping the weeds out of the soil.

crack weeder

This tool is part knife, part weeder. It's available in either long- or short-handled models and is strong and solid. The business end consists of an acutely angled steel tip that's thick and flat at its base, then tapers to a point as it curves upward. This weeder is ideal for levering shallow weeds from soil or scraping them from cracks in narrow spots between stones and in walks.

weed whip

This traditional tool was the original weed whacker. It has a wooden hand grip on a strong metal shank that's angled so its metal cutting piece is flat to the ground. The cutting piece is serrated on both edges so it cuts whether you're moving it forward or backward. Swing the whip—a mini scythe—much the way you would a golf club to cut tall rangy weeds down to size.

older ones that have well-established root systems. Make every effort to deal with weeds before they set seed. Most are easiest to pull when they are flowering and just beginning to set seed. Tools give you the satisfaction of removing weeds immediately. Unlike herbicide sprays, which take hours or days to work, mechanical devices offer instant results. The trick is to get the root. In the case of perennial weeds, any piece of root left in the soil is likely to create a new weed. Use herbicides only on extensive patches of weeds or for harmful ones, such as poison ivy.

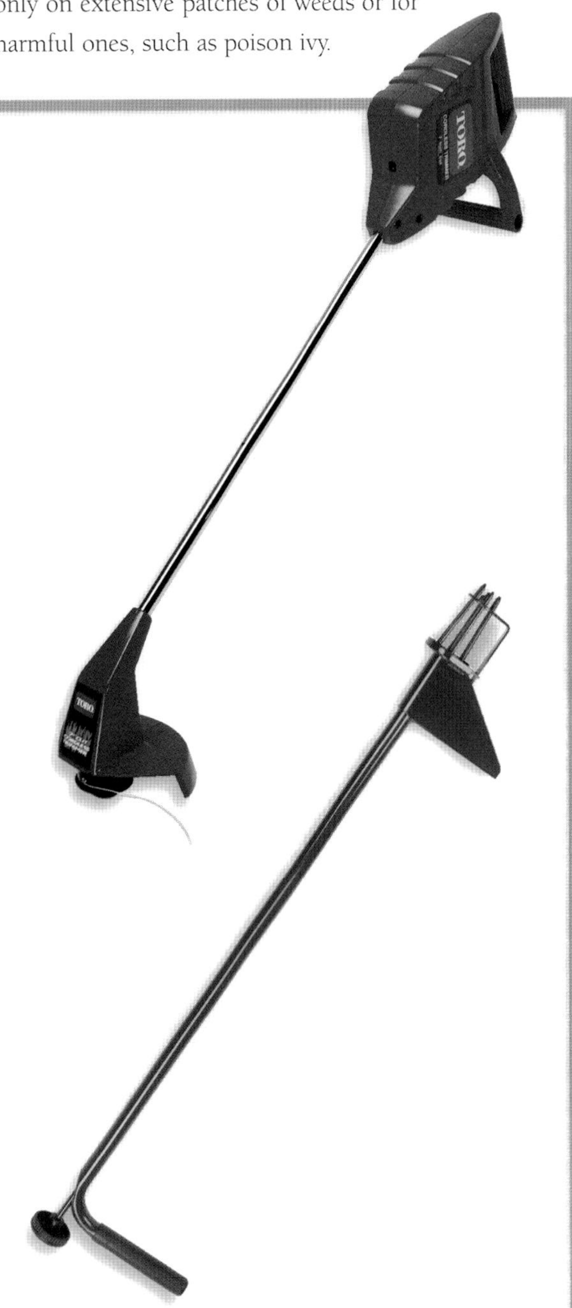

power weed trimmer

Power weed trimmers typically have an electric motor—either corded or battery-operated—but can be gas-powered, as well. They power a whirling piece of nylon string that resembles fishing line. As it continuously feeds off its spool at high speed, the line knocks off the tops of grassy weeds. It's especially effective along walls and drives. When you tilt it, this type of trimmer will edge around stepping stones and along walks. Replacement spools of nylon line are easily available. Be careful not to use it too close to trees or shrubs—it's easy to cut the bark or stems, injuring or killing the plants.

dandelion weeder

This high-tech version of the traditional fishtail weeder is easier on the back. It has a waist-high handle of wood or steel, tipped by a ring of steel prongs. Center it over the weed and apply pressure to the foot plate attached to the base of the handle. This action inserts the prongs into the soil. Then use the knob or lever mechanism at the top of the wooden handle to trip the levered action, closing the prongs and trapping the crown of the plant. Finally, tug on the handle to pop the weed out, root and all.

plant list

It's a good idea to keep track of the plants in your garden. *It helps you remember what's planted where. Photocopy this page, if you wish, to start a garden journal. Use it to keep records of each plant you buy, the date, and where you plant it. Use the comments column for any other information you want to remember—where you bought it, the date it bloomed, how long it stayed in bloom, the color of the flower, and pest or disease problems. You'll find tha this type of record-keeping is helpful as yo garden matures, allowir you to remember all its pertinent facts and history. Some people also record when (if) a plant dies and why.*

plant name	date planted	location

	comments

resources

key

(B) bulbs

(P) Plants

(S) seeds

catalog price noted

Most nursery, home, and garden centers stock the supplies you will need. If you can't find what you're looking for, here are some resources:

American Horticulture Society (AHS)
7931 East Boulevard Drive
Alexandria, VA 22308
703-768-5700
www.ahs.com
A good source for information about plant hardiness, new plant releases, and other horticultural information. Their website has an excellent list of gardening websites and other resources.

American Rose Society (ARS)
P.O. Box 30,000
Shreveport, LA 71130
318-938-5402
www.ars.org
The source for information on growing roses.

Bedding Plants International
525 S.W. 5th Street/Suite A
Des Moines, IA 50309
800-647-7742
A source for information on annuals.

Lawn Institute
1855-A Hicks Road
Rolling Meadows, IL 60008
800-405-8873
www.lawninstitute.com
A source for information on various turfgrasses.

Perennial Plant Association (PPA)
3383 Schirtzinger Road
Hilliard, OH 43026
614-771-8431
www.perennialplant.org
A source for the latest information on how specific plants perform in your region and where to acquire plants.

Mail-Order Nurseries and Seed Suppliers

Antique Rose Emporium (P) free
9300 Lueckemeyer Rd.
Brenham, TX 77833–6453
800-441-0002
www.antiqueroseemporium.com

Arena Rose Co. (P) $5
P.O. Box 3096
Paso Robles, CA 93447
805-227-4094

Brent and Becky's Bulbs (B) free
7463 Heath Trail
Gloucester, VA 23061
804-693-3966
www.BrentandBecky'sbulb.com

Burpee (S) free
300 Park Ave.
Warminster, PA 18991-0001
800-888-1447
www.burpee.com

The Cook's Garden (S) free
P.O. Box 535
Londonderry, VT 05148
800-457-9703
www.cooksgarden.com

Forestfarm (P) $4
990 Tetherow Rd.
Williams, OR 97544-9599
541-846-7269
www.forestfarm.com

The Gourmet Gardener (S) free
8650 College Blvd.
Overland Park, KS 66210
913-345-0490
www.gourmetgardener.com

Greer Gardens (P) $3
1280 Goodpasture Island Road
Eugene, OR 97401
541-686-8266
www.greergardens.com

Heronswood Nursery Ltd. (P) $8
7530 NE 288th St.
Kingston, WA 98346
360-297-4172
www.heronswood.com

Jackson & Perkins Co. (P) free
2518 S. Pacific Highway
Medford, OR 97501
800-292-4769
www.jacksonandperkins.com

J. L. Hudson, Seedsman (S) $1
Star Rte. 2, Box 337
La Honda, CA 94020
No phone

Johnny's Selected Seeds (S) free
One Foss Hill Rd.
Albion, ME 04910-9731
207-437-4395
www.johnnyseeds.com

Kurt Bluemel, Inc. (P) $3
2740 Greene Ln.
Baldwin, MD 21013–9523
800-248-7584
www.bluemel.com

Louisiana Nursery (P) $5
5853 Highway 182
Opelousas, LA 70570
318-948-3696

McClure & Zimmerman (B) free
P.O. Box 368
Friesland, WI 53935-0368
800-883-6998
www.mzbulb.com

Mountain Maples (P) $2
P.O. Box 1329
Laytonville, CA 95454
707-984-6522
www.mountainmaples.com

resources

key

(B) bulbs

(P) Plants

(S) seeds

catalog price noted

Musser Forests (P) free
P.O. Box S-91 M
Indiana, PA 15701
800-643-3819
www.musserforests.com

Niche Gardens (P) $3
1111 Dawson Rd.
Chapel Hill, NC 27516
919-967-0078
www.nichegdn.com

Nichols Garden Nursery (S) free
1190 N. Pacific Hwy.
Albany, OR 97321-4580
541-928-9280
www.gardennursery.com

Park Seed Company (S) free
One Parkton Ave.
Greenwood, SC 29647-0001
800-845-3369
www.parkseed.com

Pinetree Garden Seeds (S) free
Box 300
New Gloucester, ME 04260
207-926-3400
www.superseeds.com

Plant Delights Nursery (P)
One box of chocolates or ten stamps
9241 Sauls Rd.
Raleigh, NC 27603
919-772-4794
www.plantdelights.com

Richters (S)
Goodwood
Ontario L0C 1A0 Canada
905-640-6677
www.richters.com

Roses of Yesterday (P) $3
803 Brown's Valley Rd.
Watsonville, CA 95076
831-728-1901
www.rosesofyesterday.com

Roslyn Nursery (P) $2
211 Burrs Lane
Dix Hills, NY 11746
631-643-9347
www.roslynnursery.com

Seed Savers Exchange (S) free
3076 North Winn Rd.
Decorah, IA 52101
319-382-5990
www.seedsavers.org

Select Seeds (S) $3
180 Stickney Hill Rd.
Union, CT 06076-4617
860-684-9310
www.selectseeds.com

Stark Bros. Nursery (P) free
P.O. Box 10
Louisiana, MO 63353-0010
800-325-4180
www.myseasons.com

Thompson & Morgan, Inc. (S) free
P.O. Box 1308
Jackson, NJ 08527-0308
800-274-7333
www.thompson-morgan.com

Tranquil Lake Nursery (P) $1
45 River St.
Rehoboth, MA 02769-1395
800-353-4344
www.tranquil-lake.com

Van Bourgondien (P) free
P.O. Box 1000
Babylon, NY 11702
800-622-9959
www.dutchbulbs.com

White Flower Farm (P) free
P.O. Box 50
Litchfield, CT 06759–0050
800-503-9624
www.whiteflowerfarm.com

Woodlanders (P) $2
1128 Colleton Ave.
Aiken, SC 29801
803-648-7522

Yard and Garden Supplies

Duncraft Specialities for Birds
102 Fisherville Road
Concord, NH 03303-2086
800-593-5656
www.duncraft.com

Gardener's Supply Company
128 Intervale Road
Burlington, VT 05401
800-955-3370
www.gardeners.com

Kinsman Co.
River Road
Point Pleasant, PA 18950
803-733-4146
www.kinsmangarden.com

Lagenbach Tools free
638 Lindero Canyon Road, MSC 290
Oak Park, CA 91301-5464
800-362-1991
www.langenbach.com

Plants from the Internet

http://www.bhglive.com
http://www.garden.com
http://www.landscapeusa.com

metric conversions

US Units to Metric Equivalents

to convert from	multiply by	to get
Inches	25.400	Millimetres
Inches	2.540	Centimetres
Feet	30.480	Centimetres
Feet	0.3048	Metres
Yards	0.9144	Metres
Square inches	6.4516	Square centimetres
Square feet	0.0929	Square metres
Square yards	0.8361	Square metres
Acres	0.4047	Hectares
Cubic inches	16.387	Cubic centimetres
Cubic feet	0.0283	Cubic metres
Cubic feet	28.316	Litres
Cubic yards	0.7646	Cubic metres
Cubic yards	764.550	Litres

To convert from degrees Celsius to degrees Fahrenheit, multiply by ⁹⁄₅, then add 32.

Metric Units to US Equivalents

to convert from	multiply by	to get
Millimetres	0.0394	Inches
Centimetres	0.3937	Inches
Centimetres	0.0328	Feet
Metres	3.2808	Feet
Metres	1.0936	Yards
Square centimetres	0.1550	Square inches
Square metres	10.764	Square feet
Square metres	1.1960	Square metres
Hectares	2.4711	Acres
Cubic centimetres	0.0610	Cubic inches
Cubic metres	35.315	Cubic feet
Litres	0.0353	Cubic feet
Cubic metres	1.308	Cubic yards
Litres	0.0013	Cubic yards

To convert from degrees Fahrenheit (F) to degrees Celsius (C), first subtract 32, then multiply by ⁵⁄₉.

index

Photos in boldface italics
Projects in boldface

a

b

index

index

index

q–r

index